The Oxford Introductions to U.S. Law

Contracts

The Oxford Introductions to U.S. Law

Contracts

RANDY E. BARNETT

Dennis Patterson, Series Editor
The Oxford Introductions to U.S. Law

OXFORD
UNIVERSITY PRESS

OXFORD
UNIVERSITY PRESS

Oxford University Press, Inc., publishes works that further Oxford University's objective of excellence in research, scholarship, and education.

Oxford   New York
Auckland   Cape Town   Dar es Salaam   Hong Kong   Karachi   Kuala Lumpur   Madrid   Melbourne
Mexico City   Nairobi   New Delhi   Shanghai   Taipei   Toronto

With offices in
Argentina   Austria   Brazil   Chile   Czech Republic   France   Greece   Guatemala   Hungary   Italy
Japan   Poland   Portugal   Singapore   South Korea   Switzerland   Thailand   Turkey   Ukraine
Vietnam

Published by Oxford University Press, Inc.
198 Madison Avenue, New York, New York 10016

Oxford is a registered trademark of Oxford University Press
Oxford University Press is a registered trademark of Oxford University Press, Inc.

Library of Congress Cataloging-in-Publication Data

Barnett, Randy E.
    The Oxford introductions to U.S. law: contracts / Randy E. Barnett.
        p. cm.—(The Oxford introductions to U.S. law)
    Includes bibliographical references and index.
    ISBN 978-0-19-974018-5 (pbk. : alk. paper)
1. Contracts—United States. I. Title. II. Title: Contracts.
    KF801.B37 2010
    346.7302—dc22   2010002668

 2 3 4 5 6 7 8 9

Printed in the United States of America on acid-free paper

Note to Readers
This publication is designed to provide accurate and authoritative information in regard to the subject matter covered. It is based upon sources believed to be accurate and reliable and is intended to be current as of the time it was written. It is sold with the understanding that the publisher is not engaged in rendering legal, accounting, or other professional services. If legal advice or other expert assistance is required, the services of a competent professional person should be sought. Also, to confirm that the information has not been affected or changed by recent developments, traditional legal research techniques should be used, including checking primary sources where appropriate.

(Based on the Declaration of Principles jointly adopted by a Committee of the American Bar Association and a Committee of Publishers and Associations.)

*To Allan Farnsworth for his kindness and encouragement
when I needed it most*

Acknowledgments

I AM DEEPLY GRATEFUL TO Dennis Patterson for inviting me to contribute this volume to this impressive series, to Gregory Klass and Curtis Bridgeman for their critical and insightful comments on an earlier draft, and to Lawrence Solum for proposing the distinction between bargains and bets I discuss in Chapter 6.

Contents

Introduction

✹ I.1 The Study of Contract Law

It is only a slight exaggeration to say that no student goes to law school to learn about contracts. Few students react to their first-year schedule by thinking, "Contracts, now *this* will be interesting!" Yet many students find that contracts is indeed the most intellectually challenging and engaging subject of their first year of law school. I know I did, which is why after practicing law as a criminal prosecutor I chose contract law as the subject I most wanted to teach when I became a professor.

What makes contracts so interesting? First of all, it contains lots of really colorful and memorable cases. Pregnant cows, carbolic smoke balls, opera singers, hairy hands, ships named *Peerless*, employees diving off balconies to save their employers—the list goes on and on. The classic cases studied in contracts are not only inherently engaging, they raise fundamental questions about the nature of law and its relationship to justice. And they identify and illuminate rules of law that are still in effect today. For these reasons, these iconic cases form the basic building blocks of contract law. Judges today relate current cases to the classic ones. No literate contracts lawyer, or law professor, can afford to be unaware of them.

Secondly, contract law contains lots of law. There are ancient and very real rules to learn and apply to cases. Other than civil procedure, contracts may have the most intricate set of rules that law students encounter in their first year. The intellectual challenge is understanding how these rules fit into a "big picture" so students can fully grasp their content and how each relates to the others.

One way to answer this challenge is through history. The root of "history" is "story" and the story of contract law is fascinating. Today's contract doctrines have evolved over the centuries. The Statute of Frauds was first enacted in England in 1677. Not coincidentally, the enigmatic doctrine of consideration developed in the same period. Understanding why these and other developments occurred is of genuine assistance in understanding modern contract doctrines. Why was the doctrine of consideration transformed in the nineteenth century? How did that transformation bring about the development of promissory estoppel? The story of contract law provides accessible answers to these questions. And, these answers enlighten current contract doctrine.

A second way to grasp the big picture is with theory. Many students balk at the word "theory." "Theory may be interesting to the professor," some think, "but I just want to learn the law." Once it is explained to them, however, that theory is just a fancy way of referring to the *reasons* why the law is the way it is, then it becomes much less esoteric, and seems much more relevant. What purpose is served by the doctrine of consideration or the Statute of Frauds? Is the doctrine of promissory estoppel a substitute for consideration *within* an action for breach of contract? Or is it really a separate cause of action altogether as is tort? Contract scholars have wrestled with these issues for more than one hundred years. A body of classic writings by such scholars as Morris Cohen, Lon Fuller, and Grant Gilmore has developed to compliment the classic cases; and contemporary scholars have made significant advances on these classic works.

This book provides students with ready access to the basic doctrines of contract law, the story behind their evolution, and the rationales for their continued existence. It is organized around the principle that lies at the heart of contracts, and that distinguishes it from torts: *consent*. Whereas the duties enforced by torts may or may not be a product of the consent of the persons on whom they are imposed, every contract begins with the consent of the parties. Discerning the existence and meaning of that consent comprises the core of the study of contract.

Some scholars contend that *reliance*, and not consent, is the basis of contract law. In this book, I will examine that thesis. In the end, I think there is much to be said on its behalf, and the challenge will be to reconcile consent with reliance. Allowing one person to rely on the commitment of another is indeed one of the central purposes of contracts, but that purpose does not distinguish *when* reliance will be protected from when it will not. My thesis is that contract law provides protection to those persons who are relying on another person's consent to be legally bound. In other words, consent is the variable that tells us when reliance on the commitment of another will be protected by a legal remedy. It also tells us the extent of that remedy. But enabling reliance on the commitments of others is a prime reason for recognizing consent-based obligations.

Viewing consent as the heart of contract law also reveals the limits of contract. For one thing, there are some things to which people may not consent. Or, more accurately, there are some matters about which they are always entitled to change their mind. For another, understanding *why* consent is at the heart of contract will illuminate the rationale for contract defenses by which persons may avoid the enforcement of contracts to which it appears they consented.

Put most simply, the main reason we enforce consensual bargains is that such commitments tend to enhance the welfare of those who make them. Each party values what he receives from the other party more than what he gives up. Enforcement of these bargains enables each party to rely in confidence upon the commitment of another in making his plans and investments. By making both parties to a bargain better off, the enforcement of contracts also benefits society as a whole (provided that the rights of third parties are not violated by the transaction).

But there are identifiable circumstances in which the assumption that bargains are value-enhancing does not hold. When one party can be shown to lack the capacity to make value-enhancing choices—whether because of mental incapacitation, intoxication, infancy, or other impairment—the manifestation of that party's consent is deprived of its normal significance. The enforcement of such bargains no longer satisfies the rationale for enforcing consensual commitments. So too when one party's consent is obtained by improper means—such as by duress or misrepresentation. Understanding why consent may be set aside because one party lacked capacity or the other party obtained assent by improper means also illuminates other contractual defenses such as undue influence and unconscionability.

Finally, the limits of consent are also reached when there has been a failure of a basic assumption shared by both parties. Such defenses as mistake, impracticability, and frustration do not so much describe circumstances that deprive consent of its normal significance. Instead, such defenses can best be understood as acknowledging the limits of what can be anticipated at the time of formation. When such circumstances later arise, it can no longer accurately be said that parties truly allocated this risk when they made their agreement. The contract is no longer enforceable because, in these unanticipated circumstances, consent has run out.

Did I mention that contracts is interesting? Even this basic outline of the problems of contract law shows why. The study of contracts requires that students master a complex web of rules, and doing so is facilitated by studying their origin and rationales. The study of contracts raises compelling moral issues and is integral to the prosperity of a modern free society. What could be more interesting than all this? But as interesting as the subject of contracts may be, it can be frustrating unless one grasps the basic principles that lie at its core. The primacy of consent is the most important of these principles.

Of course, the approach presented here is not the only way to understand contracts. Other theories have been advanced, for example, the contract-as-promise theory of Charles Fried; Patrick Atiyah's theory that contract is a combination of reliance and unjust enrichment; Grant Gilmore's theory that contract law is best explained solely in terms or detrimental reliance and is no different than torts (which will be discussed below); Ian Macneil's relational theory of contract; Dori Kimel's theory that contract is a substitute for the social institution of promising; Seana Shiffrin's theory that contract law should facilitate moral conduct; or the efficiency approach associated with such law and economics scholars as Richard Posner, Alan Schwartz, Richard Craswell (and others too numerous to list) that explains and justifies contract law as maximizing aggregate social welfare.

But this book is not a survey of different contract law theories. While it would be interesting, I do not think a book about contract law theories would help students organize the otherwise confusing doctrines of contract law. Rather than being about contract law theories, this book is about contract *law* itself. My goal is to assist the law student by making sense of its otherwise disparate parts the same way I make sense of it for myself. I think I would have gotten more out of my contracts class if I had this framework with which to understand the doctrines.

Of course, to do well in a course on contracts, every student should seek to understand how his or her professor understands the subject. If your professor subscribes to one of the theories listed above, you would do well to read more about it. But many contracts professors hold no particular theory of the subject, if for no other reason than contract law is not their scholarly specialty. Students may be surprised to learn that is true of most professors who teach contracts. For this reason, students may sometimes find themselves lost at sea. This book provides a map by which to orient themselves; a map that works for me.

✐ I.2 Contract Law Has an Underlying Structure

When I practiced law, there were two judges before whom I tried cases. Although both were former trial lawyers, they were a study in contrasts. One was a mild-mannered graduate of an elite law school, who had previously been a high-ranking supervisor in the prosecutor's office. The other was much older, a graduate of a local law school who had been a lawyer for the city before becoming a judge, and who also had a fiery temper and a shock of white hair.

Their evidentiary rulings were as different as everything else about them. The younger judge seemed to be relying on his recollection of cases he had read. The problem was he frequently misremembered their holdings, and because he could not always remember the case names, it was hard to look them up to see if his memory was in error. In sharp contrast, the older cantankerous judge's rulings were invariably spot on. Why the difference?

In addition to keeping up with the cases, the older judge obviously had internalized the underlying structure of evidence law. He not only knew the rules, but their function. So he could reason his way to correct rulings, usually on the spot as typically is necessary in the heat of a trial. Because at some point in his career as a trial lawyer he had grasped the logic of evidence, the case law usually conformed to his "common sense" of the situation. In contrast, the younger judge seemed to operate by memorization and, unfortunately, sometimes his memory was faulty.

Like evidence, contract law has a structure or logic that is based on its functions. Internalize that structure and the rules make sense. Students internalize the structure of their courses in different ways. Although there are students who are eventually able to glean this from reading the assigned materials, many students want to read something extra that helps puts the material in better focus. Some save this until studying for the final to help them put it all together. Others read along as the semester proceeds to gain a better handle on class discussion. And there are few who read up on their courses even before starting law school.

If you are a student looking for a book that lays out the basic structure of contract law before, during, or after your classes, without getting lost in the weeds of detail, then this book is intended for you. My goal is to simplify without oversimplifying what can seem like an enormously complex body of rules, and to provide a short introduction to the basic structure of contract law.

🎘 I.3 The Three Core Concerns of Contracts

The law in its entirety provides a background set of rights and duties that apply by default to all persons within its jurisdiction. The principal function of contract law is to allow persons to alter or change these rights and duties to better serve their purposes. The background law of torts, for example, forbids the theft of another's property. A contract enables one person to transfer his property rights to another in exchange for something he prefers. This essential function of contracting explains three important features of the law governing contracts.

First, there is always more than one party to every contract, though most of the contracts you will study and be tested on have just two. And typically (though not always) each party is making a commitment in exchange for the commitment of the other party. Given contract's principal function of allowing the parties to serve their purposes by reordering their rights and duties to each other, the law of contracts is concerned with identifying the *will* or *intentions* of each party who enters into an agreement. These intentions define the scope of the change in the preexisting rights of the parties that results from making a contract. So the first concern of contract law is with the intentions of the parties.

Second, each party enters a contract to enable it better to count on or rely on the other party fulfilling his or her commitment. We are constantly making social commitments to each other, but almost always must trust others to fulfil their commitments. Ordinarily, we have no enforceable right to seek legal relief for their failure to perform. Contracts enhance our ability to rely on the commitment of another person by creating a right to legal enforcement of that commitment in case of its breach. So the second concern of contract law is protecting the *reliance* of each party on the commitment of the other.

Third, because the principal function of contracts is to permit persons to alter their rights and duties to each other to better achieve their purposes, a contract should ordinarily improve the situation of both parties. If you prefer owning a particular automobile than owning, say $10,000, and the seller prefers owning the $10,000 to owning the car, a contract to sell the car to you for $10,000 will leave both parties better off than they were before. This is sometimes called a *value-enhancing* exchange. A third concern of contract law is to ensure, or at least increase the chances, that a contract is value-enhancing for both parties.

Contract law consists of rules and principles. Most of these rules and principles—or what is sometimes called "doctrine"—exist to satisfy one or more of these three concerns: (1) identifying the intentions (or "will") of the parties that define the scope of the commitment, (2) protecting the reliance of each party on the commitment of the other, and (3) ensuring that these commitments are value-enhancing for both parties.

These three core concerns cannot always be satisfied at the same time. For example, an agreement may accurately reflect the intentions of the parties at the time of formation and one party may have relied on it, but after formation the other party regrets the deal so it is no longer value-enhancing for him or her. Unless the circumstances justifying one of the defenses discussed in Chapter 6 applies, however, the regret of one party will not suffice to let that party out of the deal even though it is no longer value-enhancing for both. Likewise, protecting the reliance of one party can sometimes be in conflict with the subjective intention of the other, and vice versa.

Because these concerns can be in tension with each other, cases will inevitably arise about which our intuitions may be uncertain or in conflict. Such cases that are then selected to be studied in contracts courses precisely because they play one of these concerns against the others. If you find yourself torn about the correctness of a particular case, this may be one of the reasons why. Your intuitions are in conflict. But the fact that these core concerns may sometimes conflict does not make them any less basic to contract law. Taken as a whole, the body of contract law can be viewed as mediating or compromising among these core concerns.

I.4 The Concept of Default Rules

For a long time, many of the rules of contract law were called "gap fillers" which emphasized that they applied precisely when the agreement of the parties did not address the issue governed by the rule. In short, the rules of contract law applied when there was a "gap" in the assent of the parties. By adopting this terminology, the consent of the parties could be cast as irrelevant to contract law because contract law applied precisely when the consent of the parties did not exist.

In recent years, however, this image of contract law has been supplanted to a large extent by a different image—the rules of contract law as "default rules." As such, they apply unless the parties "contract around" them by putting a different term in their agreement. The default rules of contract law are like the default margins supplied by your word-processing program that apply unless you change them. Although there are a few contract law doctrines that cannot be contracted around, the great majority of contract law rules are default rules. Indeed, most of the cases studied in contracts courses would not be there had the parties only inserted an express clause to cover the issue that later arose. Whereas the image of "gap filler" emphasized the discontinuity between contract law and the consent of the parties, the concept of default rules highlights an intimate connection. Even though the rules of contract law are provided by the courts or legislature rather than by the parties, in many cases the parties can be said to have consented to the application of those background rules by remaining silent and accepting their operation.

Some have concluded from this that the cost of contracting should be reduced by applying contract law rules to which most parties would agree, placing the onus on the minority of dissenting parties to expressly contract around the rules. While this may sometimes be a good way of selecting contract law rules, other considerations may also be taken into account. In particular, as will be discussed in Chapters 2 and 3, the background default rules can be chosen to reduce misunderstandings about the terms that will actually apply in the event of a dispute, even if that means applying default rules that all, or nearly all, parties expressly contract around. When this is the case, far from being inimical to consent, the law of contract is greatly influenced by the objective of increasing the likelihood that both parties are consenting to the same thing.

I.5 The Sources of Contract Law

The American law of contract took centuries to develop in a case-by-case fashion, first in England, and then in the United States. Most first-year courses are constructed around reading a mix of classic and more recent cases. Some cases, such as *Hadley v. Baxendale*, are famous for the rules they originated, and lawyers consult appellate court decisions to determine the law in their jurisdiction. But cases are more often studied in law school because of their facts—the more colorful and memorable the better. It is next to impossible to understand rules of law without knowing the sorts of factual problems that the rules are designed to address. This is why the readings for law school courses do not consist solely of "black letter" rules.

In addition to cases, there are two other important sources of contract law today: the Restatement (Second) of Contracts (*Restatement 2nd*) and the Uniform Commercial Code (UCC). The *Restatement 2nd* is the product of the American Law Institute (ALI), a private nonprofit select group of practicing lawyers, judges, and law professors. One of the Institute's principal projects is the production of "restatements of the law" of numerous subjects. According to the ALI, the purpose of these volumes is to "address uncertainty in the law through a restatement of basic legal subjects that would tell judges and lawyers what the law was."[1] Although these restatements are supposed to be summaries of existing law, by systematizing their subjects, they inevitably reshape the law being summarized. Sometimes a restatement also tries its hand at consciously reforming the law in response to complaints by legal scholars or practitioners or both.

Each restatement has a reporter or reporters who organize the massive task of drafting proposals, eliciting feedback, and trying to accommodate criticisms. The reporters also draft the comments, illustrations, and reporter's notes that follow each black letter rule. The first *Restatement of Contracts* was published in 1932. Its reporter was the famous Harvard contracts professor, Samuel Williston (1861–1963). The *Restatement 2nd* was commenced in 1962 and completed in 1979; it carries a 1981 publication date. Its original reporter was Harvard law professor Robert Braucher (1916–1982). When Braucher was appointed to the Supreme Judicial Court of Massachusetts in 1971, Columbia law professor E. Allan Farnsworth (1928–2005), to whom this book is dedicated, became the reporter.

The other principal source of legal doctrine we will study is the Uniform Commercial Code. A product of the nineteenth-century movement to harmonize and make uniform the laws of the fifty states, the UCC is a joint product of the ALI and the National Conference of Commissioners on Uniform State Laws (NCCUSL). The Conference has drafted more than two hundred uniform laws on numerous subjects and in various fields of law, setting patterns for uniformity across the nation. Uniform acts include the Uniform Probate Code, the Uniform Child Custody Jurisdiction Act, the Uniform Partnership Act, the Uniform Anatomical Gift Act, the Uniform Limited Partnership Act, and the Uniform Interstate

---

1. http://www.ali.org/index.cfm?fuseaction=about.instituteprojects.

Family Support Act. The legislatures of the states must then enact these laws.

In 1940 the Conference decided to address the issue of commercial relations. In 1942, Karl Llewellyn (1893–1962) of Columbia was named the principal drafter of the UCC. His assistant on the project was Soia Mentschikoff (1915–1984), who joined the faculty of the Harvard Law School in 1947 as its first female professor. In 1949, she was named associate chief reporter. The two were married in 1947 and, in 1951, both joined the faculty of the University of Chicago School of Law.

It took ten years to draft the UCC and another fourteen years to see it adopted by the legislatures of every state except Louisiana, which still uses a version of the Napoleonic Code. Article 2 of the UCC concerns the *sale* of *goods*. Students must know that if a contractual transaction is *not a sale* or *does not involve goods*, it is not covered by the UCC. So a lease of goods, a sale of land, or an employment services contract are still regulated by the common law of each state, not by the UCC. One reason for the revision of the Restatement was to incorporate the various reforms adopted in the UCC to harmonize both documents. Still, the *Restatement 2nd* is of greatest relevance to the many contracts that do not involve the sale of goods and are not, therefore, governed by the UCC.

What is the authoritative weight of these three sources of law—cases, the *Restatement 2nd*, and the UCC? A judicial decision is binding only within its relevant jurisdiction, but it may also be "persuasive" in the courts of other jurisdictions, especially when considering a matter for the first time. The UCC is a statute adopted by the legislatures of 49 states and is binding on the courts of those states; it supersedes any common law rules that are inconsistent with its provisions. By contrast, the *Restatement* is good authority in the literal sense: It is widely respected because of how it was drafted and the learned "authorities" who drafted it. For this reason, courts often adopt its provisions as the law. When a state appellate court is deciding what doctrine to adopt, following the *Restatement* is likely to be considered a safe option. Note, however, that state courts have sometimes adopted provisions of the first *Restatement* as the law in their jurisdictions, and then have not since revisited the issue after the *Restatement 2nd* was published or have even affirmatively rejected the revised approach of the second Restatement. So in these jurisdictions, the first *Restatement* still plays a role.

In discussing these sources of law, I have mentioned three of the most famous academic authorities on contract law of the twentieth century: Samuel Williston (Harvard), Karl Llewellyn (Chicago), and Allan Farnsworth (Columbia). Both Williston and Farnsworth produced highly respected and influential treatises and I still recommend Farnsworth's treatise to my students. To this list of luminaries should be added Arthur Corbin (1874–1967) of Yale Law School— indeed Yale's first full-time law professor. The author of *Corbin on Contracts*, he was slightly younger than Williston, and the two were considered rivals of a sort. Whereas the first *Restatement* reflected Williston's approach to contracts, Corbin's ideas can be seen in the second *Restatement*. He heavily influenced the drafters of the UCC, particularly Karl Llewellyn, his former student at Yale who referred to Corbin as "Dad." No scholar in the twenty-first century has yet emerged to equal the presence in contract law of these four. Perhaps no one will.

※ I.6 Basic Terminology

In this book, I will repeatedly use some basic terms that have both ordinary and technical legal meanings. I advise my students to be familiar with these definitions found in the *Restatement 2nd*:

What is a "contract"? The *Restatement 2nd*, section 1 defines a contract as follows: "A contract is a promise or a set of promises for the breach of which the law gives a remedy, or the performance of which the law in some way recognizes as a duty." Of particular note, the concept of a contract is defined in terms of a "promise." In essence, a contract is an *enforceable promise*.

What is a promise? Restatement 2nd, section 2(1) defines a promise as follows: "A promise is a manifestation of intention to act or refrain from acting in a specified way, so made as to justify a promisee in understanding that a commitment has been made." The "promisor" is the person who manifests this intention; the person to whom the manifestation is addressed is the "promisee." Notice that not just any statement of intention to do something is sufficient. It must amount to "a commitment." As we will see, this requirement of a commitment introduces an ambiguity into the definition of a contract.

What is the difference between express and implied contracts? According to *Restatement 2nd*, section 4, "A promise may be stated in words either oral or written, or may be inferred wholly or partly from conduct." Contracts in which the promises are stated in words are called *expressed*; contracts in which the promises are inferred from conduct are called *implied*. Comment a to section 4 instructs us that the distinction between expressed and implied contracts involves "no difference in legal effect, but lies merely in the mode of manifesting consent."

In later chapters, we will address the following issues: What are the consequences for breaking a contract? (Chapter 2). What constitutes a manifestation of assent? (Chapter 3). Which manifestations of assent are enforceable? (Chapter 4). What actions constitute a breach of an enforceable promise? (Chapter 5). And what defenses to the enforcement of a promise are available for parties seeking to avoid enforcement? (Chapter 6). But, to appreciate the underlying structure of modern contract law, our first order of business is to sketch the origins of this body of law.

ONE

A Short History of Contract Law

SUMMARY: This chapter briefly tells the story of the rise of the writ of assumpsit to permit the more ready enforcement of informal contracts, and how this necessitated the development of doctrines to identify which informal contracts would be enforced, and a statute requiring that some contracts be in writing. This chapter also discusses the difference between law and equity.

%% 1.1 The Common Law Writ System

Understanding today's contract law is easier if you know from where it came. Some of the older contracts cases you will read in your course refer to the action of "assumpsit." Notice the similarity between the words "assumpsit" and "assumption"—as in he or she assumed or undertook an obligation. Assumpsit was a writ or "form of action." In common law courts of England (and later America) a writ served as both a definition of the cause of action and a definition of available remedies.

A writ was an order by a legal official, such as a judge. Each writ had a name, and each writ was also a recognized justification for legal action. The jurisdiction of any court was only as extensive as the recognized writs it could issue. Until the mid-nineteenth century you could not bring a lawsuit unless you could make the facts conform to a recognized cause of action or "form of action." Originally this was an actual form.

1

There were many rigid rules that regulated the use of these forms. The main function of the forms was to order a lawsuit, for example, by determining the nature of the relief being sought and the basis of that relief. The writ system was a way of putting people, especially lawyers, on notice as to what actions had legal consequences and if a lawsuit was brought, what precisely was being alleged.

The formal system of writs avoided much of the practitioner's need for legal theory. Lawyers were trained by other lawyers, not by professors in universities. Yet the absence of theory helps explain the rigidity of the legal system and why the contortions I am about to describe were necessary to make what now seems like a rather straightforward change.

When the writ system was abolished in the nineteenth century, the need to conceptualize causes of action first arose. This is when the modern subjects of contract, tort, property, and so forth, came to be accepted as organizing categories. In his book, *The Death of Contract*,[1] Grant Gilmore was correct, but misleading, when he argued that contract was invented in the nineteenth century. *All* of these categories were invented at that time to replace the writ system. We return to this topic in Chapter 4.

⅏ 1.2 The Writs of Debt, Detinue, and Covenant

Until the sixteenth century there were three principal writs for enforcing a private agreement:

Debt—An action to gain return of a specified amount of money

Detinue—An action to regain a specified piece of property (that had been wrongfully "detained")

---

1. GRANT GILMORE, THE DEATH OF CONTRACT (1974).

Covenant—An action to gain performance of an agreement or "covenant"

The first two of these writs—*debt* and *detinue*—did not require the making of a promise to do or refrain from doing something in the future. They were based on *property* not promises: The defendant was in possession of property that properly belonged to the plaintiff. An expressed promise might be *evidence* of who owned an item of property, but it was not essential to either writ. Although the third writ—*covenant*—was based on the making of a promise or agreement, in practice, it too became property-based. Eventually the formal writing in which the promise was expressed was considered essential to maintain the action; if you lost the writing, you lost your cause of action.

What was wrong with these three causes of action? Basically, the rules that regulated the use of these three forms limited the ability of parties to get legal enforcement in ways that people wanted and that seemed justified. Debt and detinue were very specific and did not include failure to perform a promissory commitment except to pay a "sum certain" of money or tender specified goods. The way medieval lawyers got around this restriction was by the use of "penal bonds." One party would agree to transfer an amount of money to another if the promise was not performed, thereby converting a promise to a claim to property.

The writ of *covenant* was promissory but, as with the writs of debt and detinue, if the agreement was not in writing and under seal, it was subject to a defense called "wager of law." Wager of law—also called "compurgation"—was a carryover from the medieval tribal legal systems. To wager law you had to bring in eleven persons who would swear—take an oath—that you had not made the covenant or incur the debt. These compurgators—or oath-helpers as they were known—were not witnesses. They might know nothing of the facts of the case. They simply were willing to bet their eternal soul that you were telling the truth. If you could get eleven such persons to take such a risk on your behalf, then your claim was adjudged to be credible, and you had an absolute defense.

Although there was no wager of law defense to agreements that were in writing and under seal, wager of law obviously put a crimp in the enforcement of informal promises, whether to pay a sum of money, deliver a good, or perform one's promise. A person could, however, also sue in the church or ecclesiastical courts for "breach of faith" (*laesio fidei*). If successful, religious sanctions might be levied, and these types of remedies were taken quite seriously. Breach of faith actions were not uncommon, and they drained legal fees away from the common law courts to the competing ecclesiastical courts. Because the common law judges made their living from these fees, they had an economic incentive to figure out a way to enforce informal promises more effectively.

🏛 1.3 The Rise of Assumpsit

Judges and lawyers seeking to enforce informal promissory commitments in the common law courts, while avoiding the defense of wager of law, began to focus on a fourth writ: the writ of *assumpsit*. The term assumpsit resembles the term "assumption," as in someone assuming or undertaking an obligation. Assumpsit became the focus of attention because it was based on the voluntary assumption of a duty to perform and, most importantly, because the age-old defense of wager of law was not available as a defense to a simple assumpsit involving an informal promise. The theory was that you could bring an action in assumpsit on an informal agreement if some or all performance had occurred and you were alleging that you were injured because the performance was not done correctly. Consider this example: You promise to build a house and because of the way you built it, the house collapses, causing injury to you and to your property.

Assumpsit was originally a writ that we would today describe as a tort. But remember that the distinct concepts of "contract" and "tort" were only devised in the nineteenth century as a replacement for the writ system. Speaking of either "tort" writs or "contract" writs before then is anachronistic. Writs falling under the category of *trespass* were actions for harms *directly* caused by the defendant's actions. Assumpsit was a writ that fell within the category called "trespass on the case"—which were actions for harms *indirectly* caused by the defendant's actions.

As a vehicle for enforcing contracts, assumpsit had two big disadvantages. First, you could not bring an action in assumpsit if the wrong done was covered by debt or detinue. A second disadvantage was the requirement of proving *malfeasance* or bad performance. Remember that assumpsit stressed (a) the wrongful infliction of injury, (b) caused by the defective performance of the defendant. Consequently, assumpsit required malfeasance—that is the performance must have begun and been defective.

The requirement of part performance or *mal*performance explains why there was no wager of law defense to assumpsit. Wager of law was based on a sworn denial that one made a promise to perform, which was backed up by the oath helpers. Partial performance of a promise, however, was excellent evidence that the promise had been made. You could hardly deny that you promised to build a house after constructing it defectively. In other words, the requirement of part performance, or performance that was somehow inadequate, served an important *evidentiary function*. If you partially performed, there was little doubt that an agreement of some kind did exist. Nevertheless, the second big obstacle to using assumpsit for ordinary breaches of contract was that there was no action available for *non*feasance—that is, the complete failure to perform one's promise.

By 1530 the restriction that only misfeasance (or negligence) could be acted upon had been abandoned, making nonperformance of an informal agreement actionable as well. The theoretical argument made by lawyers, and finally accepted by judges, was that you could be just as harmed by a complete lack of performance as you were by a partial, but defective performance. Then, in

Slade's case (1602) it was held that the complainant could choose either debt or assumpsit as a cause of action. This effectively did away with the action of debt to enforce informal agreements and, eventually, formal agreements as well.

After 1602, assumpsit became the principal way of bringing a suit for breach of informal contracts. Instead of suing on the debt owed or goods retained, you sued on the promise to pay the debt owed or to deliver the goods. The lucrative business of enforcing breach of faith actions in the ecclesiastical courts was wiped out. And, as parties seeking the enforcement of informal agreements selected assumpsit instead of debt, detinue, or covenant, the traditional defense of wager of law eventually died out as well.

▨ 1.4 The Doctrinal Implications of this Story

The story of the rise of the writ of assumpsit is important background to understanding two contract law doctrines that remain with us to this day.

First, when the defense of wager of law to the enforcement of informal promises was eliminated, there quickly arose the problem of fraudulent claims of promises that had never really been made. This led to Parliament passing—in 1677—a bill known as the *Statute of Frauds,* which required that, to be enforced, certain specified promises had to be in writing (although not under seal), thereby restoring some of the formality that had previously accompanied the writs of debt and detinue. Every state today still has a statute of frauds that takes much the same form as the original.

Second, with actions based on promises supplanting actions based on property, there arose a need to identify *which* promises would be enforced and which would not. After all, the action of assumpsit could conceivably apply to any informal promise the nonperformance of which caused injury. In formal agreements, lawyers had long cited the "considerations" or reasons for the making of a contract. From this practice, common law courts developed what came to be known as the *doctrine of consideration* to define the promises that were legally actionable based on the reasons why the promise was made. Although its content has changed, students must still struggle with understanding the modern doctrine of consideration.

Both the Statute of Frauds and the doctrine of consideration have led to countless theoretical, doctrinal, and practical problems ever since they were devised to handle the problems created by the rise of assumpsit.

▨ 1.5 Law and Equity

The distinction between law and equity originated long before the rise of assumpsit, dating back at least to the ancient Greeks. In Book V of the *Nicomachean Ethics*,[2] Aristotle identifies "the equitable" as "a corrective of what is legally just." The reason why the law requires correction by equity is "that all law is universal, but there are some things about which it is not possible to speak correctly in universal terms." When "it is necessary to speak in universal terms but impossible to do so correctly, the law takes the majority of cases, fully realizing that it misses the mark." In those situations in which "the case at issue happens to fall outside the universal formula," Aristotle described "equity" as rectifying "the omission and mistake of the lawgiver due to the generality of his statement. Such a rectification corresponds to what the lawgiver himself would have enacted if he had known (of this particular case)."

The English legal system reflected the distinction between law and equity by developing two different court systems. The common law courts were considered to be courts *of law* that adjudicated the rights of the parties before them, based on general rules and principles.

---

2. ARISTOTLE, THE NICHOMACHEAN ETHICS 141–42 (Martin Ostwald, ed., Prentice Hall, 1999).

Side-by-side with this system, the Chancellor of England employed the royal authority of the King to dispense "equity" in cases where he deemed the remedies available at law to be inadequate. Eventually, a regular Court of Chancery was established to hear pleas for relief from the rules of the common law. Thus, not only were the common law courts in competition with the ecclesiastical courts of the Church of England, so too were they in competition with the Chancery courts.

The courts of law and equity exercised different powers because of their differing types of authority. The common law judges issued legal *judgments* identifying the rights of the parties before them. For example, the judgment that A owed B $500; or A rather than B owned a piece of land. The enforcement of these judgments was left to the parties to seek. Because the authority of the Chancery courts derived from the King, they could issue coercive *orders* and punish those who disobeyed by imprisonment for contempt.

The theoretical difference between courts of law and equity resulted in the following practical differences in their approaches to contract law that we will consider at greater length in the next chapter.

1. Remedies available at law were considered to be *the rule;* remedies in equity were considered *exceptional.*

2. Only the remedies given at law were available as a matter *of right.* In principle at least, the remedies given in equity were available only as a matter *of discretion* (although equity too became somewhat rule bound about when its exceptional relief would be granted).

3. The differing authority and powers of these legal systems explains the different remedies they enforced for breach of contract. Courts of law were limited to issuing judgments assessing *money damages.* Only Chancery courts of equity could order injunctive relief—especially injunctions commanding specific performance—and then hold a party in contempt and imprison him or her for failing to obey the injunction to perform.

4. All this meant that, in practice, equity provided remedies when the common law did not.

One way to understand the distinction between law and equity is that, where "law" provides a general rule, "equity" makes exceptions. But law has always recognized exceptions to its general rules. The defenses to contract we discuss in Chapter 6, for example, could each be considered exceptions to the general rule that bargained-for commitments are enforceable. So a more precise way to view the distinction might be that equity provides exceptions that cannot be reduced to a general rule. But even this does not reflect how equity was practiced. Chancery courts developed their own rules as to when they would intervene in a dispute and when they would refrain. So the line between law and equity was always in contention.

Maintaining a separate legal system to dispense equity often meant that parties had to go through years of litigation in one system only to be told to start over in the other. For this reason, by the end of the twentieth century, most jurisdictions had abolished the formal distinction between law and equity. Now most circuit court judges have a general jurisdiction to issue both legal judgments and equitable orders; however some jurisdictions still preserve law and chancery divisions that specialize in different forms of relief of the sort that used to be handled by distinct court systems. Yet even where this is not the case, every practitioner must still know the difference between legal and equitable relief because "equity" still defines exceptional relief, albeit relief that is now available in a single lawsuit *within* a unitary court system.

TWO

The Enforcement of Contracts

SUMMARY: Understanding the different ways to calculate money damages—the expectation, reliance, and restitution measures—is of great assistance in appreciating otherwise difficult-to-grasp doctrines such as promissory estoppel. The chapter begins by explaining the difference between legal relief in the form of money damages and equitable relief in the form of specific performance. It then discusses how to calculate money damages, the limits on what damages can be collected, and the availability of specific performance. Cases discussed include: *Hawkins v. McGee, Sullivan v. O'Connor, Shaheen v. Knight, Jacob & Youngs v. Kent, Groves v. Wunder, Peevyhouse v. Garland Coal Mining Company, Hadley v. Baxendale, Globe Refining Co. v. Landa Oil, Chicago Coliseum v. Jack Dempsey, Anglia Television v. Robert Reed*, and *Lumley v. Wagner*.

※ 2.1 Why Read about Contract Remedies Before Contract Formation?

Logic seems to suggest that one should read about how a contract is formed and broken before reading about what happens when a contract is breached. But deciding which promises are enforceable is influenced by the consequences of enforcement. Suppose that breach of contract resulted in the death penalty. Would that not influence which promises courts have held to be enforceable and which they have not? More importantly, there are different ways to calculate money damages. When we get to the doctrines on formation—especially the doctrine of promissory estoppel discussed in Chapter 4—it will be useful to already know about these different measures of damages. The fact that one measure rather than another is used to assess damages will provide important clues as to why or whether a promise was held to be enforceable. So we need to read about them first.

⁂ 2.2 Money Damages: The Presumptive *Form* of Remedy for Breach of Contract

There are two possible forms of relief: money damages and injunctive relief. Money damages consist of a judgment that the party in breach owes the other party a sum of money. (How one goes about actually enforcing the judgment and collecting that money is a matter that is beyond the scope of most contracts classes.) Injunctive relief is an order by a court that the party in breach must specifically perform or refrain from performing a particular act, or face possible jailing for contempt. As discussed in Chapter 1, judgments for money damages historically were considered *legal* relief available as a matter of right; coercive injunctions were considered *equitable* relief available as a matter of discretion, and these labels are still used. The basic structure of remedies for breach of contract is straightforward:

Money damages are the presumptive form of relief for breach of contract and are the remedy that *every party* has a right to receive.

Injunctions for specific performance, or to order an action not be performed, are exceptions that are only available if money damages are, for some reason, inadequate.

A claim for money damages raises two distinct legal issues:

1. how should the amount of money damages be computed?

2. Do any limitations on the availability of money damages apply?

   We will examine these issues in the next two sections.

🕮 2.3 Money Damages

When assessing money damages, a host of issues arise. This section focuses on identifying the differing ways that money damages could be calculated, and why one measure is generally favored over the others.

2.3.1 Measures of Money Damages

In 1936, Lon Fuller and William R. Perdue, Jr. published their article *The Reliance Interest in Contract Damages*.[1] Harvard law professor Lon Fuller (1902–1978) was one of the giants of twentieth-century contract law theorists; William Perdue was his research assistant. Their hugely influential article identified three different ways to measure contract damages. These measures have since been incorporated into the *Restatement (Second) of Contracts*

1. *Expectation:* The amount of money it would take to put the victim of the breach in the same position as the victim would have been *had the contract been performed.*
2. *Reliance:* The amount of money it would take to return the victim of the breach to the position the victim would have been in *had the contract not been made.*
3. *Restitution:* The amount of money it would take to return the party in breach to the position the breaching party would have

---

1. Lon L. Fuller & William R. Perdue, Jr., *The Reliance Interest in Contract Damages* (Part 1), 46 YALE L.J. 52 (1936).

been in *had the contract not been made*—that is, make the breaching party discourge any benefits he or she received from entering into the contract.

The expectation interest is the presumptive measure of contract damages. It will be awarded unless one of the three limitations on damages—foreseeability, certainty, and avoidability—discussed in the next section applies; in which case a court would most likely award the reliance measure (although, as will be explained in section 2.4.2, some contend that, even then, the court is still awarding the expectation measure, as that measure should be understood). The restitution measure is most likely to be used when the contract is *rescinded* as a result of a successful defense of the sort discussed in Chapter 6.

2.3.2 The Expectation Measure of Contract Damages

A widely studied case in which the expectation interest was awarded is *Hawkins v. McGee*,[2] involving a doctor who failed to completely restore the plaintiff's scarred hand by a skin grafting procedure as the doctor had allegedly promised. The court there affirmed that the purpose of contract law is to "put the plaintiff in as good a position as he would have been in had the defendant kept his contract." How the court analyzed the jury instruction on the issue of damages computation is instructive. The instruction read as follows: "If you find the plaintiff entitled to anything, he is entitled to recover for what pain and suffering he has been made to endure and for what injury he has sustained over and above what injury he had before."

---

2. 84 N.H. 114, 146 Atl. 641 (1929).

The appellate judge interpreted this instruction to mean that the jury was erroneously told to consider two elements of damage: (1) the "pain and suffering due to the operation" and (2) the "positive ill effects of the operation upon the plaintiff's hand." The term, *damages*, he explained, means "compensation for breach measured in terms of the contract." The purpose of awarding damages is "to put the plaintiff in as good a position as he would have been in had the defendant kept his contract." The proper measure of recovery, therefore, "is based upon what the defendant should have given the plaintiff, not what the plaintiff has given the defendant or otherwise expended."

This last sentence refers to all three measures of contract damages identified by Fuller and Perdue: "what the defendant should have given the plaintiff" is a way of expressing the expectation measure; "what the plaintiff has given the defendant" is a way of expressing the restitution measure and that portion of the reliance measure which benefitted the party in breach; and "otherwise expended" is a reference to any additional reliance measure by the victim of the breach that did not benefit the other party.

The judge in *Hawkins* affirmed that the expectation measure is the normal measure of contract damages. Applied to the facts of the case, the "true measure of the plaintiff's damage" is the difference between the value to the plaintiff of a good hand; and the value to the plaintiff of the hand as it is, including "any incidental consequences fairly within the contemplation of the parties when they made their contract." (This last qualifier is a reference to the foreseeability limitation on contract damages discussed in section 2.4.) "Damages not thus limited," wrote the judge, "although naturally resulting, are not to be given."

Why did not the plaintiff's pain and suffering figure into the calculation of damages? The court stated that the "pain necessarily incidental to a serious surgical operation was a part of the contribution which the plaintiff was willing to make to his joint undertaking with the defendant to produce a good hand." Put another way, "[i]t represented a part of the price which he was willing to pay for a good hand, but it furnished no test of the value of a good hand or the difference between the value of the hand which the defendant promised and the one which resulted from the operation."

One of the reasons why *Hawkins v. McGee* seems problematic has nothing to do with the measure of damages that the court is attempting to apply to the facts. Rather it is the seeming arbitrariness of assigning any monetary value, however computed, to the damages done to a person's hand. In today's dollars, would this injury be worth $10,000? $100,000? $1,000,000? There seems to be no principled way to decide this. This is a question that goes to the very heart of a legal system that awards money damages as compensation for the violation of rights. I will address this issue below when discussing the "uncertainty" limitation on the collection of the expectation interest. For now, suffice it to say that this problem is pervasive throughout the law. Tort law awards monetary compensation for personal injuries every day. I suppose the least we can say on behalf of this remedy is that some compensation is better than none.

The case of *Sullivan v. O'Connor*[3] adopts a different approach than *Hawkins*. In *Sullivan*, the plaintiff, an entertainer, underwent plastic surgery to modify the prominence of her nose. As a result of the surgery, the appearance of her nose was greatly worsened. The trial judge instructed the jury that they could take into account the plaintiff's out-of-pocket damages plus compensation for her pain and suffering; the judge denied her plea to recover the difference in value between the nose as promised and the nose as it appeared after the operations. On appeal, the plaintiff withdrew her objection to the judge's denial and asked the court to uphold the jury's award of $13,500.

Judge Benjamin Kaplan, who had been a student of Karl Llewellyn and a distinguished Harvard law professor, upheld the jury verdict. Although his opinion rested, at least in part, on the plaintiff's waiver

---

3. 363 Mass. 579, 296 N.E.2d 183 (1973).

of her claim for more money, he also emphasized the questionable nature of the underlying claim against the doctor. In *Shaheen v. Knight*,[4] for example, a court refused to enforce a "warranty of cure" against a doctor who had allegedly promised that the operation would be successful because allowing claims based on such a promise was against public policy. In *Sullivan*, Judge Kaplan adopted a compromise position that allowed a cause of action for promises by physicians but limited the scope of damages. "The factors," he wrote, "which have made the cause of action somewhat suspect, also suggest moderation as to the breadth of the recovery that should be permitted."

Judge Kaplan also stressed the uncertainty of trying to measure the full expectation damage: "To attempt, moreover, to put a value on the condition that would or might have resulted, had the treatment succeeded as promised, may sometimes put an exceptional strain on the imagination of the fact finder." As will be shown in section 2.4.2, when expectation damages are uncertain, courts are said to switch to the reliance measure of damages. *Sullivan* can be understood as an example of this type of switch.

2.3.3 Why Favor the Expectation Measure?

Why do courts use the expectation measure rather than the reliance or restitution measures? After all, in tort law, courts try to restore a victim of a tort to the position the victim would have been in had the tort not been committed, which closely resembles the reliance measure. For some, it seems odd that contract damages are aimed at putting the victim in a better position than he or she would have been in had the victim not entered into the contract. Fuller and Perdue's article became famous for the paradoxical answer they gave to the question of why courts do this: Courts award the

---

4. 11 Pa. D. & C. 2d 41 (1957).

expectation measure, they claimed, to protect what they called the "reliance interest in contract damages."

Fuller and Perdue began their analysis by ruling out three alternative reasons for awarding an expected gain that a promisee had never possessed. The first is psychological: A breach of promise arouses in the promisee a sense of injury. Because the promisee has formed an attitude of expectancy, upon a breach the promisee feels *deprived* of something. Fuller and Perdue rejected this explanation because the law does not enforce all promises, and which promises are enforced does not depend on the degree of deprivation or resentment engendered by the breach.

The second reason is based on the *will* of the parties: If there has been a promise to pay $1000, the promisor is compelled to pay this sum because the agreement, which is the product of the will or intentions of the parties, calls for this payment. Fuller and Perdue rejected this explanation because most contracts say nothing about what should happen if they are breached, and the parties have no intention or will with respect to the measure of damages. (The exceptions are those contracts with liquidated damages clauses.) So it is vain to look to a will theory for a solution to the problem of measuring damages.

The third reason is what Fuller and Perdue called *economic* or *institutional*: The essence of a credit economy is to eliminate the distinction between present and future (promised) goods. Expectation of future values become, for purposes of trade, present values. An enforceable promise is a kind of property and a breach of promise does injury to that property. They reject this explanation as circular. A promise of future performance only has value because it is enforceable. The fact it is valued cannot, therefore, be used to justify its enforceability.

The reason for awarding the expectation interest Fuller and Perdue ultimately adopted is what they called *juristic*, but we would today call *policy*: Enforcement depends on some policy pursued by the courts or other lawmakers that yields better consequences than alternative measures. And the particular consequence they emphasized was the protection of the reliance "interest" of the promisee. They contended that reliance was better protected by computing damages according to the expectation measure than to the reliance measure.

Although the reliance measure is typically calculated by looking at the out-of-pocket expenditures of the promisee that were made in reliance on the promise, this does not reflect the promisee's true reliance interest, which consists of giving up the next most attractive alternative. For example, your true reliance cost for choosing admission to a particular law school was passing up the next most attractive acceptance you received. You gave up the opportunity to attend your second choice in reliance on the promise of admission of your higher choice. When selling your car, your reliance interest is the next best offer you passed up to accept the offer you did. The term economists use for this form of reliance loss is *opportunity costs.*

But the law does not compensate for opportunity costs because they are ephemeral and therefore hard to prove with certainty. (The certainty limitation on contract damages is examined below.) The next best opportunity forgone *never happened* and is therefore difficult to establish. For this reason, courts limit the reliance measure to demonstrable out-of-pocket expenses that may not equal the true reliance interest of the promisee. (Remember this, as it will be important in section 2.4.2.) The expectation interest is the value of the first best choice that was lost as a result of the breach. By awarding enough money to compensate for the loss of the expected gain, one is assured of awarding enough to compensate for the second best opportunity, which by assumption was worth less to the promisee. And, unlike opportunity costs, the first best opportunity is known to the court because it is the very performance promised in the contract.

Also, the protection of expectancy may more effectively deter breaches of contract because it may be a more severe sanction, and one that is easier to administer. By providing a higher and more reliable recovery than out-of-pocket reliance expenditures—and by fully compensating for opportunity costs—the expectation measure facilitates greater reliance by individuals upon each other, to the benefit of society.

For these reasons, Fuller and Perdue concluded that "[t]o encourage reliance we must therefore dispense with its proof." To the extent a promisee senses the "difficulties in proving reliance and subjecting it to pecuniary measurement," he "would hesitate to rely on a promise in any case where the legal sanction was of significance to him." For this reason, Fuller and Perdue conclude, "it has been found wise to make recovery on a promise independent of reliance," in two senses. First, "in some cases the promise is enforced though not relied on (as in the bilateral business agreement)," and second in some cases "recovery is not limited to the detriment incurred in reliance."

There are several possible responses to Fuller and Perdue's argument that the expectation measure is grounded on the reliance interest of the promisee. To begin with, just because the three alternative justifications may not, each considered on its own, provide a sufficient justification for awarding the expectation measure, this does not mean these reasons ought to be dismissed as justifications altogether. A reason for a particular rule that is not dispositive standing alone, may still be an argument in favor of that rule, when combined with other reasons that support the same conclusion.

Furthermore, although Fuller and Perdue were correct that most contracts do not stipulate the measure of damages, this does not mean that no measure is silently intended or willed by the parties. If the expectation measure is known to be what the courts typically award, the parties do not need to mention the issue of damages in their contracts unless they want to limit or expand the measure below or above the expectation measure default rule. In other words, they may accept the expectation measure by default the way most accept the default margins automatically set by their word-processing program. Relatedly, courts refuse to enforce what they deem to be penalty clauses in contracts that stipulate an amount of damages above the expectation measure. Given this, there is no reason for parties to waste time bargaining over inserting in their agreement an unenforceable clause to increase damages.

More fundamentally, Fuller and Perdue accepted the view that the expectation interest is puzzling because, unlike damages in torts, "we 'compensate' the plaintiff by giving him something he never had," which they characterize as "a queer kind of 'compensation.'" But there is another way of looking at this matter. A tort can be conceived of as violating the preexisting rights of the victim. A contract can be conceived as *altering* or changing the preexisting rights of both parties. Later, when a breach occurs, it too is violating the preexisting rights of the victim *as modified* by the contract in the very same way as tortious conduct does. The difference is that, unlike a tort, the contract that precedes a breach changed the entitlements of the victim, which is why a breach did indeed deprive the promisee of something to which he or she was already entitled.

Nor is it circular to view the preexisting entitlements arising from the contract, which are themselves a product of a legal system, as justification for a legal entitlement to the expectation measure. After all, the "loss" for which a tort victim is compensated is also assessed with reference to the preexisting legal entitlements of the victim of a tort. Indeed, one reason a legal system defines "rights" or entitlements is to enable it to differentiate between a compensable loss and other sorts of harms for which a person may not claim compensation from a particular defendant.

For example, if I become sick and come to you to pay my medical bills, you may well ask: "Why me? Of all the persons in the world, why should *I* be the one who pays your medical bill?" But if you are an insurance company, the answer is "because you promised to pay in a legally enforceable contract." The contract between the policy holder and the insurance company changes the normal or preexisting rights and duties of the parties by giving one party a new entitlement to have his or her medical bills paid by the other party. That this is a legally enforceable commitment entails that there be a remedy for breach. The expectation measure is an attempt to assess money damages to "compensate" for the deprivation of the right that was created by the contract.

Of course, this argument assumes that, by entering into a contract, the parties are exercising a legally effective power to alter their respective rights. Ironically, this was a view that was later defended by none other than Lon Fuller in his equally famous 1941 article, *Consideration and Form*.[5] "Among the basic conceptions of contract law the most pervasive and indispensable is the principle of private autonomy," wrote Fuller. By "private autonomy" he meant "that the law views private individuals as possessing a power to effect, within certain limits, changes in their legal relations. The man who conveys property to another is exercising this power; so is the man who enters a contract." In this article, Fuller equated the power of private parties to make law for themselves with the power of the legislature. "This power of the individual to effect changes in his legal relations with others is comparable to the power of a legislature." Indeed, it is "only a kind of political prejudice which causes us to use the word 'law' in one case and not in the other . . . , a prejudice which did not deter the Romans from applying the word *lex* to the norms established by private agreement." There is nothing "queer" about compensating for the "lost" value of a right that resulted from the exercise of this private law making power.

2.3.4 The Concept of Efficient Breach

Another reason that has been given for awarding the expectation interest is based the concept of *efficient breach*. A party will have an incentive to breach a contract when doing so makes that party better off than performing. For example, a seller might have found a

---

5. Lon L. Fuller, *Consideration and Form*, 41 COLUM. L. REV. 799 (1941).

second buyer for a good who is willing to pay more than the original contract price with the first buyer. As long as the seller is required to put the first buyer in as good a position as the buyer would have been had the contract been performed, then the first buyer is, by assumption, no worse off. Yet the seller is better off because he can pocket the difference between the amount he must pay the first buyer and the higher amount he collects from the second buyer. Under these circumstances, therefore, a breach can be *efficient* insofar as one party (the seller) is made better off, the other party (buyer one) is no worse off, and the good ends up in the possession of the person (buyer two) who values it most highly (as evidenced by the willingness to pay a higher price).

The suggestion that it is all right for a party to breach a contract so long as the breaching party monetarily compensates the victim of the breach for its lost expectancy challenges the intuitions of most students. Perhaps this is one reason why contracts professors like to teach efficient breach whether or not they personally agree with the argument. Understanding why the efficient breach argument is right or wrong reveals a lot about why we compensate for breaches of contract, the limits of the remedy of money damages, and when we might compel specific performance instead. Some criticisms of the efficient breach argument will be considered when the equitable remedy of specific performance is discussed in sections 2.3.6 and 2.5.2.

2.3.5 How to Compute the Expectation Measure

Having identified the expectation measure as the presumptive measure of contract damages, we need to know how to compute these damages. The *Restatement 2nd*, section 347 provides that "the injured party has a right to damages based on his expectation interest as measured by (a) the loss in the value to him of the other party's performance caused by its failure or deficiency, plus (b) any other loss, including incidental or consequential loss, caused by the breach, less (c) any cost or other loss that he has avoided by not having to perform." In short:

$$\text{The expectation measure} =$$
$$\text{Loss in value} + \text{Other loss} - \text{Cost avoided} - \text{Loss avoided}$$

Typically, the *loss in value* is the market price of obtaining the lost performance from another provider. If the contract calls for the sale of a good for $1000 that would cost $1200 to replace from another source, then the promisee would collect $1200. If the price of the substitute was $800, then this would be the loss in value even though the contract price was $1000. To the loss in value would then be added any *other loss* incurred, such as the extra costs of obtaining a substitute performance or any incidental reliance expenditures that are rendered worthless because of the failure of the other party to perform (subject to the limitations discussed in section 2.4).

In other words, the expectancy is computed by establishing the lost value of the promised performance and then adding any *incidental* reliance costs. We ignore the cost to the promisee of performing his end of the deal under the contract. For example, when I promise to buy your car for $10,000 and pay you the money, I cannot collect both for the lost value of the car *and* also my $10,000 out-of-pocket cost. Fuller and Perdue called the cost of performing one's duties under the contract one's *essential* reliance. "Certain acts of reliance are in a loose sense the 'price' of whatever benefits the contract may involve for the plaintiff," they explained. If these essential reliance costs are less than the loss in value, then enforcing the contract by awarding the expectation interest results in a net gain or profit. If the essential reliance costs are greater than loss in value, then the contract is a losing one, but not because the breach took place. "We will not in a suit for reimbursement for losses incurred in reliance on a contract," they wrote, "knowingly put the plaintiff in a better position than he would have occupied had the contract been fully performed."

But compensating for "other loss" that *was* caused by the breach (in addition to the loss in value) is another matter. Consider the 1664 case of *Nurse v. Barnes*,[6] in which the defendant promised to give the plaintiff the use of certain premises for a period of six months in return for a rent of £10. Relying on this promise the plaintiff laid in a stock of goods. The defendant then failed to perform his promise. Because his expenditures for goods were thus rendered useless, the plaintiff lost £500 which he was permitted to recover from the defendant. As Fuller and Perdue explained, "[h]ere there was nothing to indicate that the plaintiff entered a losing bargain; on the contrary it was expressly found that the lease was worth just what the plaintiff agreed to pay for it." The £500 spent for the stock of goods was not part of the performance required of the plaintiff under the contract as the price for receiving the defendant's performance in return. Therefore, it would be compensated under the Restatement formula as *other loss*.

To put the promisee in as good a position as the promisee would have been had the contract been performed also requires subtracting from the loss in value plus other loss whatever costs or losses the promisee avoided. The "cost avoided" is that portion of the promisee's *essential* reliance that was not paid. Suppose a promisee is paying $1000 for a good that would cost $1200 to replace but at the time of the breach has only paid $300 of the contract price with the balance of $700 payable on delivery. When the promisor breaches, the promisee thus *avoids* the essential reliance *cost* of $700, and this amount would then be deducted from the *loss in value* of $1200 to yield an expectation amount of $500 ($1200 + 0 − $700 − 0). If this $700 were not deducted, the promisee would be that amount better off than if the contract were fully performed because only $300 would have been paid for a good worth $1200, whereas the promise had contractually agreed to pay $1000.

---

6. Sir T. Raym 77 (King's Bench, 1664).

In the next section, we shall see that a party may not collect damages for losses that he or she might have reasonably avoided. Suppose that the promisor agrees to pay $10,000 for a car from a private seller. After making a $100 deposit, the buyer breaches. The "loss in value" to the seller is the $10,000 purchase price less the $100 deposit or $9900. But the seller remains in possession of the automobile that the seller was going to transfer to the buyer under the terms of the agreement. Suppose the car can be resold to another buyer for $9000. This amount of "loss avoided" needs to be deducted from the $9900, or the seller will be in a better position than he would have been had the promisor paid the $10,000 and taken delivery of the car as agreed. If the additional cost to the seller of making the second sale was $50, then this is an "other loss" caused by the breach. Therefore, the amount of recovery would be $9900 (loss in value) + $50 (other loss) – cost avoided ($0) – loss avoided ($9000) = $950.

Note that each of the examples in this section involve a sale of goods and would therefore be computed with the rules provided by the Uniform Commercial Code (UCC).[7] These rules reach the same result but are more specific depending on whether the buyer or seller is in breach, and they address additional complexities that can arise in such cases.

2.3.6 Subjective Cost and Money Damages

Measuring damages to *compensate* monetarily for *loss* sounds far more precise than it is. Although, as shown below, some damages such as lost profits or opportunity costs are considered too uncertain to assess, it is important to remember the problem of uncertainty is

---

7. *See, e.g.,* § 2-703 ("Seller's Remedies in General"); § 2-708 ("Seller's Damages for Non-Acceptance or Repudiation"); § 2-709 ("Action for the Price"); § 2-711 ("Buyer's Remedies in General").

far more pervasive than this. *Any* assessment of legal damages attempts to quantify or objectify that which is actually *subjective* and essentially unmeasurable, especially the degree to which the benefit of a bargain to a party exceeds its costs, which is most commonly referred to as a *profit.*

Profits are normally thought of as objective—that is, the difference between the value expected and the essential reliance costs required to receive that value. In his treatise, *Human Action,*[8] economist Ludwig von Mises disputed this. What is called *gain* or *profit,* is the "difference between the value of the price paid (costs incurred) and that of the goal attained." Mises famously contended that a profit "is purely subjective, it is an increase in the acting man's happiness, it is a psychical phenomenon that can be neither measured nor weighed. There is a more and a less in the removal of uneasiness felt; it cannot be established and determined in an objective way."

Moreover, as mentioned in section 2.3.3, the true cost of any choice is not any out-of-pocket expenses but the opportunities forgone, which are both subjective and ephemeral. Cost is *subjective* because it depends entirely on the particular situation or alternatives that are available to an actor at the time of the action and the valuation placed on these alternatives by the actor. Cost is *ephemeral* because the alternative opportunities were mere potentialities; they never actually happened.

Mises also noted that how strongly we value a particular activity or object is *unmeasurable.* How much I value something cannot be directly compared to how much you value the same thing. When we measure length, we can divide the object being measured into standard units and add them up. But our feelings and preferences cannot be unitized in this way, because there is no standard against which the intensity of our desires can be measured. "Preferring always means to love or desire *a* more than *b.* Just as there is no

---

8. Ludwig von Mises, Human Action, 3rd ed. (Henry Regnery Co. 1966), p. 97. 204–205.

standard and no measurement of sexual love, of friendship and sympathy, and of aesthetic enjoyment, so there is no measurement of the value of commodities." For example, "[i]f a man exchanged two pounds of butter for a shirt, all that we can assert with regard to this transaction is that he—at the instant of the transaction and under the conditions which this instant offers to him—prefers one shirt to two pounds of butter."

It makes no literal sense to say I like chocolate chip ice cream, "twice as much" as you, since there is no unit of measurement to measure your love of ice cream or mine. "[P]sychic quantities can only be felt," Mises explained. "They are entirely personal, and there is no semantic means to express their intensity and to convey information about them to other people. There is no method available to construct a unit of value." When she was little, my daughter used to say "I love you all around the world and a thousand." This was as good a way to "measure" her affection as any other, but it is a metaphorical rather than truly a quantitative measurement.

Although we cannot measure our desires, we can often rank order them. Desiring one thing more than another is called a preference. For example, at one moment I may prefer to have a scoop of chocolate chip ice cream to a dollar in my wallet. After I have eaten it, I prefer keeping the other dollar in my wallet to having another scoop. If we could not order our preferences we could never improve our subjective well-being by making choices.

Economists distinguish two kinds of preferences: stated preferences and demonstrated preferences. *Stated* preferences are what we *say* we prefer; for example, I say, "I would give a dollar or a hundred dollars for a scoop of chocolate chip ice cream." Preferences are constantly in flux so stated preferences are rarely reliable even when they are sincere. There is little, if any, way for an observer to know whether I am stating my preferences accurately until I am given a chance to demonstrate my preferences by actually making a voluntary exchange. *Demonstrated* preferences are those that are reflected by our actions. For example, the act of exchanging one dollar for a scoop of chocolate chip ice cream demonstrates my preference for a scoop of chocolate chip ice cream over my one dollar.

The contract prices and terms to which the parties have agreed represent their demonstrated preferences. We know that at the time they agreed, each party valued what it was to receive more highly than what it was to give up in return, which is what motived each to enter into the exchange. (Although when facts exist to support contract defenses involving lack of capacity or obtaining consent by improper means—discussed in Chapter 6—this may not truly be the case.)

Just like a tort, a breach of contract can be considered a *forced exchange* of a party's rights. The victim of a breach is deprived of something to which the victim is entitled without the victim's consent. When we try to rectify any forced exchange by awarding money damages, we are trying to substitute an amount of money for what was taken without the benefit of a demonstrated preference as to its value to the victim. There is no reliable substitute for the demonstrated preferences revealed by a free exchange. How much did the plaintiff in *Hawkins v. McGee* value a repaired hand in monetary terms? How much did the plaintiff in *Sullivan v. O'Connor* value the anticipated improvement to her nose? Because a free exchange is no longer possible, these questions are literally unanswerable.

Given that, in our legal system, the presumptive form of relief is money damages, what does the problem of subjective cost suggest for contract damages? For one thing, it supports calculating money damages using the expectancy measure. Because the promisee valued the performance more highly than any known alternative (or else the promisee would have chosen the alternative), giving a monetary substitute for this value is more likely to compensate the promisee for his or her next most desirable alternative and preserve the subjective benefit expected by the promisee than will awarding a substitute for the promisee's reliance.

But the moral of this story is that we must never forget how deficient this type of remedy truly is, which is one reason why the concept of "efficient breach"—described above in section 2.3.4—challenges our intuitions. The concept of efficient breach assumes that the victim of the breach is fully compensated by being paid an amount of money equal to the expectation measure. But this is not always the case, and we cannot be entirely confident when it is and when it is not.

Because of the uncertainty of compensating for the loss of a subjective value with money, both contract law and torts adopt surrogates with the aim of avoiding complete arbitrariness. So, for example, one might collect the *market value* of a particular good. A market price represents the demonstrated subjective preferences of others who entered into their own exchanges at a particular price. Using this measure assumes that the victim of a breach or a tort is typical, unless shown to be otherwise. Yet sometimes this assumption is not the case. For example, if someone preferred the market value of his house to continuing to own it, he would sell. This means that, at any given time, many if not most home owners subjectively value their homes more than they value the price they could get in the market. If their home was destroyed, awarding the market price would undercompensate them.

Then why rely on a surrogate such as market price? When administering a system of justice, we must be concerned with overcompensation—which constitutes an injustice to the party in breach—as well as undercompensation. But, given that actual losses are subjective, we should be willing to adjust the damages upward when special circumstances are shown that would distinguish a particular promisee from other persons in the market. Perhaps the promisee's costs were different. This will be the case, for example, when there was no ready substitute available to the promisee on the market.

Although the subjectivity of costs generally supports the existing rule favoring the expectation measure of contract damages, the uncertainty of reducing subjective costs to an amount of money also supports the enforcement of *liquidated damage clauses* in which parties specify the damages for breach. Although such clauses are enforceable today, courts still suspiciously scrutinize them to ensure that they are not penalties for nonperformance. The ready enforcement of liquidated damage clauses encourages the parties themselves to reveal or demonstrate their subjective preferences with respect to money damages at the time of formation before any forced exchange has occurred.

Finally, the subjectivity of costs argues in favor of changing contract law to make specific performance, rather than money damages, the presumptive form of relief at the option of the promisee. Giving a party the actual performance that was promised, rather than a monetary substitute, where this is what the promisee still wants to receive, would better ensure that any subjective value attached to the performance would be protected. Specific performance will be discussed in section 2.5.

2.3.7 Measuring Damages by Cost of Completion or Diminution in Value

The expectation measure is the amount of money it would take to put the promisee in as good a position as the promisee would have been in had the contract been performed as promised. Sometimes there is more than one way to do this. Ordinarily, a party may seek the amount of money it would take to finish the promised performance so he ends up with what he bargained for. This is the *cost of completion*. However, a few cases have instead awarded the difference between the market value of what was promised and what was delivered so the promisee is made whole for his loss. This is the *diminution in value*. These two approaches reflect two different conceptions of the expectation measure: what would provide exactly what was promised versus what would compensate for the reduction of value because of incomplete performance. Ordinarily, these two measures should be about the same. In three commonly taught cases, however, they diverged, giving rise to differing results and conflicting intuitions.

In *Jacob & Youngs v. Kent,*[9] a builder failed to install Reading pipe—the brand of iron plumbing pipe that had been specified by the homeowner's architect in the contract. When the homeowner refused to pay the balance due under the contract, the builder sued. The court found for the builder on the ground that the cost to demolish the walls of the building to replace the pipe was grossly in excess of any diminution in the value of the house caused by installing the wrong brand of pipe. "It is true that in most cases the cost of replacement is the measure," wrote Judge Cardozo. "The owner is entitled to the money which will permit him to complete, unless the cost of completion is grossly and unfairly out of proportion to the good to be attained. When that is true, the measure is the difference in value."

The facts of *Jacob & Youngs* are peculiar. So far as we can tell, the architect specified Reading pipe in the contract, not because the homeowner attached any subjective value to owning this particular brand of pipe, but as a standard by which the quality of the pipe could be assured. As it turned out, there seems to have been no difference whatsoever between the quality of the Reading pipe specified and the Cohoes-brand pipe that was installed. So, whether considered objectively or subjectively, there was apparently no real damage at all. Relations between the builder and homeowner had become highly acrimonious, and it may well be that the court suspected that the homeowner seized on the "trivial" error to justify withholding the significant balance due the builder (amounting to about 5 percent of the entire contract). Given the facts of the case, there is little reason to believe that the owner would have used the amount of money saved on the house to replace the pipe. One suspects that, had there been any demonstrable reason to prefer Reading pipe to pipe made by Cohoes, the court might well have awarded the amount it would have taken to replace the pipe.

---

9. 230 N.Y. 239, 129 N.E. 889 (1921).

In *Groves v. John Wunder Co.*,[10] Groves leased some land to Wunder. Wunder was to pay $105,000 to use the land and take sand and gravel from it but was supposed to leave the property at a "uniform grade, substantially the same as the grade now existing at the roadway." After removing only "the richest and best of the gravel," Wunder surrendered the premises, not substantially at the grade required by the contract "nor at any uniform grade." Instead, the ground was "broken, rugged, and uneven." To complete its performance, 288,495 cubic yards of overburden would need to be excavated, taken from the premises, and deposited elsewhere, at a cost in excess of $60,000. If, however, the defendant had fully performed, the reasonable value of the property would have been only $12,160. The Supreme Court of Minnesota reversed the trial court's award of the diminution of value, and awarded the cost of completion. It distinguished *Jacob & Youngs* on the grounds that, in that case, the breach was inadvertent and there had been substantial performance. In this case, the breach was deliberate and there was no substantial performance.

Another difference between the cases may well affect our intuitions about the result. In *Jacob & Youngs*, there is no reason to believe that the cost of the Cohoes pipe was any less than that of the Reading pipe. So the builder incurred its full cost of performance contemplated by the performance and was not enriched by its breach. In *Groves*, the lessor obtained the full benefit of the lease at a greatly reduced cost than it had bargained for. "To diminish damages recoverable against him in proportion as there is presently small value in the land would favor the faithless contractor," stated the court; "[i]t would also ignore and so defeat plaintiff's right to contract and build for the future. To justify such a course would require more of the prophetic vision than judges possess."

---

10. 205 Minn. 163, 286 N.W. 235 (1939).

Finally, consider *Peevyhouse v. Garland Coal Mining Company*,[11] where a coal-mining company leased land from a farmer and his wife whose home was adjacent to the excavation. The farmer had bargained for the mining company to fully restore the land but, after strip-mining the coal, the company failed to restore the land. Whereas the cost of completion was about $29,000, the diminution in the value of the land was put at $300. In awarding the lesser amount, the Supreme Court of Oklahoma rejected the approach of *Groves v. Wunder.* "[U]nder the 'cost of performance' rule, plaintiffs might recover an amount about nine times the total value of their farm. Such would seem to be 'unconscionable and grossly oppressive damages, contrary to substantial justice.'" The court contended that "it can hardly be denied that if plaintiffs here are permitted to recover under the 'cost of performance' rule, they will receive a greater benefit from the breach than could be gained from full performance."

The court also accepted the coal company's argument that spending $29,000 to obtain a benefit worth $300 constituted "economic waste," an argument the court in *Groves* had rejected. But the economic-waste argument is a red herring. Although it could be considered wasteful to spend $29,000 worth of scarce resources to obtain a $300 benefit, paying the Peeveyhouses $29,000 is simply a transfer of wealth. No resources are "wasted" by the payment of money damages. One party is simply made wealthier and the other less wealthy. The $29,000 worth of resources it would take to reclaim the land will only be expended if the Peeveyhouses subjectively value the improvement to the land next door to where they live more than they value saving the money or spending it in another way. But if they do this, then it would not be economically wasteful, notwithstanding the trivial increase in the market value, because the value of the expenditure to the Peeveyhouses is greater than the

---

11. 382 P.2d 109 (1963).

price paid for restoration. The market value of the farm is simply a guess based on other transactions about how much someone else would pay for the restored farm land. It does not measure the subjective benefits to the Peevyhouses of restoring the adjacent land.

Of course, the Peeveyhouses could *state* that they prefer the restored land to the $29,000; they would only *demonstrate* their preference by actually spending the money this way. They may not even know what they prefer until they actually have to incur the subjective cost of their choice. The court's claim that the Peeveyhouses "will receive a greater benefit from the breach than could be gained from full performance," however, assumes that they will subjectively value the $29,000 in excess of the subjective benefit they will receive from restoring the land and, consequently, they will keep the money. But even if this is true, no economic waste will result so long as the Peeveyhouses have a choice of whether to spend the money on restoring the land or keeping it to spend on something else they value more highly. The only way to discover whether this is true, however, is by awarding the $29,000 to the Peeveyhouses and seeing how they choose to spend it.

This reveals that there are five potentially conflicting factors that affect our intuitions about these cases, which is why they stimulate interesting classroom discussion: (1) victims of breach of contract are ordinarily entitled to sufficient funds to obtain substitute performance from elsewhere; (2) no one contemplates they will have to pay an amount in damages that grossly exceeds a trivial diminution in value; (3) contract breakers should not be enriched as a result of their breach; (4) but neither should victims of a breach knowingly be put in a better position than they would have been had the contract been performed; and yet (5) parties should be compensated for their loss of subjective value even where it exceeds market value. Our intuitions matter because they reflect the tacit assumptions of contracting parties in the absence of an express clause to the contrary.

Here is a possible damage rule that attempts to reconcile these potentially conflicting intuitions and thereby capture the tacit understanding of the parties:

1. The normal expectation measure is the amount of money it would take to complete performance.
2. However, where the cost of completion greatly exceeds the diminution of market value, the diminution of market value will be awarded, unless
   a. The contract expressly stipulates the cost of completion measure even when it greatly exceeds the diminution in value; or
   b. The victim of the breach is likely to attach subjective value to the complete performance; or
   c. The party in breach would gain the full benefit of the contract while avoiding its essential reliance cost.

How would this rule apply to the three cases just discussed? Assuming substantial performance had occurred (which may be questionable in *Groves*), in all of these cases the cost of completion greatly exceeded the diminution in value caused by the breach; in none of the cases was there an expressed clause to address the proper measure of damages. So the analysis would shift to the issues of subjective detriment to the victim of the breach or benefit to the party in breach. In *Jacob & Youngs v. Kent*, the owner attached no subjective value to the specified pipe, and the installed pipe cost the same as the specified pipe, so this case was rightly decided. In *Groves v. Wunder*, although there is no evidence that the victim of the breach attached a subjective value to the restored land, the breaching party did not expend what they were required to under the contract and were therefore benefitted by their breach, so this case was rightly decided. In *Peevyhouse v. Garland Coal Mining*, the Peeveyhouses likely attached a subjective value to receiving the promised performance, *and* the mining company did not expend what the contract required therefore it benefitted from its breach—so for two reasons this case was wrongly decided.

Separating the different considerations this way helps to isolate our intuitions about these three puzzling cases. Of course, if you object to any part of this proposed damage rule, you would decide these cases differently. For example, according to an "efficient breach" approach, it is perfectly all right that the promisor is made better off by avoiding its essential reliance costs so long as the victim of the breach is made whole. If you accept this argument, then you would omit the above (2)(b) from your analysis and would then conclude that both *Groves* and *Peeveyhouse* were wrongly decided. Lacking any proof of subjective value, the cost of completion was the wrong measure of damages in *Groves*, whereas in *Peeveyhouse* the probable existence of subjective value made the diminution of market value the wrong measure of the expectancy.

With all this in mind, we now turn our attention to the three limitations on the recovery of expectation damages. The concept of subjectivity of value will play a role in understanding some of these doctrines as well as many others discussed throughout the rest of this book.

✄ 2.4 Three Limitations on Contract Damages

The right of the promisee to collect damages that would put the promisee in as good a position as he would have been in had the contract been performed is limited in three ways:

1. The "other loss" actually incurred must not have been remote or unforeseeable.
2. The damages claimed (whether "loss in value" or "other loss") must be certain enough to be capable of calculation.
3. The losses incurred must not have been avoidable by the promisee.

Note that, if any of these three circumstances are shown to exist, the promisee could be left in a worse position than if the contract had not been made, but there are reasons why contract law may nevertheless allow this result. We will consider each of these limitations and their rationales in turn.

2.4.1 Remoteness or Foreseeability of Harm

The first limitation on contract damages was mentioned in *Hawkins v. McGee* where the court announced that the "true measure of the plaintiff's damage" is the difference between the value to the plaintiff of a good hand; and the value to the plaintiff of the hand as it is, including "any incidental consequences *fairly within the contemplation of the parties when they made their contract.*" This limitation on contract damages dates back to one of the most famous of all contracts cases—the 1854 English case of *Hadley v. Baxendale.*[12]

In *Hadley*, the plaintiffs owned a mill in which they used a steam engine to clean grain, grind it into meal, and dress it into flour, sharps, and brans. The steam engine's crank shaft broke, preventing the engine from working. The plaintiffs ordered a new crank shaft from W. Joyce & Co. of Greenwich. To make a new shaft, W. Joyce & Co. needed the old shaft as a model so the new one would fit the other parts of the engine. The defendant was a common carrier of goods and chattels for hire between Gloucester and Greenwich. The plaintiffs' employee went to the defendant's office to arrange its delivery to Greenwich. He told the defendant's clerk that the mill was stopped and that the shaft must be sent immediately. When asked when the shaft would be taken, the clerk replied that, if the shaft was brought to them by noon, it would be delivered to Greenwich the following day. The next day, before noon, the plaintiff's employee delivered the broken shaft to the defendant's office

---

12. 9 Ex. 341. 156 Eng. Rep. 145 (1854).

and paid £2, 4s. for the carriage. The defendant's clerk was told that a special entry should be made, if required, to hasten its delivery. The delivery of the shaft to Greenwich was delayed. As a result, the plaintiff received the new shaft five days later than it otherwise would have.

The court held that the £300 worth of lost profits and wages paid during the shut down—what the *Restatement* calls "other loss"—that resulted from the delay were not recoverable. In reaching this conclusion, the court announced what came to be known as the "two rules" of *Hadley v. Baxendale.* "Where two parties have made a contract which one of them has broken, the damages which the other party ought to receive in respect of such breach of contract should be," first, "such as may fairly and reasonably be considered either arising naturally, i.e. according to the usual course of things, from such breach of contract itself," or second, "such as may reasonably be supposed to have been in the contemplation of both parties, at the time they made the contract, as the probable result of the breach of it."

The court then explained how the second rule can expand liability beyond the ordinary or "natural" results of a breach to include losses that are extraordinary. If "the special circumstances under which the contract was actually made were communicated by the plaintiffs to the defendants," then such unusual circumstances would become "known to both parties" and therefore "the damages resulting from the breach of such a contract, which they would reasonably contemplate, would be the amount of injury which would ordinarily follow from a breach of contract under these special circumstances so known and communicated."

In sum, to be recoverable, the damages incurred by the promisee must be *foreseeable* to the promisor. And there are two ways that damages are foreseeable. First, they are the ordinary or natural result of such a breach. Second, they are unusual, but the breaching party was put on notice that they might result. In either event, these damages are then said to be within the contemplation of the parties at the time of formation.

There is some dispute in the reports of this decision on what exactly the defendant's clerk was told by the plaintiff's employee about the consequences of delay. The reported facts seem to indicate that the clerk was put on notice that the mill was shut down, but the appellate judges seemed to doubt that the communication was adequate to convey the information that the mill was shut down on account of the broken shaft. Richard Danzig has speculated that this discrepancy may have occurred because limited liability corporations had not yet arisen and the owners of a company such as the shipping firm would be personally liable for its obligations. Indeed, the suit was against Baxendale, the owner, not his firm. Danzig speculates that, to shield owners from such expansive liability because of their agent's misconduct, the court was skeptical about whether the information given an agent of the firm was sufficient to put the firm on notice that so substantial a damage might result from a delay.[13]

This ambiguity in the facts can cause some students to become unduly distracted by the adequacy of notice rather than focusing on the foreseeability rule announced by the court, which is the reason why *Hadley* is assigned, and which has largely been adopted by the *Restatement*:

§ 351. UNFORESEEABILITY AND RELATED LIMITATIONS ON DAMAGES

(1) Damages are not recoverable for loss that the party in breach did not have reason to foresee as a probable result of the breach when the contract was made.

(2) Loss may be foreseeable as a probable result of a breach because it follows from the breach

    (a) in the ordinary course of events, or

---

13. *See* Richard Danzig, *Hadley v. Baxendale: A Study in the Industrialization of the Law*, 4 J. LEG. STUD. 249 (1975).

(b) as a result of special circumstances, beyond the ordinary course of events, that the party in breach had reason
to know.

(3) A court may limit damages for foreseeable loss by excluding recovery for loss of profits, by allowing recovery only for
loss incurred in reliance, or otherwise if it concludes that in the
circumstances justice so requires in order to avoid dispropor-
tionate compensation.

The two rules described by *Hadley* for establishing foreseeability
are stated in section 351 (2)(a) and (2)(b).

Notice that the foreseeability doctrine entails that *un*foreseeable
losses that *did* occur would not be compensated. That is, a breach
causes real loss but, because "the party in breach did not have
reason to foresee [these losses] as a probable result of the breach
when the contract was made" they are not recoverable by the victim
of a breach. In other words, someone who breached a contract and
caused real but unforeseeable injury to the other party does not
need to pay for this injury. Why not?

One answer to this question involves efficiency. In the absence
of notice, denying recovery for unusual losses creates an incentive
for the party with knowledge of its special circumstances to notify
the other party who would otherwise be unaware of them. Only if
the other party has this information can it increase its efforts to
ensure performance; and (having been informed) only if it is held
liable for damages for these unusual circumstances would it have
the incentive to take make the extra effort. For example, the rule in
Hadley creates both an incentive for the mill owner to let the shipper know about his special circumstances and an incentive for the
shipper to act on this knowledge to avoid the delay.

Another answer involves consent. It begins by distinguishing
between the obligation of performance and the extent of liability for
nonperformance. These are by no means the same things. Suppose
I promise to deliver a lecture at a law school. The scope of my obligation is the giving of the lecture. Now suppose that I breach and

fail to perform. The scope of my liability for this breach will be to pay money damages. How much money damages? Enough to put the school in as good a position as it would have been had I given the lecture, as qualified by the doctrines of foreseeability, certainty, and avoidability. The extent of my liability is simply a different act (the payment of damages) than the contractual obligation (delivery of the lecture).

In Chapter 4, I will propose that the existence of a contractual obligation is founded on consent—in particular, a manifested assent to be legally bound to perform. I am legally obligated to deliver the promised lecture because I somehow manifested to the school that invited me that I assented to be held legally responsible should I fail to perform as promised. This makes the origin of contractual obligation distinct from obligations in torts that are imposed on persons regardless of whether they consented to them or not. The obligation to respect the person and property of another does not depend on whether you consented to do so. Should you violate your duties to respect the person and property of others, you will be held responsible in tort without any need to show that you consented to this obligation.

Not all contracts professors agree with this theory. Some think that contractual obligation is founded on the reliance of the promisee rather than the consent of the promisor. We shall examine this disagreement in Chapter 4. But one can hold that the obligation to perform arises from the consent to be legally bound by the promisor, and still think that the remedy for breach is not founded on consent, but is rather imposed on the parties in the same way as are remedies for tortious conduct. In other words, even if the origin of a contractual obligation differs from obligations defined by torts in that the former is grounded on consent and the latter is imposed by the legal system, the remedies for breach of both sorts of obligation could still be imposed by the legal system for reasons of public policy.

This seems to have been the position held by Lon Fuller. Fuller both affirmed in *Consideration and Form* that one source of contractual obligations was an exercise of "private autonomy," while he denied in *The Reliance Interest in Contract Damages* that the remedy for breach of this obligation was based on the "will" of the parties (contending instead that remedies were based on "juristic" reasons of public policy). I suspect that even some contracts professors who accept that contractual obligations are consensual, unlike obligations in tort, think remedies for breach of either types of obligation are imposed on the parties for policy reasons.

The foreseeability doctrine, however, suggests that the extent of liability for breach of a contractual obligation may also be founded on the consent of the promisor. When one consents to be legally bound to perform one's promise, that liability to which one is consenting has limits, just as the obligation to perform has limits. Suppose you go to a car dealership and sign a formal written purchase agreement. If the dealer asks whether you are consenting to be legally bound should you renege, you reply, "Of course, that is what I thought I was doing when I signed the agreement." Now suppose you breach because your plans changed and you no longer need a car. You admit that the contract was perfectly valid and that you have breached the contract. A court then decides to impose the death penalty. Would you not respond: "Whoa! Although I did agree to be legally bound and understood that I would be liable for any breach, I certainly did *not* agree to the remedy of death!"

The same reasoning can be applied to the amount of money damages owed for breach. Did your consent to be legally bound imply your consent to forfeit all your property? If not, what *did* it imply? The most obvious answer is that it implied a duty to compensate the dealer for the injuries that resulted from your breach. But *any* injury whatsoever? Would you have signed the contract had you been told that if your failure to take delivery on the car resulted in the bankruptcy of the dealership, and you would be responsible to the owner of the dealership for having to sell his vacation home to satisfy his creditors? More realistically, would you have signed had you been told that you were responsible for any harm caused by your breach no matter how remote? Probably not.

The foreseeability doctrine can be understood as reflecting the *common sense* or basic tacit assumption of both parties concerning their extent of liability for breaching their obligations. They will be held responsible for all the natural, usual, and ordinary consequences of breach. If they are to be held responsible for unusual and extraordinary consequences, they must at least be put on notice at the time of formation that such consequences could occur so that they will be within their contemplation when they consent to be bound.

The second rule of *Hadley* embodied in section 351(2)(b) requires the party in breach at the time of formation to have "reason to know" of any unusual special circumstances. In *Hadley* the reason to know was allegedly provided by the mill owner's employee notifying the shipper's clerk of the special circumstances of the idled mill. But, if the extent of liability is based in the implicit consent of the parties, is mere notice enough to justify extending liability for breach beyond the harms that would ordinarily or naturally occur?

In the 1903 Supreme Court case of *Globe Refining Co. v. Landa Oil*,[14] Justice Oliver Wendell Holmes contended that mere notice was not enough. Instead, the extra liability that might result from the special circumstances "must be brought home to the party sought to be charged under such circumstances that he must know that the person he contracts with reasonably believes that he accepts the contract with the special condition attached to it." At least one state, Arkansas, follows the Holmes approach and requires some additional evidence that the party in breach has *tacitly assented* to extended liability.

In *Morrow v. First National Bank of Hot Springs*,[15] the plaintiff had applied to a bank for a safe deposit box, and the bank promised to inform him when one became available, which it failed to do. When the plaintiff was burgled and his coins stolen, he sued the bank for

---

14. 190 U.S. 540 (1903).

15. 261 Ark. 568, 550 S.W. 429 (1977).

the loss of the coins worth $32,000 caused by its breach of its promise. In refusing to hold the bank liable for the loss even though it knew that the plaintiff planned to use the box to store his coins, the court relied on the following passages from a 1904 Arkansas decision: "It seems then that mere notice is not always sufficient to impose on the party who breaks a contract damages arising by reason of special circumstances." After quoting Holmes in *Globe Refining*, the 1904 case continues:

> [W]here the damages arise from special circumstances, and are so large as to be out of proportion to the consideration agreed to be paid for the services to be rendered under the contract, it raises a doubt at once as to whether the party *would have assented to such a liability had it been called to his attention at the making of the contract* unless the consideration to be paid was also raised so as to correspond in some respect to the liability assumed. (emphasis added)

After again quoting from Holmes, the 1904 decision concludes that, where there is no express contract to pay such special damages, the "facts and circumstances in proof must be such as to make it reasonable for the judge or jury trying the case to believe that the party at the time of the contract tacitly consented to be bound to more than ordinary damages in case of default on his part." As a result, the court in *Morrow* refused to hold the bank liable for the loss.

The official comments to UCC section 2-715 explicitly reject the "tacit assent" test, which means that, even in Arkansas, it would not apply to a sale of goods (as distinct from the rental of a safe deposit box). So too has the *Restatement 2nd*. Arkansas may be the only state in which this approach survives. Does this repudiation undermine the theory that the extent of liability for breach of a contractual obligation is based on consent? Not necessarily. The enormous difficulty in proving "tacit" assent to enhanced liability would bar a lot of recoveries where one party *had* assumed a greater obligation, but where this extra proof is lacking.

Most contracts will be silent on the issue of extent of liability. A court seeking to enforce the terms that most parties would expect to be enforced might well figure that most parties expect to be liable for any losses that are foreseeable at the time of formation. Requiring additional proof of this expectation would lead to systematic under-enforcement, because such proof is so difficult. This sounds a bit like Fuller and Perdue's argument that "to protect reliance we dispense with its proof." Putting the burden on the minority of parties to express their dissent from the general expectation by expressly disclaiming extended liability would allow both parties to know where they stand.

Indeed, consider this disclaimer from a modern express delivery company in a clause entitled, "Limitations on Our Liability and Liabilities Not Assumed."

> Our liability in connection with this shipment is limited to the lesser of the actual damages or $100, unless you declare a higher value, pay an additional charge, and document your actual loss in a timely manner. You may pay an additional charge for each $100 of declared value. The declared value does not constitute, nor do we provide, cargo insurance.
>
> In any event, we will not be liable for any damage, whether direct, incidental, special, or consequential, in excess of the declared value of a shipment, whether or not [Federal Express] has knowledge that such damages might be incurred, including but not limited to loss of income and profits.

Most commercial contracts, drafted by lawyers familiar with the rule of *Hadley v. Baxendale*, contain such disclaimers.

When consumers bring their packages to Federal Express, they are not going to hire a lawyer to explain FedEx's extent of liability for its advertised promise to "absolutely positively" deliver their packages overnight. They will likely assume FedEx is responsible for all foreseeable losses caused by their breach. If the law adopted the tacit assent test, FedEx would know its liability was limited because its lawyers would tell it so, but consumers would not because they would have no lawyers and such a rule is unexpected. As a result, at the time of formation, there would likely be a misunderstanding between the parties on this matter. Adopting the foreseeability rule of *Hadley*, which conforms to the common-sense expectation of ordinary persons, places the onus on repeat players such as Federal Express, who are knowledgeable about the background law of contracts, to inform consumers that their liability is limited. In this way, contract law increases the likelihood that both parties are more likely to be consenting to the same thing, and reduces the chances of a misunderstanding.

This example suggests a more general approach to contract law. As was mentioned in the Introduction, most of the rules of contract law are "default rules"—that is, rules that the courts will apply unless the parties expressly stipulate something different. Think of the default margins applied by your word-processing program unless you specify something else. Some contracts scholars contend that these default rules should be what a majority of parties would select to govern their relationship, putting the onus on those who disagree to incur the expense of contracting around the default rule by inserting an express clause that differs. So if most contracts contain disclaimers of the sort in the Federal Express contract—as probably 99.9 percent of all commercial contracts do—then this should be the default rule, in which case Federal Express could remain silent on this issue, and the onus would be on the consumer to bargain for a different term.

But the analysis of foreseeability I just presented suggests that this "majoritarian" approach to setting default rules is wrong. To be sure, default rules should be chosen to reflect the consent of the parties, but they should also reduce the instances of misunderstandings between the parties about the scope of their respective obligations and liabilities to which they are consenting. It is rational for repeat players such as Federal Express who enter into thousands of the same sorts of transactions every day, to hire a lawyer to inform them of what the law of contract says about these transactions.

In contrast, it would be irrational for "one-shot players" such as ordinary consumers to hire a lawyer to inform them about their contractual rights for most small transactions.

Therefore, with respect to the scope of the parties' liability for breach, courts should adopt default rules that reflect the *common sense* of ordinary consumers because, by so doing, the onus will fall on repeat players to include express provisions that deviate from what the consumers might reasonably expect. In this way, there is less likely to be a fundamental misunderstanding between the parties. And this is true even if every consumer ends up accepting Federal Express's disclaimer of liability.

2.4.2 Certainty of Harm

A second limitation on contract damages applies when damages cannot be proved with reasonable certainty. For example, a company might claim that, as a result of a delay in construction that postponed the opening of its store, it lost profits on sales it might have made if the store had opened on time. Unlike the loss of profits caused by the closure of the mill in *Hadley*, such a loss would arise naturally from the delay in opening the store on time. In a 1906 case,[16] the Supreme Court of North Carolina rejected a claim based on lost sales because such profits "are shadowy, uncertain, and speculative and therefore incapable of legal computation." Claims based on transactions that did not occur because of the breach should be rejected as an item in the calculation of damages because the existence of these transactions "are subject to too many contingencies and are too dependent upon the fluctuations of markets and the chances of business to constitute a safe criterion for an estimate of damages."

---

16. Winston Cigarette Mach. Co. v. Wells-Whitehead Tobacco Co., 141 N.C. 284, 53 S.E. 886 (1906).

Then the North Carolina court offered a more general justification for denying damage claims that cannot be proven with reasonable certainty. Although the law may not always do perfect justice, this is not by design. Allowing juries to award damages that were speculative "would tend not only to make the law itself odious, but to corrupt its administration, by fostering a disregard of the just rights of parties." In contracts cases, courts have found it safer to adopt definite rules for the jury to use to estimate damages, although this may risk falling short of the actual damages. These rules are based on "such elements of certainty" presented by a case, while excluding those further damages that may have been suffered, but can only be "estimated as a matter of opinion." The court expressed concern that giving such "unbridled discretion" to a jury would "bring ruin upon the party in default," even though "no such loss was contemplated." Instead, parties should "expressly provide for such enlarged responsibility. This they may do by liquidating the amount when the damages cannot be otherwise ascertained and are such as the law will not allow because of their uncertainty."

When courts cannot compute the loss in value because some or all of the loss is too speculative, they commonly compute money damages by using the reliance measure instead. Earlier in this chapter, we saw an example of this in *Sullivan v. O'Connor*. But this can also lead to problems. Consider the case of *Chicago Coliseum Club v. Dempsey*,[17] in which Jack Dempsey, the heavyweight champion of the world, breached his contract to fight Harry Wills so he could fight Gene Tunney instead. Although it found that Dempsey had breached the contract, the court held that the company promoting the fight could not recover its lost profits because they were too uncertain. Nor could it recover for expenditures incurred prior to Dempsey signing the contract, although all of these expenditures were rendered worthless because they were not incurred in reliance on the not-yet-executed contract with Dempsey. Nor could they collect

---

17. 265 Ill. App. 542 (1933).

any post-breach expenditures to enforce the contract because these too could not have been made in reliance on a contract they already knew Dempsey had breached. Because the court had shifted its focus from the expectation measure to a reliance measure, the plaintiff ended up collecting only its out-of-pocket losses incurred between the formation of the contract and Dempsey's breach. In this manner, the plaintiff collected next to nothing for Dempsey's flagrant refusal to perform his obligation under the contract.

Now compare the *Chicago Coliseum* case with the English case of *Anglia Television Ltd. v. Reed,*[18] in which actor Robert Reed breached his contract to appear in the teleplay "The Man in the Wood." There the English court allowed the production company to recover "the expenditure incurred before the contract, provided that it was such as would reasonably be in the contemplation of the parties as likely to be wasted if the contract was broken." The court justified this on the principle that "when Mr. Reed entered into this contract, he must have known perfectly well that much expenditure had already been incurred on director's fees and the like." Reed "must have contemplated—or, at any rate, it is reasonably to be imputed to him—that if he broke his contract, all that expenditure would be wasted, whether or not it was incurred before or after the contract. He must pay damages for all the expenditure so wasted and thrown away."

Can the reasoning in *Anglia* be reconciled with the proposition that, when the expectation measure is too uncertain, the courts will shift their analysis to the reliance measure? Yes, but only if the reliance measure includes opportunities forgone in reliance on the contract. In *Anglia*, the precontractual expenditures were wasted when the production company relied on Reed's promise, *rather than entering a contract with another actor* who would have performed as promised. But we have already learned that, because opportunity costs are often highly speculative, the reliance measure is typically

---

18. 3 All E.R. 690 [Court of Appeal, Civil Division, 1971].

limited to out-of-pocket expenditures, as were awarded in *Dempsey*.

As in *Dempsey*, the plaintiff in *Anglia* did incur substantial out-of-pocket expenses, but they were expended before entering the agreement with Reed. In this way, limiting recovery to the reliance measure, if limited to out-of-pocket expenditures, fails to compensate for any potential reliance in the form of lost opportunities to enter into the next best contract. Perhaps in *Dempsey*, the plaintiff had no other opportunities to forgo; but this might not have been true for Anglia Television.

Professor Michael Kelly has proposed a solution to this problem that would, at the same time, simplify the rules governing the measure of contract damages.[19] Courts are wrong, he contended, to shift their focus from the expectation measure to the reliance measure just because some elements of the expectation measure, such as lost profits, are too uncertain to calculate. Instead, courts should still attempt to put the parties in the position they would have been had the contract been performed. When lost profits are too uncertain to collect, the courts should presume that the contract would have broken even—that is, revenue would have covered costs, and the victim of the breach can collect his proven expenditures. Kelly called this the *expectancy of zero profits*. If the victim of the breach can also prove lost profits, then these profits can be added to the expenditures; conversely, if the party in breach can prove that the contract would have lost money, then these losses will reduce the amount owed in damages below that which was expended to perform.

Under Kelly's approach, *Chicago Coliseum* was wrongly decided because it used the reliance measure of damages. *Anglia* was correctly decided but the court really used an expectation measure, while assuming that the plaintiff would have broken even. It attempted to put the production company in as good a position

---

19. *See* Michael B. Kelly, *The Phantom Reliance Interest in Contract Damages*, 1992 WISC. L. REV. 1755.

as it would have been had the contract been performed, given the uncertainty of proving that it would have made a profit and how much that profit would have been.

The *Restatement 2nd* appears to adopt the traditional approach, but it fudges a bit.

§ 349. DAMAGES BASED ON RELIANCE INTEREST

As an alternative to the measure of damages stated in section 347, the injured party has a right to damages based on his reliance interest, including expenditures made in preparation for performance or in performance, less any loss that the party in breach can prove with reasonable certainty the injured party would have suffered had the contract been performed.

Although this section speaks of the reliance interest, it allows the recovery of "expenditures made in preparation for performance." Does it mean only those expenditures incurred in reliance on the contract, as in *Dempsey*, or all expenditures, as in *Anglia?* If it is serious about basing damages "on his reliance interest," then, as in the *Chicago Coliseum* case, these should not include precontractual expenditures. But at the end, the section allows a deduction for any losses that "the party in breach can prove with reasonable certainty the injured party would have suffered had the contract been performed."

This seems a lot like Kelly's approach. Recover for *all* expenditures made in preparation to perform (as in *Anglia*), which would assume that the victim would have covered its expenditures and broken even, while allowing the breaching party to prove any loss the injured party would have suffered had the contract been performed. Because all of this is the prospective approach of the expectation measure, not the retrospective approach of the reliance measure, it would seem that the focus of the inquiry remains the expectation measure even though some elements of expectation damages are too uncertain to collect.

Finally, let me note a point to which I will return in Chapter 4. The reliance *interest* of which Fuller and Perdue wrote is not necessarily the same as the reliance *measure* of contract damages. Assume that Kelly is correct that courts should think of themselves as awarding the expectation measure and not switch to a reliance measure because the expectation measure is too remote. Nevertheless, enforcing the manifested consent of the parties may well be justified on the ground that it serves *both* the will of the promisor and the reliance interest of the promisee.

2.4.3 Avoidability of Loss

Can a victim of a breach recover for losses that the victim might have taken steps to avoid but did not? Contract law says "No." Consider the case of *Rockingham County v. Luten Bridge Co.*[20] There, Rockingham County, North Carolina, contracted with the Luten Bridge Company to build a bridge across a river. After much public opposition to the expense of the bridge, the county breached its contract by repudiating it and notifying the bridge company to stop performing. After receiving this notice, the company continued to finish the bridge and sought its damages for the full contract price. The court rejected its claim, allowing it to collect only those reliance expenditures it had incurred up to the point it was notified of breach together with its "net" profit on the entire contract. It could not collect its expenditures incurred after the breach to finish the bridge.

Why not? Because the county notified the bridge company of its repudiation, the loss of expenditures incurred after its notice were not "caused" by its breach. They were caused by the refusal of the bridge company to accept the repudiation. More fundamentally, the avoidability doctrine is said to prevent the waste of scarce resources.

---

20. 35 F.2d 301 (1929).

The finished bridge is a waste of resources because the county no longer wants it, and the victim of the breach can be made whole by compensating it for its lost expenditures incurred up until the repudiation plus lost profit on the whole transaction.

The avoidability limitation on the collection of damages—sometimes called the "duty to mitigate" damages—thus relates to the third principal rationale of contract law: allowing persons to make exchanges that are value-enhancing for both parties. At the time of formation, the county subjectively valued having a bridge more than it valued the money to pay for it. The bridge company subjectively valued the money it would receive more than what it would cost to construct the bridge. But because of an intervening election of the county board, the valuation of the county changed. It no longer desired the finished bridge more than whatever additional amount it would cost to complete it.

Of course, every breach of contract involves a change of the valuation of the party in breach. Every breaching party no longer values the performance it has yet to receive more highly than the performance it has yet to render. Enforceable contracts exist precisely to allow a promisee to rely on receiving performance even if the other party's valuation changes. So a later change in valuation by a promisor is no defense to the enforcement of his promise.

Even so, any further expenditures incurred after the repudiation of the contract can be considered a "waste" of scarce resources because two things are true: (a) the completed performance is no longer subjectively valued more highly than the cost to receive it; *and* (b) the other party can be made whole by paying its expenditures up to the point of repudiation together with its lost profit or "net expectancy" for the entire contract, including the profit on that portion of the contract that is yet to be performed.

Put another way, although the contractual agreement was value enhancing for both parties at the time of formation, because the value of one party changed, stopping performance at this point improved the welfare of the party in breach while compensation rendered the victim of the breach in the same position as it would have been in had the contract been performed and, therefore, no worse off. When it is said that the avoidability limitation is meant to prevent waste, what is really meant is that it is attempting to preserve a value-enhancing transaction for both parties after the values of one of the parties has changed.

This analysis of avoidability assumes, however, that the victim of the breach is made whole by monetary damages. Although often the case, it is not always so. Sometimes the victim subjectively values performing the contract more highly than it values the money it would receive from the breaching party. A case that may illustrate this situation is *Parker v. Twentieth Century Fox Film Corp.*[21] There, actress Shirley MacLaine entered into a written contract with a film studio to make a musical comedy, *Bloomer Girls*, about the suffragette movement. At some point, the studio no longer wished to make the picture and offered MacLaine the leading role in a Western, *Big Country, Big Man.* MacLaine refused the part and sued for the amount due to her under the contract. In accepting her claim, the Supreme Court of California rejected the studio's objection that MacLaine had failed to avoid or mitigate the loss caused by its breach by accepting the part in the other film.

In a famous article,[22] Professor Mary Jo Frug explained this result by hypothesizing that Shirley MacLaine might have valued the promised role more highly than the substituted role. Whereas *Bloomer Girls* portrayed earlier feminists in a favorable light, a traditional Western would put MacLaine's character in a subordinate role to the male lead. If Frug's speculations are correct, then the substitute part would not have put MacLaine in as good a position as she would have been in had the contract been performed.

---

21. 3 Cal. 3d 176, 89 Cal. Rptr. 737, 474 P.2d 689 (1970).

22. Mary Joe Frug, *Shirley MacLaine and the Mitigation of Damages Rule: Re-Uniting Language and Experience in Legal Doctrine*, 34 Am. U. L. Rev. 1065 (1985).

At least part of the reason for this is that the reputation and career of an actor depends greatly on the roles they play, not just the money they receive for playing them. Moreover, acting is a form of self-expression. For this and other reasons, MacLaine might not value performing in a Western as highly as the musical comedy. Indeed she may have loathed the idea. On this assumption, she cannot be penalized for refusing to accept the lesser and inferior job which was forced upon her by the studio's breach.[23]

The *Parker* case also illustrates a complication with applying the avoidability doctrine in the context of labor contracts. If Shirley MacLaine is allowed to collect the entire amount of the contract, she is very likely to be made better off than she would have been had the contract been performed. This is because she is collecting the full contract price without having to perform her end of the contract. It would be like the bridge company collecting the full contract price without even starting to build the bridge. She would then get, in effect, a year's paid vacation. For this reason, the film company would be entitled to a deduction for the amount she earned from another project during the time of the original contract. This would enable MacLaine to accept a lower paying role in a film she subjectively valued, while still earning the full contract price. Still, unless a court scrutinizes her choices (as they did her choice to turn down *Big Country, Big Man*), she could opt for a paid vacation by turning down any alternate projects that came her way, which would make her potentially far better off than had the contract been performed.

Victor Goldberg offered an alternative justification for requiring the studio to pay the entire amount without any deduction for a substitute project.[24] In the contract was the following

---

23. As it happens, MacLaine played the lead in *Two Mules for Sister Sarah*, a Western costarring Clint Eastwood, that was released the same year as the California Supreme Court's opinion about the *Bloomer Girls* project.

24. *See* VICTOR GOLDBERG, FRAMING CONTRACT LAW: AN ECONOMIC PERSPECTIVE 281–84 (2006).

clause: "We [the studio] shall not be obligated to utilize your [plain-tiff's] services in or in connection with the Photoplay hereunder, our sole obligation, subject to the terms and conditions of this Agreement, being to pay you the guaranteed compensation herein provided for." Although the existence of this clause did not figure in the court's reasoning, and is therefore sometimes overlooked in classroom discussion of the case, Goldberg characterized the agree-ment as a "play or pay" contract. In other words, as a result of this clause, while Shirley MacLaine assumed the risk that there might be no film at all, the studio assumed the risk of having to pay MacLaine even if the film was not made. By this clause, the parties had contracted around the default rule provided by the avoidability doctrine, and there was no need for the court to concern itself with whether the substitute part offered to MacLaine by the studio was inferior to the one in *Bloomer Girls*.

Let us consider one final twist on avoidability. In *Neri v. Retail Marine Corp.*,[25] a buyer of a boat breached his purchase agreement and later claimed that the boat dealer could not collect damages for the amount it received from reselling the boat to another buyer. The court, however, rejected the buyer's claim that the subsequent sale mitigated the loss caused by his breach. Why? Presumably, if the seller is in the business of selling boats and had a ready supply of these boats from the manufacturer, it could always have sold *both* boats. If the buyer's damages are reduced by the amount of the second sale, the dealer is made worse off because it would receive the profit on only one sale rather than the two sales it made. This is known as the "lost volume" doctrine. It does not apply to the sale of a unique good where there could not be two sales of the same item; it also does not apply to sellers who have only one item to sell because are not in the business of buying and selling in volume. (Recall the hypothetical car sale in section 2.3.5 in which I assumed the seller of the car was a private party.) In both of these situations,

---

25. 334 N.Y.S.2d 165, 30 N.Y.2d 393, 285 N.E.2d 311 (1972).

a second transaction is made possible by the breach—there could be no second transaction without the breach—whereas in *Neri* the dealer could have sold a second boat regardless of whether the first buyer breached.

2.5 Specific Performance

As we have just seen, an award of money damages is the presumptive form of remedy for breach of contract. This presumption can be rebutted, however, by proof of exceptional circumstances that require equitable relief in the form of specific performance of the promise. Put simply, specific performance is available when money damages are shown to be inadequate. Over the years, certain circumstances have come to be accepted as sufficient reasons for substituting specific performance for money damages. To understand these circumstances, it is useful to distinguish between contracts for land, contracts for goods, and contracts for personal services and consider each in turn.

2.5.1 Contracts for Land

Historically, each parcel of land was considered to be unique in the literal sense of "one of a kind." What differentiates one parcel from another is what realtors refer to as "location, location, location." No two pieces of land can be located in exactly the same place. One side of a street gets sun, the other does not. One parcel has good soil, the other does not. Think about that street corner where no gas station can seem to stay in business (and eventually became a convenience store), while the one directly across the intersection thrives.

Money damages are obviously inadequate when money cannot buy the same thing. Because this is largely true with land, courts have traditionally presumed that money damages are inadequate for enforcing land contracts. This means that, with land contracts, the presumption favoring money damages is reversed, and specific performance becomes the presumptive form of relief.

This traditional rule is consistent with the concept of subjective value discussed above. If land is unique, a victim of a breach is likely to prefer receiving the promised parcel over receiving money damages with which he can buy a different parcel. Of course, no one compels a plaintiff to seek specific performance when money damages will do fine. Suppose the delay caused by the breach has led a buyer no longer to want a particular parcel of land because his business use for that parcel is no longer feasible. The buyer may opt for his legal right to money damages rather than pursue his relief in equity for the land itself.

2.5.2 Contracts for Goods

In contrast with land contracts, for which money damages are presumed to be inadequate, with contracts for goods, the inadequacy of money damages must be established by a victim of a breach before specific performance will be awarded. With most goods, others just like it are available on the market, so awarding money damages in an amount sufficient to buy a replacement should put the victim of the breach in as good a position as he would have been had the contract been performed.

Suppose a replacement is not available on the market? If this can be shown by the promisee, then money damages are inadequate, and the presumption in favor of money damages is rebutted. This exception used to be limited to contracts involving literally unique or one-of-a-kind goods, such as a painting. Nowadays, the rule has been expanded to goods that, although numerous, are simply not available on the market. The UCC section 2-716 says that "[s]pecific performance may be ordered where the goods are unique *or in other proper circumstances*" (emphasis added). Establishing an inability to *cover*—which means obtaining a substitute performance—is now considered sufficient to rebut the presumption favoring money damages.

Some economists have used the efficient breach concept discussed in section 2.3.4 to defend the traditional presumption favoring money damages on the grounds that, under some circumstances, it is value-enhancing—or *efficient*—for the promisor to breach provided that the expectation measure is awarded to the promisee. By his actions, the promisor demonstrates that he would prefer not to perform over paying money damages to the promisee, so allowing him to breach and pay damages makes him better off, while awarding the expectancy measure, by definition, puts the promisee in as good a position as she would have been had the contract been performed, so she is no worse off.

Suppose a second buyer is willing to pay more than the amount of expectation damages. By breaching, the seller is better off, the second buyer is better off, and the first buyer is no worse off. Therefore, overall, the world is a better place if we allow breaches under these circumstances. Of course, if money damages are shown to be inadequate because of an inability to cover, limiting recovery to money damages would not be value-enhancing for both parties. In this way, the concept of efficient breach explains both the rule and its exception.

The idea of efficient breach has been widely criticized. Daniel Friedmann has argued that, if specific goods are identified to the contract, in a real sense, they belong to the buyer.[26] When a second buyer comes along and is willing to spend more for the item, the seller is attempting to sell something that no longer belongs to him. Suppose after you buy a car and drive off, a new buyer offers the dealer more for it. Should the dealer be able to come to your home and repossess the car from you provided he is willing to pay you expectation damages? After all, the car is yours now, not his. Friedmann contends that the rationale supporting efficient breach

---

26. *See* Daniel Friedmann, *The Efficient Breach Fallacy*, 18 J. LEG. STUD. 1 (1989).

could just as easily support the idea of "efficient theft." Law and economics scholar Alan Schwartz has denied that awards of specific performance are less efficient than money damages.[27] And Seana Shiffrin has argued that the efficient breach argument, along with the preference for money damages, directly conflicts with the moral duty to keep one's promises.[28]

The argument on behalf of efficient breach purports to be consistent with the idea of subjective value. The world is a better place because the promisor subjectively prefers to sell to the second buyer after paying damages to the first buyer, the second buyer subjectively prefers to pay the higher price for the goods than to find them elsewhere, and the first buyer is no worse off subjectively than had the contract been performed. But how do we know the last claim is true? One way to find out would be to give the promisee the option of freely choosing damages or specific performance. By making this choice, the promisee would be demonstrating his preferences in the same way that the promisor and second buyer are. If forced to accept money damages, however, there is no reliable way of knowing that the expectation measure really does leave the promisee no worse off.

A flaw in the efficient breach analysis is that, while we *know* the promisor and second buyer are better off because they have demonstrated their preferences, we can only *assume* that the expectation measure leaves the first buyer no worse off. Money damages are calculated by others; the amount of money damages is not a price that is consented to by the promisee thereby demonstrating his subjective preferences. Recall as well that, to prevent overcompensation, actual contract damages are limited by the requirement that they be calculable with a reasonable degree of certainty. Yet this

---

27. *See* Alan Schwartz, *The Case for Specific Performance*, 89 YALE L.J. 271 (1979).

28. *See* Seana Shiffrin, *The Divergence of Contract and Promise*, 120 HARV. L. REV. 70 (2007).

will inevitably lead to undercompensation in those cases where damages, such as lost profits, cannot be so calculated.

The efficient breach analysis purports to justify the traditional rule favoring money damages, but when subjective value is fully considered, it would seem that, as with land, a victim of a breach should be given the option of specific performance or money damages. This reform could be qualified by allowing promisors to show why specific performance is unduly onerous and money damages are adequate, but this is not the current approach. At present, a failure of proof redounds to the advantage of those who have breached their contract, rather than to the victim of a breach.

2.5.3 Contracts for Personal Services

If an inability to cover when a particular good is one of a kind rebuts the normal presumption favoring money damages, the same reasoning would also seem to justify the specific performance of contracts for personal services. What could be more unique or special than the services of a particular singer, athlete, scientist, salesman, or executive? Yet, contract law has generally refused to compel the specific performance of personal services, without even permitting a showing of an inability to cover by obtaining the services of another. Of course, the remedy of expectation damages provides some incentive to performing personal services. But the closest the courts have come to compelling performance of such services is to issue a "negative injunction" forbidding the promisor from performing elsewhere upon penalty of contempt.

What explains the courts' refusal to compel specific performance of personal services contracts notwithstanding the fact that money damages are inadequate? Two explanations are usually advanced. The first is practical. Courts just do not want to get into the business of evaluating whether personal performance was rendered well or poorly. Remember, imprisonment for contempt of court would follow a deficient performance. In contrast, it is easy to discern whether a person has performed for another contrary to a negative injunction or has refused to pay money damages. Indeed, courts are not in the business of seeing that promisees collect money damage awards; parties are on their own in obtaining enforcement of judgments.

But moral concerns are also responsible for the reluctance of judges to compel personal services. These concerns were movingly summarized in the 1821 Indiana case of *In re Mary Clark, A Woman of Color:*[29] "Whenever contracting parties disagree about the performance of their contract, and a Court of justice of necessity interposes to settle their different rights," observed the Indiana justice, "their feelings become irritated against each other; and the losing party feels mortified and degraded in being compelled to perform for the other what he had previously refused." This mortification is only magnified with contracts for personal services where "that performance will place him frequently in the presence or under the direction of his adversary." And this is as true of the ordinary employee as it is in the case of an actor or athlete. "But this state of degradation, this irritation of feeling, could be in no other case so manifestly experienced, as in the case of a common servant, where the master would have a continual right of command, and the servant be compelled to a continual obedience."

In this regard, promises to deliver external objects such as land or goods are inherently different than promises to specifically perform services. "Many covenants, the breaches of which are only remunerated in damages, might be specifically performed, either by a third person at a distance from the adversary, or in a short space of time." But contracts for service, "if performed at all, must be personally performed under the eye of the master; and might, as in the case before us, require a number of years." Compelling specific performance of services "would produce a state of servitude as degrading and demoralizing in its consequences, as a state of

---

29. 1 Blackf. 122 (Ind. 1821).

absolute slavery; and if enforced under a government like ours, which acknowledges a personal equality, it would be productive of a state of feeling more discordant and irritating than slavery itself." Therefore, the court concluded, even "if all other contracts were specifically enforced by law, it would be impolitic to extend the principle to contracts for personal service."

The practical and moral differences between enforcing personal services and contracts for external objects such as land and goods are captured by the distinction between alienable and inalienable rights. Recall the Declaration of Independence's famous invocation of "unalienable rights" among which "are Life, Liberty and the pursuit of Happiness." Although an alienable right—such as a right to a car or house—can be freely transferred by consent to another person, the right to one's own person cannot be transferred, even with consent. In contrast with compelling someone to perform a service for another, the award of money damages for nonperformance merely requires the transfer of alienable rights.

Although it is common to distinguish between personal and property rights, there is no reason why the rights to control one's body cannot be considered a property right. John Locke, the classical natural rights theorist, affirmed that "every Man has a Property in his own Person. This no Body has any Right to but himself. The Labour of his Body, and the Work of his Hands, we may say, are properly his."[30] Indeed, American abolitionists characterized slavery as "man theft" because it deprived people of their property in their own persons. So the difference is not so much between personal and property rights, but between those alienable property rights that can be specifically enforced and those inalienable property rights that can only be enforced by the payment of money damages.

---

30. JOHN LOCKE, SECOND TREATISE CONCERNING CIVIL GOVERNMENT § 27 (1690).

What does this analysis suggest for the availability of negative injunctions preventing a promisor from performing for someone else? It is worth noting that this remedy was accepted only gradually and fitfully. In the classic 1852 case of *Lumley v. Wagner*,[31] while the English court refused to compel the opera singer Johanna Wagner to sing in the plaintiff's opera house, they did forbid her from singing in the rival opera house that had offered her more money to sing there. Yet even here the court justified its ruling by noting the existence of a negative covenant saying that "Mademoiselle Wagner engages herself not to use her talents at any other theater, nor in any concert or reunion, public or private, without the written authorization of Mr. Lumley." So rather than indirectly enforcing the duty to sing, the court in *Lumley* could be said to have specifically enforced *this* clause pledging not to sing for another.

American courts initially rejected even this restriction on what was called "free labor." In 1865, a Philadelphia court in *Ford v. Jermon*[32] expressed the view that *Lumley* "should be regarded as a warning rather than followed as a precedent." In *Jermon*, the Court contended that "a contract for personal services thus enforced would be but a mitigated form of slavery, in which the party would have lost the right to dispose of himself as a free agent, and be, for a greater or less length of time, subject to the control of another." And this was true despite the existence of a negative covenant of the sort that was in Johanna Wagner's contract. "Otherwise the court might be compelled to transcend the limits within which its jurisdiction ought to be confined, and engage in a contest where the sympathies of mankind would be all with the weaker party."

Yet in the twentieth century, negative injunctions gradually came to be available when money damages were inadequate even where the agreement contained no negative covenant. Undoubtedly, the

---

31. Ch., 1 De G., M. & G. 604, 42 Eng. Rep. 687 (1852).

32. 6 Phila. 6 (Dist. Ct. 1865).

comparative ease of discerning compliance with the order eliminated one traditional objection to such enforcement. And there seems to be a qualitative difference between compelling someone like Johanna Wagner to work for another and stopping her from working for someone else. Even so, with expressed covenants not to compete—which sometimes accompany the sale of a business or the disclosure of confidential information to employees—courts will scrutinize such agreements to ensure that they are limited by type of activity, by geographical area, and by time so as not to exceed the legitimate purposes for which they were included in the agreement.

There is another practical reason for enforcing negative injunctions, even in cases not involving celebrity performers. Employees often are not worth their salaries until they have been trained. Firms who provide this training hope to get back their investment in "human capital" over time by entering into an employment contract under which they pay more than the employee is "worth" during the early years and somewhat less than a fully trained employee is worth during the later years. If trained employees are allowed to breach their agreements by accepting a higher salary elsewhere before a firm recaptures its investment, employers would have greatly reduced incentives to provide on-the-job training coupled with a decent salary.

Still, even here there is an alternative to enforcing an absolute negative injunction. A court could instead allow the employee to leave but require them to disgorge any salary increase to the first employer. If such an order could be crafted to avoid evasion, this would potentially eliminate any financial incentive to leave the first job, while confining the form of relief to payment of money damages that would reiumburse the first employer for the cost of providing training. Appreciating the moral problem with compelling personal services helps justify adopting such an alternative where it is feasible.

THREE

Mutual Assent

SUMMARY: This chapter covers the first of the two basic elements of a contract—the existence of mutual assent. Among the topics discussed are the objective theory of contract (with its generally hidden "subjective twist"), the offer-acceptance method of reaching assent, the difference between bilateral and unilateral contracts, and how to discern the meaning of the agreement. This chapter also considers why it is the objective manifestation of consent, rather than subjective assent, that is generally enforced by contract law, and when and why subjective assent becomes relevant. Finally, we consider whether form contracts that some call "contracts of adhesion" should be enforceable and, if so, to what extent, as well as what happens when the forms of the parties conflict. Cases discussed in this chapter include: *Embry v. Hargadine, McKittrick Dry Goods, Lucy v. Zehmer, Leonard v. Pepsico, Dickenson v. Dodds, Carlill v. Carbolic Smoke Ball, Peterson v. Pattberg, Fragiliment v. B.N.S International Sales, Sun Printing & Publishing v. Remington, Spooner v. Reserve Life Insurance Co., Wood v. Lucy, Lady Duff-Gordon, ProCD, Inc. v. Zeidenberg, Hill v. Gateway 2000,* and *Klocek v. Gateway.*

Formation of a contract requires two basic elements: (1) the mutual assent of the parties and (2) enforceability. In this chapter we study the first of these two elements. The next chapter discusses what makes a promise enforceable.

⁊ 3.1 The Objective Theory of Assent

There was a time when, to form a contract, it was said there needed to be a "meeting of the minds." In the 1874 English case of *Dickinson v. Dodds*,[1] Lord Justice James advanced the proposition that "[i]t must, to constitute a contract, appear that the two minds were at one at the same moment of time . . ."; and that "the existence of the same mind between the two parties . . . is essential in point of law to the making of an agreement." Taken literally, a meeting of the minds is no longer a requirement to make a contract, if it ever was. Indeed, the first of Lord James' two statements: "[i]t must . . . *appear* that the two minds were of one . . ." introduces an ambiguity into his discussion. One party could *appear* to be assenting without actually holding that particular state of mind.

In contract law, the terms *subjective* and *objective* are used to describe this distinction. "Subjective" refers to what is in one's head; "objective" refers to what one manifests or communicates to another person. Contract law is said to have adopted the *objective theory* of assent insofar as it is not necessary that there be a subjective meeting of the minds between the parties. Although both parties need not subjectively assent to a contract for it to be enforceable, contract law has a sometimes hidden *subjective twist.*

The subjective twist is illustrated by the case of *Embry v. Hargadine, McKittrick Dry Goods Co.*[2] There, a salesman named Embry went into the office of McKittrick, his boss and the president of his company, and demanded an extension of his written employment contract or he would quit. According to Embry, McKittrick asked him a few questions about how his department was operating and then said: "Go ahead, you're all right; get your men out and don't let that worry you." Embry then returned to work. About two months later, Embry was fired.

---

1. 2 Ch. D. 463 [1874].

2. 127 Mo. App. 383, 105 S.W. 777 (1907).

After a jury found for McKittrick, Embry appealed claiming that it was error for the trial judge to instruct the jury that a contract existed "if you (the jury) find *both parties thereby intended* and did contract with each other for plaintiff's employment for one year from and including December 23, 1903, at a salary of $2000 per annum (emphasis added)." On appeal, the appellate court rejected this requirement that both parties intend to contract with each other.

The court conceded that "[j]udicial opinion and elementary treatises abound in statement of the rule that to constitute a contract there must be a meeting of the minds of the parties, and both must agree to the same thing in the same sense." However, while "[g]enerally speaking, this may be true, … it is not literally or universally true." In other words, it is *false*. A literal meeting of the minds is *not* required. The court then rejected a subjective theory of assent: "[T]he inner intention of parties to a conversation subsequently alleged to create a contract, cannot either make a contract of what transpired or prevent one from arising, if the words used were sufficient to constitute a contract." It then affirmed an objective approach: "In so far as their intention is an influential element, it is only such intention as the words or acts of the parties indicate; not one secretly cherished which is inconsistent with those words or acts."

The meaning that is objectively communicated is the meaning that *a reasonable person* in the relevant community would attach to the other party's words or conduct. The court in *Embry* quoted with approval the following passage from another case: "The law imputes to a person an intention corresponding to the reasonable meaning of his words and acts. It judges his intention by his outward expressions and excludes all questions in regard to his unexpressed intention." It then asked "whether or not the language used was of that character, namely, was such that Embry, as a reasonable man, might consider he was re-employed for the ensuing year in the previous terms and act accordingly." It concluded that "no reasonable man would construe [McKittrick's] answer to Embry's demand that he be employed for another year, otherwise than as an assent to the demand."

Yet in its holding affirming an objective theory, the court then added a subjective twist (indicated by the italicized passage):

> [W]e hold that, though McKittrick may not have intended to employ Embry by what transpired between them according to the latter's testimony, yet if what McKittrick said would have been taken by a reasonable man to be an employment, *and Embry so understood it*, it constituted a valid contract of employment for the ensuing year (emphasis added).

At the end of its opinion it reiterated the twist: "It was only necessary that Embry, as a reasonable man, had a right to *and did* so understand" (emphasis added). In other words, although it was not necessary for *McKittrick* to subjectively think *he* was contracting, it was necessary that *Embry* subjectively think that *McKittrick* was contracting. Understanding why the objective theory has a subjective twist requires us to identify the rationale for favoring an objective over a subjective theory of assent in the first place.

As was noted in Chapter 1, contract law allows the parties to alter their preexisting legal rights. In a typical contract, each party transfers a right he has in exchange for the right of the other. So I transfer to you my rights to $10,000 in exchange for your right to your car, and vice versa. Both of us are made better off by this exchange, on the assumption that we each subjectively prefer what we receive more than what we give up in exchange. So to ensure that contracts are welfare enhancing—that is, they improve the welfare of *both* parties—both parties must consent to the exchange.

Yet there is another fact of human life that now assumes importance: We cannot read each other's minds. Personally, I think this is a good thing. Life would be miserable if we could know what everyone else was secretly thinking—especially life as a law professor. Whether we like it or not, unless we are in the world of science fiction, parties to a contract cannot peer through each other's forehead to see if they are subjectively assenting. Moreover, with most contracts, at least one party is a legal entity, such as a corporation, lacking a single mind to read. Such entities are represented by their agents, who speak for the company without being the company itself. Asking what a company as a whole subjectively desired is a non sequitur.

This brings us to another of the three core concerns discussed in Chapter 1: the need each person has to rely on the commitments of others. To ensure that a rights transfer is value enhancing for *both* parties, both parties must assent to transfer their rights to each other. After this occurs, each party then needs to be able to count on or *rely upon* the transfer that has just taken place. Your agreement to sell me your car for $10,000 is only value enhancing to you if, having consented to the deal, you can then rely on my actually paying you the $10,000. We enter into contracts precisely to increase the chances that the other person will perform as promised, so that we may today rely more safely upon receiving that performance in the future.

Given that we cannot read each other's minds, our reliance can only be based on the appearance of assent created by another party. For this reason, contract law eschews a literal meeting of the minds—or subjective agreement—in favor of the objective appearance of subjective agreement. In other words, each party has a right to rely on the appearances created, whether intentionally or not, by the other party and vice versa.

How does this analysis explain the subjective twist? The objective theory allows each party to rely on the appearances created by the other. But before someone can be held responsible for his manifested commitment, the subjective twist requires that the other party really *did* rely on the commitment. So it was not enough that McKittrick appeared to a reasonable person to be agreeing to extend Embry's contract. Embry must have actually or subjectively relied on McKittrick's apparent consent. To protect the right of the other party, like Embry, to rely on the appearances, we hold parties like McKittrick responsible for commitments they may not have intended to be binding. For this reason, the subjective twist requires that Embry did indeed rely on McKittrick's objective manifestation.

Conversely, the subjective twist does not require that McKittrick read Embry's mind at the time of formation, which would reintroduce the problems associated with subjective assent. McKittrick remains responsible for the appearance he creates regardless of whether he subjectively meant to bind himself contractually. The subjective twist only allows him to avoid the obligation that ordinarily follows the appearances if court finds that Embry did not in fact rely on these appearances.

Studying why there is an objective theory of contract, and also why it is qualified by a subjective twist, provides an opportunity to step back and view the big picture. As will be discussed at greater length in Chapter 4 (section 4.1), the law of contracts, property, and torts can be viewed as defining boundaries within which people may make their own choices in pursuit of their own happiness. You are allowed to do what you wish with what is yours (as defined by property law), provided that you do not infringe (as defined by tort law) on the property of others—including the inalienable property rights one has in one's own body. Contract law provides the means by which people can transfer their property to another by their consent.[3]

So contracts, property, and torts—along with other subjects such as restitution—can be viewed as providing the legal boundaries defining the scope of individual liberty and distinguishing rightful from wrongful conduct. To act rightfully is to remain within these boundaries; conduct is wrongful when it crosses over into another's rightful domain. These boundaries do not presuppose an

---

3. Note, however, that wholly gratuitous transfers or *gifts*, as distinguished from transfers that are a part of an exchange, are traditionally considered to be an aspect of property law, not contracts. To be enforceable, gifts typically require actual or constructive delivery.

atomistic individualism in which each person is an island. Instead, they address the interconnected nature of human social life by distinguishing those actions that are permissible *even if they do somehow affect others* from those that are not. In this way property rights define private jurisdictions within which persons are able to pursue their own happiness while living in society with others that are analogous to the borders of a nation within which each government is free to pursue its own policies while living in peace with other nations.

If the law is doing its boundary-defining job, each person should know, or be able to find out, what physical resources belong to him for his use, and what belongs to others, as well as how to use what is his without interfering with the like rights of others. In this way, these legal boundaries or limits on rightful conduct provide vital information to all those who might wish to avoid disputes and respect the rights of others. Potential conflicts between persons who might otherwise vie for control of a given resource are thus avoided, and society as a whole is rendered more harmonious.

In contract law, this informational or boundary-defining function is served by requiring that consent to alienate or transfer one's rights be *manifested* or communicated by one party to the other. Without a manifestation of assent that is accessible to all affected parties, the law will have failed to identify clearly and communicate to both parties (and to third parties) the rightful boundaries that all must respect. Without such communication, parties to a transaction (and third parties) cannot accurately ascertain what constitutes rightful conduct and what constitutes a commitment on which they can rely. Disputes that might otherwise be avoided will occur, and the attendant uncertainties of the transfer process will discourage beneficial reliance.

This analysis explains why, generally, one's consent to transfer rights depends not on one's subjective opinion about the meaning of one's words or conduct, but on the ordinary meaning that is attached to them. If the word "yes" ordinarily means *yes*, then a subjective and unrevealed belief that "yes" means *no* is generally immaterial.

Only a general reliance on objectively ascertainable assertive conduct will enable a legal system to perform its boundary-defining function.

Of course, because one of the core concerns of contract is that the actual or inner subjective welfare of each party be increased, contracts are interpreted with an eye toward honoring the actual intentions of the parties. In the main, genuinely consensual exchanges are value enhancing. Nevertheless, where the subjective intentions of one party have not been manifested or communicated to the other, only the reasonable or objective interpretation of the commitment will establish the clear boundaries that are required for people to pursue happiness without interfering in the like pursuit by others of their happiness.

There is nothing novel or revolutionary about contract law's concern for protecting reliance by promisees. One of the most important functions of the institution of property rights is to legally protect certain expectations of rights holders so that they may rely on the continued use of certain resources. For example, owners of land rely on their titles when they invest in building houses or factories upon it, because they expect that their titles will be honored by a legal system in the future. They also rely on their titles when they leave town on vacation, expecting their property to still be theirs when they return.

But, to return to the subjective twist, such reliance is only protected *where it actually exists*. In *Embry*, the employee must have actually relied on the appearance of a commitment by his employer. If he did not, there is no reliance to protect, so Embry must show not only that a reasonable person would have thought that McKittrick assented but that he, Embry, subjectively thought this too.

When we reach the topic of interpreting the meaning of the words of a contract, we will find another subjective qualification of the objective approach: where both parties can be shown to have subjectively understood words to have a particular meaning, this meaning will be enforced regardless of whether a reasonable person would have interpreted the meaning another way. But first, we need to consider some doctrines that have developed to identify whether or not assent has been manifested.

𝕄 3.2 Reaching an Agreement

Contract law has developed a number of doctrines for identifying when people have objectively manifested their assent to enter into a contract with each other. In law school, considerable time is often spent studying the rules governing *offer and acceptance.* Before considering some of these rules, it is worth noting that modern contract law does not require that the element of mutual assent be reached solely by means of an offer followed by an acceptance. Most major business transactions take place after extensive negotiations between agents of companies, followed by their lawyers working out the legal details. By the time a formal agreement is drafted it is no longer possible to identify who made the offer and who accepted it. At the time of formation there is simply a lengthy agreement that is signed by representatives of both parties. Still, many contracts are formed by offer and acceptance, for example, when buying a house or car. And examining the theoretical puzzles posed by the doctrines governing offer and acceptance helps students come to grips with the underlying structure of contract law.

3.2.1 Offers versus Preliminary Negotiations

One issue that can arise in practice is the need to distinguish preliminary negotiations from an offer that the other side can and did accept. For example, *Texaco v. Pennzoil,*[4] one of the biggest contracts disputes of all time, involved whether Texaco had tortiously interfered with a contract for Getty Oil to purchase Pennzoil by

---

4. 729 S.W.2d 768 (1987).

offering Pennzoil owners a higher purchase price for the company than Getty offered. Texaco alleged that, because Getty and Pennzoil were still engaged in preliminary negotiations there was no contract with which they could interfere. Getty maintained that their offer had already been accepted and that they were just working out some details. When the Texas Supreme Court accepted Getty's argument, Texaco was on the hook for $8.5 *billion*.

Appreciating the difference between a true offer and preliminary negotiations provides important insights into the underlying structure of contract law. Section 24 of the *Restatement 2nd* defines an offer as "the manifestation of willingness to enter into a bargain, so made as to justify another person in understanding that his assent to that bargain is invited and will conclude it." Section 26 then distinguishes preliminary negotiations from an offer "if the person to whom it is addressed knows or has reason to know that the person making it does not intend to conclude a bargain until he has made a further manifestation of assent."

A manifestation of assent to enter into a bargain is an offer rather than preliminary negotiations if its terms are so definite or complete that all the other side has to do is say "yes." As in *Embry*, the issue is whether an offeree had *reason to believe* that an offer was intended by the purported offeror, not whether the offeror had the subjective intention to make a legally binding commitment.

How does *completeness* indicate or manifest a willingness to enter into a legally binding bargain? At issue is whether it appears to the offeree that the offeror intends to be bound upon acceptance, that is, with no more negotiations over terms. If the terms are perfectly clear then no further negotiations are required and all that remains to be done is accept. The more complete the offer, the more it is clear to the offeree (1) what the terms of a bargain are, (2) that the offeror does not anticipate further negotiations, and therefore (3) that a particular bargain is being proposed that is ripe for acceptance.

Consider the *Restatement's* definitions of contract and promise that were quoted in the Introduction. In section 1, the *Restatement* defines a contract this way: "A contract is a promise or a set of promises for the breach of which the law gives a remedy, or the performance of which the law in some way recognizes as a duty." In essence, a contract is an enforceable promise. In section 2, it then defines a promise as "a manifestation of intention to act or refrain from acting in a specified way, so made as to justify a promisee in understanding that a *commitment* has been made" (emphasis added). An offer is not yet a promise for it is not a commitment until it is accepted.

To constitute an offer, the terms communicated must be certain or definite enough to constitute a commitment upon the other party saying "yes." Although *Restatement* section 33(1) says this is true "[e]ven though a manifestation of intention is intended to be understood as an offer," the lack of certain terms suggests that a communication was not intended to be an offer. According to section 33(3): "The fact that one or more terms of a proposed bargain are left open or uncertain may show that a manifestation of intention is not intended to be understood as an offer or as an acceptance."

When we turn to the Uniform Commercial Code (UCC) we can better understand why the uncertainty of terms undermines the existence of a commitment. According to section 2-204(3): "Even though one or more terms are left open a contract for sale does not fail for indefiniteness if the parties have intended to make a contract and there is a reasonably certain basis for giving an appropriate remedy." Of particular significance is the fact that the parties "intended to make a contract." Notice that, in the UCC, indefiniteness is an indication of the parties' lack of intent to enter into a contract. The Official Comment to section 2-204 says: "The more terms the parties leave open the less likely it is that they have intended to conclude a binding agreement." Therefore, section 2-204 enforces contracts that still have some terms to be worked out but which are not so indefinite as to negate intent to make a contract.

We may now see what separates an offer from preliminary negotiations: the intent to make a contract. When the certainty of terms being conveyed manifests this intent, the communication is characterized as an offer that may be accepted by the other party. When accepted, an offer then becomes a commitment that may be enforced. When the terms are too uncertain, we cannot conclude that they manifest the intent to enter into a contract if accepted, and we characterize the communication as preliminary negotiations.

3.2.2 Offers versus Jests

That to be an offer a communication must convey an intent to contract is illustrated by the doctrine governing alleged offers made in jest. In the classic case of *Lucy v. Zehmer*,[5] the seller tried to get out of a sale by claiming that he had only been joking when he agreed to sell his farm. The court rejected his claim on the ground that, whatever might have been in the seller's mind, the buyer had no reason to doubt the seriousness of the offer: "[A] person cannot set up that he was merely jesting when his conduct and words would warrant a reasonable person in believing that he *intended a real agreement*" (emphasis added).

Similarly, in the more recent case of *Leonard v. Pepsico*,[6] the court rejected the plaintiff's claim that the defendant had made an offer to exchange a $23 million Harrier jet airplane for seven million "Pepsi Points" because, the court concluded, the alleged offer was really made in jest. The court relied on the following statement from *Corbin on Contracts:* "What kind of act creates a power of acceptance and is therefore an offer? It must be an expression of will or intention. It must be an act that leads the offeree reasonably to conclude that *a power to create a contract* is conferred" (emphasis added). It then examined numerous factors undermining the

---

5. 196 Va. 493, 84 S.E.2d 516 (1954).

6. 88 F. Supp. 2d 116 (1999).

reasonableness of interpreting the advertisement as conveying an intention to enter into a legally binding agreement.

3.2.3 Bilateral versus Unilateral Contracts

That a manifestation of assent or promise involves a *commitment* also helps us to understand the traditional distinction between bilateral and unilateral contracts. A classic case of unilateral contract is *Carlill v. Carbolic Smoke Ball Co.*[7] There the seller advertised that if a buyer contracted influenza after using the Carbolic Smoke Ball, it would pay a reward of £100. When the buyer, Mrs. Carlill, contracted influenza and claimed the reward, the company contended that acceptance of its offer required her to notify the company. The court rejected the company's contention and found that she had accepted the offer by performing the act of buying and using the smoke ball as directed. In other words, Mrs. Carlill accepted the offer by her performance, rather than by making her own promise to perform.

Modern contracts scholars eventually came to believe that the only difference between a bilateral and unilateral contract was the mode of acceptance. With a bilateral contract, an offer is accepted by a promise. So my offer to buy your car for $10,000 is accepted by your promise to sell it to me. With a unilateral contract, an offer is accepted by the performance of the act requested in the offer. So my offer to pay a reward of $500 for the return of my lost dog is accepted, not by your promise to find my dog, but by the act of actually finding and returning it to me.

Consequently, to avoid the impression that they were two different kinds of contracts, rather than merely referring to two different modes of accepting an offer, the concepts of bilateral and unilateral contracts were omitted from the *Restatement 2nd*. Comment f to section 1 explained: "[T]he original Restatement defined unilateral

---

7. 1 Q.B. 256 (1893).

and bilateral contracts. It has not been carried forward because of doubt as to the utility of the distinction, often treated as fundamental, between the two types."

But, this new approach led to a problem. Offers may be freely revoked up until the time they are accepted. Performance constituting acceptance has never been defined as *partial* performance of the requested act or acts. The consideration requested is *complete* performance. Although the offer of a reward is certainly made to induce people to search, the reward is for actually finding the dog, not for searching for it. So, if an offer is revoked before it has been accepted by complete performance, when performance is finally completed, no recovery may be available.

What happens if the offeree invests substantial resources in partially performing or preparing to perform, but the offer is withdrawn just before performance is completed? Because the offer may be withdrawn up until the time that performance is complete, when performance entails considerable expense and trouble in preparation, the person who is in the process of performing when the offer is revoked may be out a good deal.

Could this problem be fixed by deeming partial performance to be an acceptance of the offer, thereby rendering it irrevocable? If partial performance counts as an acceptance, however, more than the offeree's reliance is protected. The offeree is now bound as well and can be held in breach for failure to complete performance, which may not be at all what the offeree wants. If acceptance requires completing performance, the offeree retains its discretion to cease performance at any time without liability. Just as the offeror may revoke, the offeree can decide to quit.

The authors of the *Restatement 2nd* attempted to address these complications by restricting the power of offerors to revoke their offers. Section 45(1) provides: "Where an offer invites an offeree to accept by rendering a performance and does not invite a promissory acceptance, an *option contract* is created when the offeree tenders *or begins* the invited performance or tenders a beginning of it" (emphases added). An option contract limits the power of an offeror to rescind an offer, while the offeree retains *the option* of accepting or not. An option can be thought of as a subsidiary contract to keep an offer open.

Options are a very important and useful type of commercial contract. For example, there is an international market in options for the future delivery of commodities. But option contracts are entirely one sided. While the offer is irrevocable for a period of time, the offeree is completely free to accept or not. For this reason, options are normally paid for. The *Restatement* tries to mitigate this problem of one-sidedness by suspending the offeror's duty of performance until the complete performance is received. Section 45(2) says that "[t]he offeror's duty of performance under any option contract so created is conditional on completion or tender of the invited performance in accordance with the terms of the offer." Until it receives performance, the offeror is not required to perform its end of the deal, but neither can it revoke its offer and find someone else to do the job. Having made the offer, it must wait for a performance that may never arrive. To protect itself from being bound by an option contract, an offeror should require a return promise from the offeree, However, offerees may not want to commit themselves in advance to fully performing. This is all very complicated.

A Defense of the Traditional Distinction Between Bilateral and Unilateral Contracts

Could it be that some of these complications result from eliminating the traditional distinction between bilateral and unilateral contracts? One scholar who thinks this was a mistake is Peter Tiersma. In a fascinating article,[8] he observed an important difference between the speech act of a *promise* and that of an *offer*, two terms that are often used interchangeably even by contracts professors

---

8. Peter Tiersma, *Reassessing Unilateral Contracts: The Role of Offer, Acceptance, and Promise*, 26 U.C. DAVIS L. REV. 1 (1992).

and the courts. Whereas a promise is a commitment, an offer is only a commitment *if accepted*. An offer is not a promise until after it is accepted, whether by counter-promise or performance.

This difference is even reflected in the *Restatement's* own definitions. Section 2 defines as promise as "a manifestation of intention to act or refrain from acting in a specified way, so made as to justify a promisee in understanding that *a commitment has been made*" (emphasis added). By contrast, section 24 defines an offer as "the manifestation of willingness to enter into a bargain, so made as to justify another person in understanding that his assent to that bargain is invited and *will conclude* it." So whereas an offeror's commitment is conditioned on it being accepted by an offeree, a promisor has, by definition, made a commitment by promising.

Did the Carbolic Smoke Ball Company make an *offer* conditioned on acceptance by Mrs. Carlill's performance, or did it make a *promise* requiring no acceptance at all? The words of the advertisement were not conditioned on any acceptance by the buyer; nor can such a condition fairly be implied. Of course, while it was not conditioned on acceptance, the promise to pay the reward was conditioned on Mrs. Carlill using the smoke ball as directed and contracting influenza. But these conditions were satisfied.

The modern account treats offers as though they were promises and suggests that the only difference between bilateral and unilateral contracts is the mode of acceptance, which implies that both bilateral and unilateral contracts involve offers. But Tiersma's analysis suggests that promises are not offers and, unlike offers, promises require no acceptance to constitute commitments. Whereas bilateral contracts involve offers requiring acceptance to become commitments, unilateral contracts involve promises that are commitments without any acceptance. In *Carlill*, there was no acceptance because there was no offer. Instead there was a promise.

According to Tiersma, whether or not a unilateral commitment or promise is legally enforceable is a question to be addressed by the second element of a contract to be discussed in Chapter 4: the element of enforceability. If his analysis is correct, then sometimes a

MUTUAL ASSENT 83

contract can be formed even though there was only a unilateral assent. Although the smoke ball company made a unilateral promise, Mrs. Carlill was not obligated to buy or use the smoke ball, and was certainly under no obligation to contract influenza; nor was she obligated to make a claim for the reward. Only the company was unilaterally obligated to pay the reward provided that Mrs. Carlill bought the ball, used it as directed, and got sick anyway.

Contracts based on unilateral promises are made to induce reliance that is desired by the promisor. As Tiersma explains, the "primary purpose of unilateral contracts, such as reward offers or promises to pay a commission to a real estate broker, is to motivate the offeree to do the requested act." In other words, "their goal is to induce reliance." Consider the examples of an offer to pay someone to paint a fence or find a lost dog. Any such offer "provides precious little inducement if it remains freely revocable until full performance." By unilaterally committing himself when making his promise, the offeror is most likely to induce the reliance he seeks. "He can only do this by the speech act of promising, rather than offering." It is the promissor's unilateral commitment in the form of a promise that justifies the promisee's preparation or initial performance. "If the law truly believes that the offeror is the master of his offer, it should recognize that when he truly wants the promisee to perform a particular act, he will make a promise, thus binding himself from the inception."

So, according to Tiersma's analysis, the question in *Carbolic Smoke Ball* is not whether the Carbolic Smoke Ball Company made an offer that became a (bilateral) commitment if Mrs. Carlill accepted by her performance of buying and using the smoke ball, as the modern *Restatement* approach defines the issue. The question is whether the Carbolic Smoke Ball company made a (unilateral) promise or commitment not requiring an acceptance of any kind— although its duty to perform its commitment was conditioned on Mrs. Carlill buying and using the ball as directed and then getting sick.

True, as with option contracts, the commitment of a unilateral promise is one-sided. So the practical result is similar to the compromise provided by the option contract approach of section 45. But it is a commitment that is based on the unqualified words of the promise, rather than fictionally imputing to an offeror a promise not to revoke its offer. Tiersma's analysis focuses our attention on whether the words and deeds amounted to a unilateral commitment or "promise" as defined in *Restatement 2nd*, section 2, or an "offer" as defined in section 24, an issue concealed by the *Restatement's* singular concern for offers that are accepted by either counter-promise or performance.

To repeat, assuming a commitment has been made, whether bilaterally or unilaterally, there still remains the question of whether it is the type of commitment that should be enforced, an issue addressed by other doctrines to be discussed in Chapter 4. Although this is not how contract law currently understands this type of transaction, the difference between the speech acts of promising and offering nevertheless exists in the real world and affects our intuitions about these cases. Appreciating this difference will help you navigate the perplexities of unilateral contracts, should the subject arise in class, and qualifies the first element of a contract that requires mutual assent.

✺ 3.3 Interpreting the Agreement

Once we are satisfied that there was mutual assent (or that there was a unilateral promise), we must still ascertain its meaning. The meaning of the words used to express an agreement can be *ambiguous* or *vague*. "Ambiguity, properly defined, is an entirely distinct concept from that of vagueness."[9] According to Allan Farnsworth, "[a] word that may or may not be applicable to marginal objects is vague." For example, when we say an object is "light" in weight, the dividing line between light and heavy is fuzzy. "But a

---

9. E. Allan Farnsworth, *Meaning in the Law of Contracts*, 76 YALE L.J. 939, 953 (1967).

word may also have two entirely different connotations." Referring to a feather as "light" can mean either that it is light in weight or light in color. Without more information, the word "light" in this context is ambiguous.

As with identifying the manifestation of assent, an objective approach is also used to interpret the language used to express the terms of a contract and address issues of ambiguity and vagueness. Perhaps the most famous and rhetorically extreme statement of the objective theory was made by Judge Learned Hand:

> A contract has, strictly speaking, nothing to do with the personal, or individual, intent of the parties. A contract is an obligation attached by the mere force of law to certain acts of the parties, usually words, which ordinarily accompany and represent a known intent. If, however, it were proved by twenty bishops that *either* party when he used the words intended something else than the usual meaning which the law imposes on them, he would still be held, unless there were mutual mistake or something else of the sort.[10]

Yet, as with *Dickenson v. Dodds*, there may be a bit less to Hand's objectivist claim than this statement seems to suggest. In the very next sentence, often omitted from quotations, he offers an important qualification: "Of course, if it appear by other words, or acts, of the parties, that they attribute a peculiar meaning to such words as they use in the contract, that meaning will prevail, but only by virtue of the other words, and not because of their unexpressed intent." Just as the court in *Dickenson* softened its affirmation of a subjective meeting of the minds with a reference to the appearance of such a subjective agreement, so too did Learned Hand qualify his affirmation of an objective approach with a subjective element. Where *both* parties can be shown to have subjectively attached an idiosyncratic meaning to a particular term, it is the idiosyncratic

---

10. Hotchkiss v. National City Bank, 200 F. 287, 293 (S.D.N.Y. 1911) (emphasis added).

meaning and not the meaning as understood by a reasonable person that governs their relationship. This subjective element of contract interpretation is different than the subjective twist discussed above concerning the existence of assent to contract. With manifesting assent, the twist is that a reasonable person must have understood the promisor to be assenting, and the promisee subjectively understood it as well. The promisor need not have subjectively understood that he was binding himself. With interpretation, the meaning that a reasonable person would attach to the terms is what governs the agreement, unless *both parties* can be shown to have subjectively meant something different. In other words, the subjective understanding shared by both parties will trump the objective meaning.

So when does the objective meaning apply? It applies if the parties do *not* share the same subjective understanding of the meaning of the terms. When this happens, the party whose understanding corresponds to the objective meaning will prevail. Why? For the same reason that the objective theory of assent was adopted: because we cannot read each other's minds, each party is entitled to rely on the objective appearances created by the other. But where it turns out that both parties did indeed share an idiosyncratic meaning of the terms, then neither party relied on the objective meaning and enforcing that meaning would conform to the understanding of neither party. But what if the parties' understandings differ and neither party's understanding conforms with a single objective meaning because the term is ambiguous, which means it has more than one meaning?

3.3.1 Resolving Ambiguity

This unusual situation arose in one of the most famous of the classic contracts cases: *Raffles v. Wichelhaus.*[11] In *Raffles*, the defendant

---

11. 2 Hurl. & C. 906, 159 Eng. Rep. 375 (Ex. 1864).

agreed to buy and the plaintiff agreed to sell 125 bales of Surat cotton "guaranteed middling fair merchant's Dhollorah ... to arrive ex 'Peerless' from Bombay." When the goods arrived at Liverpool on the *Peerless*, the defendant refused to accept or pay for them. The defendant claimed that he thought the goods were arriving on a different ship named *Peerless* that had previously arrived in port. After the plaintiff's lawyer conceded, for the sake of argument, that the defendant had intended a different ship named *Peerless*, the defendant's lawyer argued that there had been no "consensus ad idem" or meeting of the minds. The court then stopped him from further argument, declaring that "[t]here must be judgment for the defendants."

Although *Raffles* surely looks to be a case of subjective disagreement, in his book, *The Common Law*,[12] Oliver Wendell Holmes, Jr. claimed it was entirely consistent with an objective theory of contractual interpretation. Holmes began by affirming the objective approach. "The law has nothing to do with the actual state of the parties' minds. In contract, as elsewhere, it must go by externals, and judge parties by their conduct." So, if "If there had been but one 'Peerless,' and the defendant had said 'Peerless' by mistake, meaning 'Peri,' he would have been bound." But then Holmes offered the following somewhat mysterious explanation: "The true ground of the decision was not that each party *meant* a different thing from the other, as is implied by the explanation which has been mentioned, but that each *said* a different thing. The plaintiff offered one thing, the defendant expressed his assent to another."

In his influential and entertaining little book, *The Death of Contract*,[13] Grant Gilmore famously ridiculed Holmes's reasoning: "The magician who could 'objectify' *Raffles v. Wichelhaus* ... could, the need arising, objectify anything." The issue, however, is not

---

12. OLIVER WENDELL HOLMES, JR., THE COMMON LAW 242 ([1881] Howe ed. 1963) (emphases added).

13. GRANT GILMORE, THE DEATH OF CONTRACT 40–42 (Ohio State Univ. Press, 1974).

whether the court in *Raffles* was applying a subjective meeting-of-the-minds approach, which it seems clearly to have done. The issue is whether the outcome in *Raffles* is *also* consistent with an objective approach. Contrary to Gilmore, Holmes was right to claim it was. Seeing why illuminates how the objective approach, with its subjective element, operates.

Suppose that both parties had in mind the December *Peerless* even though "ex 'Peerless' from Bombay" might well have applied to the October *Peerless* as well: What result and why? There is a contract for delivery on the December *Peerless*. The term "Peerless" in the contract is ambiguous from an objective point of view. I shall call such a term "objectively ambiguous" by which I mean that no single reasonable meaning can be attached to it. Both October and December meanings are equally reasonable; a reasonable person could be referring to either ship. Assuming, however, that *both* parties subjectively meant the December *Peerless*, then the subjective understanding of both parties will prevail over the objectively ambiguous meaning.

Why? As previously explained, the objective approach was developed in recognition of a person's need to rely on the stated words of others. Where the parties are in subjective agreement, however, the enforcement of an objective meaning is unnecessary. In this hypothetical, there is no conflict between the parties' subjective understanding of the term. Nor is there any conflict between that understanding and the objective meaning, which is ambiguous and thus includes the intended meaning. Therefore, the parties' mutual intention is the subjective meaning (December), and this is the meaning that governs. So too says section 201(1) of the *Restatement 2nd*: "Where the parties have attached the same meaning to a promise or agreement or a term thereof, it is interpreted in accordance with that meaning."

Although potentially ambiguous terms are common, the context usually narrows the reasonable meaning to just one. The existence of an objective ambiguity when two meanings are equally reasonable is rare. Proof of subjective agreement in the face of such ambiguity is even rarer—or perhaps is just rarely litigated. The more common of these abnormal cases arising out of the objective ambiguity of a term is one in which there is a genuine misunderstanding between the parties as to the meaning of the term—that is, each party understands the term to have a different meaning. For example, one party thinks "Peerless" refers to the October *Peerless*, whereas the other thinks it refers to the December *Peerless*. In such a situation, which interpretation should prevail? To answer this, we need more facts.

Suppose now that there is a genuine subjective *misunderstanding* of an objectively ambiguous term, and one party (and only one party) actually knows (1) that the other party attaches a different meaning to the term and (2) the substance of that meaning. For example, the seller subjectively intends December, and buyer subjectively intends October, but the buyer knows (perhaps from something the seller says) that the seller means December. What result? There is a contract on the seller's terms, that is, the December *Peerless*. Why? The reason why we have an objective theory—to protect the unavoidable reliance on the appearances because of limited access to subjective intentions—is inapplicable in the situation where one party actually knows that an objectively ambiguous term is not subjectively being given the same meaning by the other party. Therefore a party is not justified in relying on the objective meaning when the other party's subjective meaning of a term is known to him. In other words, the objective theory is superfluous. In accord is section 201(2)(a) of the *Restatement 2nd*:

> Where the parties have attached different meanings to a promise or agreement or a term thereof, it is interpreted in accordance with the meaning attached by one of them if at the time the agreement was made ... that party *did not know* of any different meaning attached by the other, and the other *knew* the meaning attached by the first party (emphases added).

Now what if each party attached a different meaning to the objectively ambiguous term, "Peerless," and neither party actually knew what the other party thought "Peerless" meant, but one party had *reason to know* that the other party meant December. What result? Although this is a closer case, there is a contract for the December *Peerless*, just as there was when one party somehow had actual knowledge of the subjective understanding of the other. Once again, the objective approach is adopted because parties cannot read each other's thoughts and are normally entitled to rely on the appearances. But, in this variation, one party has reason to know that the other might have adopted an idiosyncratic meaning. The existence of this reason to know undermines the reasonableness of relying on one of the normal meanings of the ambiguous term. Here too, the *Restatement 2nd* agrees. Section 201(2)(b) specifies that

> Where the parties have attached different meanings to a promise or agreement or a term thereof, it is interpreted in accordance with the meaning attached by one of them if at the time the agreement was made . . . that party had *no reason to know* of any different meaning attached by the other, and the other had *reason to know* the meaning attached by the first party (emphases added).

Now suppose that the dominant custom in this business when a common ship name was designated was to accept delivery from the first ship by that name to enter port. In such a case, the objective meaning of the term "Peerless" would be established. In other words, the term is no longer objectively ambiguous because a reasonable person would know what it meant in this type of contract. Therefore, under the objective approach, if one of the parties subjectively meant this ship, its understanding would prevail, even if the other party did not share this understanding. As section 202(3)(a) of the *Restatement 2nd* states: "Unless a different intention is manifested, where language has a generally prevailing meaning, it is interpreted in accordance with that meaning." And section 202(3)(b) says that "technical terms and words of art are given their technical meaning when used in a transaction within their technical field."

Finally, we are in a position to return to the actual (assumed) facts of *Raffles v. Wichelhaus* where (1) the term "Peerless" was objectively ambiguous; (2) each party attached a different meaning to the term; (3) neither party knew of the other's meaning; and (4) neither party had reason to know of the other party's meaning. The result was a failure of mutual assent. Why? If the terms could not be given a singular objective meaning by the parties, then the court could not determine what the terms of the agreement were. In short, there was no *objective* agreement. After the fact, therefore, one party may not seek to have one of the two reasonable meanings enforced when there was no single reasonable meaning in existence at the time of formation, and both parties did not subjectively share a single meaning.

The *Restatement* agrees. Section 201(3) says that "neither party is bound by the meaning attached by the other, even though the result may be a failure of mutual assent." If all of these techniques for ascertaining meaning are unavailable, the contract may simply be unenforceable for lack of mutual assent. Comment d to section 201 concurs: "Where the rules stated in [s]ubsections (1) and (2) do not apply, neither party is bound by the understanding of the other. The result may be an entire failure of agreement or a failure to agree as to a term."

So Holmes' objective reading of *Raffles* was not as crazy as Gilmore suggested. From an objective standpoint, by using the same term, each party manifested or "said a different thing" because the term each used was objectively ambiguous. And it was this ambiguity that led to a subjective misunderstanding (if you believe the defendant). The moral of this story is that the objective approach, as actually used, does not represent the complete overthrow of a subjective approach in the way that those who selectively quote Learned Hand suggest. Instead, the shared subjective understanding of the parties will be honored unless there is no meeting of the minds, in which case either party is entitled to rely on the unambiguous reasonable meaning of the terms that were expressed. However, where there is *both* no subjective agreement and no unambiguous reasonable meaning, the agreement will fail.

3.3.2 Resolving Vagueness

Suppose a disagreement arises between the parties not over the meaning of an ambiguous term, but over whether a term includes or excludes a particular item. This is a problem of vagueness. A famous example of vagueness is provided by the case of *Fragiliment Importing Co. v. B.N.S. International Sales Corp.*,[14] in which the contract called for the delivery of "chicken" of specified sizes and weights. When the defendant delivered stewing chicken or "fowl" rather than young chicken suitable for broiling and frying, the plaintiffs objected. The word "chicken" that gave rise to the dispute in this case was not ambiguous in the sense that it had two entirely different meanings that either or both parties intended to employ. Instead, the dispute arose over how the word was meant to apply beyond its agreed core meaning. Did it include all sorts of chicken, including stewing chicken or, under the circumstances, was its scope limited to young chicken suitable for frying or broiling?

In *Frigaliment*, each party testified concerning his subjective understanding of the word "chicken." The court concluded that "it is clear that defendant believed it could comply with the contracts by delivering stewing chicken in the 2 1/2-3 lbs. size." As discussed in the previous section, the court affirmed that the defendant's "subjective intent would not be significant if this did not coincide with an objective meaning of 'chicken.'" Of course, this statement is accurate only if there is a subjective misunderstanding between the parties about the scope of the word "chicken." Had the plaintiff been able to prove that there was a shared, limited, subjective

---

14. 190 F. Supp. 116 (1960).

understanding about the scope of the term "chicken" as it was used in their agreement, this understanding would apply regardless of whether it coincided with an objective meaning.

The case is also interesting because of the diversity of sources the court examined to discern the term's objective meaning to see if it sided with one or the other party's subjective understanding. Judge Henry Friendly concluded that the defendant's meaning "did coincide with one of the dictionary meanings, with the definition in the Department of Agriculture Regulations to which the contract made at least oblique reference, with at least some usage in the trade, with the realities of the market, and with what plaintiff's spokesman had said."

The plaintiff too introduced evidence of trade usage that "chicken" had a narrower meaning. The court thought this usage was not so well established that the defendant could be expected to know it especially given that he was new to the business. Indeed one of the plaintiff's witnesses admitted that, in his own contracts, he used "broiler" when he wanted younger birds and "fowl" when older were acceptable. From all this, Judge Friendly concluded that "the plaintiff has the burden of showing that 'chicken' was used in the narrower rather than in the broader sense, and this it has not sustained." Judge Friendly's distinction between narrow and broad senses of the term show that the problem here was one of vagueness not ambiguity.

3.3.3 The Hierarchy of Evidence of Meaning

There is a hierarchy of issues that courts consider when ascertaining the meaning of an agreement:

First, we try to establish if both parties subjectively attached the same meaning to the term—that is, we see if there was a subjective understanding. Courts begin with other provisions in the contract itself to see if they inform the meaning of the term in question. They also look for evidence of subjective understanding to the parties' negotiations, their course of performance, and their course of other dealings. If such an understanding can be shown, there is no misunderstanding in fact. There is an agreement or mutual assent and the enforceable term is the meaning subjectively held by both parties.

Second, if no subjective agreement can be shown—that is, each party subjectively attached a different meaning to the term—there is a *misunderstanding*. We then see if one party knows or has reason to know that the other party has attached a different meaning to the term and what that meaning is. If so, the enforceable term is the meaning held by the party who was ignorant of the misunderstanding.

Third, failing this, we look to objective meaning of the terms. If an objective meaning of the words of the parties can be determined—for example, by looking to usage of trade—and one of the parties mistakenly interprets a word with an objectively ascertainable meaning, he is bound nonetheless. For example, if a promisor said "Peerless" while subjectively meaning "Peri," if the promisee understood the promisor to mean *Peerless*, and *Peerless* is also the reasonable meaning, then the promisee wins. This is the type of case in which it makes a difference that courts adopt an objective theory of interpretation rather than requiring a subjective meeting of the minds. A party has the right to rely on the objective meaning manifested by the other party, so long as he was not subjectively aware that the other party attached a different meaning to the term.

Conversely, if there is no unique or objective meaning, then the term is objectively ambiguous. This is the same as saying that "Peerless" and "Peri" are both reasonable meanings. With this sort of misunderstanding, there is no agreement or manifested assent. There was no objectively manifested mutual assent. What was objectively manifested was ambiguous, and there was only the appearance of mutual assent. But this defect can sometimes be cured by one party agreeing in a timely manner to be bound by the term subjectively held by the other party—thereby waiving the ambiguity. This is called "cure by concession."

This hierarchy of issues results in a corresponding hierarchy of evidence:

Words of the Contract → Prior Negotiations → Course of Performance → Course of Other Dealings → Usage of Trade

Notice that all but the last of these can be used to show either a subjective understanding or that one party knew or had reason to know of the meaning attached to a term by the other party. If the parties' subjective understanding is like a stone thrown in a pond, each type of evidence in the hierarchy represents ripples moving away from the parties' subjective intent until it reaches the last—usage of trade—which is not about the parties' subjective understanding but instead establishes the objective meaning a reasonable third person would attach to the term.

🕊 3.4 Filling Genuine Gaps in the Agreement

Up until now, we have considered how to interpret the words that parties used to express their agreement when these words are ambiguous or vague. But it is impossible to include expressed terms that will cover every possible contingency. For this reason all manifestations of assent are inevitably incomplete. Another way of characterizing this problem is that every expression of consent contains "gaps." What do we do when we discover the existence of a gap in the parties' agreement? Do we refuse to enforce the contract as we do when there is a genuine misunderstanding between the parties about an objectively ambiguous term?

Because we cannot know the parties' intentions, providing terms that "fill the gaps" in the manifested intentions would seem to violate the parties' freedom of contract. If so, how do we justify such gap-filling? Is the pervasiveness of gaps and gap-filling evidence that undercuts the importance of consent in the formation of contractual obligation? And how exactly do we do it? Do we choose gap-fillers according to some principle or policy? We now turn to contract law doctrines that handle the problem of filling gaps, and evaluate the relationship of these doctrines to contractual freedom or consent.

3.4.1 Agreements with Open Terms

Traditionally, so-called "agreements to agree" are considered unenforceable. Yet the fact that an agreement has one or more open terms to be agreed on after formation does not always render it unenforceable. The majority and dissenting judges in *Sun Printing & Publishing Association v. Remington Paper & Power Co.*,[15] presented opposing views on the enforcement of contracts with open terms. There the plaintiff agreed to buy and the defendant to sell 1000 tons of paper per month for 16 months. Although the price for the first 4 months of the contract was specified, for the remaining 12 months of the contract, it was defined as follows:

> [T]he price of the paper and the length of terms for which such price shall apply shall be agreed upon by and between the parties hereto fifteen days prior to the expiration of each period for which the price and length of term thereof have been previously agreed upon, said price in no event to be higher than the contract price for news print charged by the Canadian Export Paper Company to the large consumers, the seller to receive the benefit of any differentials in freight rates.

In essence, at the time of formation, the parties agreed to agree later on the pricing that would apply during the last 12 months of the contract.

Delivery was made for the first four months. In advance of the time that the new price and its duration were to be agreed on, the seller gave notice that it considered the contract to be imperfect,

---

15. 235 N.Y. 338, 139 N.E. 470 (1923).

and that it disclaimed any obligation to deliver in the future. Each month during 1920, the buyer repeated its demand that the seller deliver the specified quantity at the price being charged by the Canadian Export Paper Company. The seller persisted in its refusal.

In an opinion by Judge (and future Supreme Court Justice) Benjamin Cardozo, the New York Court of Appeals found that the agreement failed. True, the Canadian standard price each month, which was the maximum price under the contract, could be determined. But even so, the number of months that this price was to be in effect was also to be agreed on by the parties, and there was no way to establish this time period. The seller was not under a duty to accept a "reasonable" period of time in default of agreement. To so hold would be "to make the contract over." According to Cardozo, "the defendant reserved the privilege of doing business its own way, and did not undertake to conform to the practice and beliefs of others." The parties were free to make a contract with these terms, but they did not. In Cardozo's famous words, "[w]e are not at liberty to revise while professing to construe."

Judge Frederick Crane vehemently dissented from this conclusion. He argued that the parties both thought they were making a contract for the purchase and sale of 16,000 tons of newsprint. The contract was on a form provided by the seller, who then took the position that this document meant nothing, "that it was formally executed for the purpose of permitting the defendant to furnish paper or not, as it pleased." But surely these two intelligent parties did not execute a document that "was useless and amounted to nothing." For this reason, wrote Crane, "the court should spell out a binding contract, if it be possible."

Judge Crane then contended that the contract itself set out a sufficient "standard by which to measure the amount the plaintiff would have to pay": the Canadian standard price. But what about the number of months that this price was to run? Crane observed that there are many answers to this. "As the Defendant has broken the contract it can be held to deliver the balance of the paper at the price set on December 15." Or "you could set the price according to the Canadian standard each month." Or "if the evidence shows that the Canadian contract price is for a certain period, you could hold the price for that period, or you can apply the rule of reason and compel parties to contract in light of fair dealing." The court could hold this defendant to the Canadian price "for a period which is reasonable under all the circumstances and conditions as applied in the paper trade."

Crane's ability to articulate numerous different ways of filling in the gap unintentionally supported Cardozo's conclusion that this contract was too indefinite to be enforced. Although Crane claimed to be enforcing an agreement of the parties, the price to be applied to that transaction could not be determined *with reference to that agreement.* Each of Crane's suggestions would yield a different result, but none are compelled by the wording of the contract and none can be excluded by the terms either. Therefore the court would be inventing a term or, in Cardozo's words, "revis[ing] while professing to construe."

Like Cardozo, Crane concluded his dissent by invoking the primacy of freedom of contract: "To let this defendant escape from its formal obligations when any one of these rulings as applied to this contract would give a practical and just result is to give the sanction of law to a deliberate breach." Crane felt that parties who entered into an agreement that calls for further negotiations should not be able to exploit such a clause to get out of their agreement if a court can possibly prevent it. Allowing this will only encourage parties to refuse to negotiate if, during the contractual period, they discover that they can get a better price elsewhere. This option runs against their manifested intention to be legally bound throughout the whole duration of the contract. Whatever else you may think of reliance, parties should be able to rely on agreements that were clearly intended to be legally binding.

Freedom of Contract and Contracts with Open Terms

So who was right about "freedom of contract": Cardozo or Crane? As it turns out, the term "freedom of contract" is ambiguous. It can mean one or both of two propositions. Cardozo was unwilling to impose terms of an agreement on an unwilling seller. Call this "freedom *from* contract": Persons should not have contracts imposed upon them without their consent. Conversely, Crane was unwilling to let the seller get out of an obligation it freely assumed to the detriment of the other party who was entitled to rely on the contract. Call this "freedom *to* contract": When persons consent to contractual obligation, the courts should enforce their commitments. Both freedom *from* and freedom *to* contract are aspects of freedom *of* contract. For this reason our intuitions are torn between Cardozo and Crane in *Sun Printing*.

Can this conflict be reconciled? The concept of a default rule may help. Sometimes, so far as freedom of contract is concerned, it does not matter what the gap-filling rule is, so long as the parties have access to the rule. It is rational for repeat players such as the commercial parties in *Sun Printing* (or one-shot players in large transactions) to learn the content of the default rule through their lawyers. By remaining silent they have consented to *whatever* term the law supplies as a gap-filler, and the conflict between freedom from and freedom to contract is ameliorated. If a court or legislature were to adopt any of Crane's suggestions prospectively, parties who do not contract around this default rule could be said to have consented to it.

But the default rules supplied by contract law will also apply when one or both parties are "rationally ignorant," a concept that will be discussed further in section 3.5.2 in the context of form contracts. It is rational to remain ignorant of the background rules of contract law when the cost of hiring a lawyer to find out the rules that will be supplied by a court is greater than the risk of agreeing to an undesired term. When this is the case, if courts "fill the gap" with a term that rationally ignorant parties would expect, the agreement is likely to be consistent with their consent. For this reason, as was previously discussed in Chapter 2 in the context of the forseeability limitation on money damages (section 2.4.1), contract law should confine itself to common-sense default rules that unsophisticated parties would expect.

When both parties are one-shot players, a common-sense default rule will likely reflect their tacit intentions. Repeat players who do not like the default rule may contract around it by inserting an express clause to the contrary in the agreement. By doing this, they will put the other party on notice that the term actually governing the transaction is not one that it would ordinarily expect. In this way, default rules reflecting the conventional understanding of the less sophisticated party will induce contracting behavior by repeat players that will minimize latent subjective disagreements from occurring, and thereby reduce the likelihood that the court will inadvertently impose on the parties a term one of them did not expect.

The UCC and Contracts with Open Terms

With this analysis in mind, we can better appreciate the approach taken by the UCC to the problem of open terms. The UCC supplies numerous gap-filling default rules where the parties are silent. For example, section 2-305 allows parties to "conclude a contract for sale even though the price is not settled" if the parties "so intend." When this happens, the price is "a reasonable price at the time for delivery" if (a) "nothing is said as to price," or (b) "the price is left to be agreed by the parties and they fail to agree," or (c) "the price is to be fixed in terms of some agreed market or other standard as set or recorded by a third person or agency and it is not so set or recorded." Under the UCC, then, *Sun Printing* is wrongly decided.

Note however that you only get to the UCC default rules such as section 2-305 by passing through section 2-204, which permits the enforcement of a contract if "one or more terms are left open," but only "if the parties have intended to make a contract." In this way, like Judge Crane, the UCC comes down on the side of protecting freedom *to* contract. At the same time, however, the common sense nature of the gap-fillers it supplies helps facilitate the parties' freedom *from* contract. By conforming to the expectations of one-shot players, they protect them from having unexpected terms imposed on them. Where repeat players want something unexpected, they are free to contract around the off-the-rack terms with which they disagree by including an express term to the contrary in the agreement.

3.4.2 Illusory Promises

Gaps in the parties' consent can arise with so-called "illusory" promises. A promise is thought to be illusory when it leaves complete discretion to perform or not in the hands of the purported promisor. In *Spooner v. Reserve Life Insurance Co.*,[16] for example, an insurance company appeared to promise its salesmen generous bonuses if they met certain targets. But the announcement concluded with the following disclaimer: "This renewal bonus is a voluntary contribution on the part of the Company. It is agreed by you and by us that it may be withheld, increased, decreased or discontinued, individually or collectively, with or without notice." With an illusory contract, one or both sides—depending on whether the contract is unilateral or bilateral—purport to be making a promise, but because the alleged "promise" allows the purported promisor to decide whether or not to perform at its discretion, it is not truly a commitment and, therefore, not truly a promise.

Sometimes when a promise appears illusory, courts will imply a commitment from the silence of the parties. For example, in *Wood v. Lucy, Lady Duff-Gordon*,[17] a fashion designer entered a contract with Otis Wood in which Wood was given an exclusive power to act as her agent in marketing her endorsements. When the designer sought to escape the contract, she alleged that it was void for want of mutuality. In particular, she alleged that the contract did not obligate Wood to do anything in particular on her behalf.

---

16. 287 P.2d 735 (1955).

17. 222 N.Y. 88, 118 N.E. 214 (1918).

In his opinion for the majority, Judge Cardozo analyzed the defendant's claim that the plaintiff did not promise to do anything. While conceding that the plaintiff does not "in so many words" express the intention to use reasonable efforts to place the defendant's endorsements and market her designs, he concluded that "such a promise is fairly to be implied." He observed that "[t]he law has outgrown its primitive stage of formalism when the precise word was the sovereign talisman, and every slip was fatal. It takes a broader view today. A promise may be lacking, and yet the whole writing may be 'instinct with an obligation,' imperfectly expressed." If this is the case, then "there is a contract."

Cardozo examined a number of factors from which a duty to perform can be implied. Because the agreement made the plaintiff the exclusive representative of the defendant for a whole year, it was unreasonable to think that this right would have been given in exchange for nothing. The agreement recited the plaintiff's ability to place endorsements, thus implying that this ability would be so employed. Given the fact that the defendant was to be paid a percentage of what the plaintiff's efforts produced, unless such a promise was involved, the defendant must have been agreeing to the possibility of receiving nothing for an entire year. Such an intention cannot be supposed. Finally, the plaintiff was required by the terms of the agreement to account to the defendant for all moneys received by him and to acquire patents and copyrights. If there was no duty to market the product, such requirements were of no value, but Cardozo thought these requirements evidenced an intention or promise to market the product.

Contrast Cardozo's treatment of the gap in this contract with his opinion in *Sun Printing* where, over Judge Crane's dissent, he refused to imply a term that would have rendered the contract sufficiently definite. What makes this case different? Perhaps the implied obligation is so obvious that it had to be in the minds of the parties at the time of formation. Perhaps the very obviousness of the commitment was a reason why it was not specifically stated. "It went without saying" goes the expression. This does not appear to be true of the agreement in *Sun Printing* where no default price term was implicit if the parties failed to reach agreement on the price. In short, the terms and surrounding circumstances may have permitted Cardozo to do in *Wood* what he was unable to do in *Sun Printing*: discern an actual unexpressed, but implied-in-fact, term of the agreeement. Nevertheless, a frustrated Judge Crane dissented in *Wood* citing Judge Cardozo's opinion in *Sun Printing*.

With contracts for the sale of goods, the UCC section 2-306 codifies the outcome in *Wood*: "A lawful agreement by either the seller or the buyer for exclusive dealing in the kind of goods concerned imposes unless otherwise agreed an obligation by the seller to use best efforts to supply the goods and by the buyer to use best efforts to promote their sale." Although reaching the same result as *Wood*, this section eliminates any requirement that a court go through the effort made by Cardozo to imply such a duty on the part of the defendant. Why?

Perhaps the authors of the Code thought that, whenever such an agreement is entered into, this must be the intention of the parties. So absent some indication to the contrary, this intention will be presumed. We have here a rebuttable presumption or default rule in place of a fact-finding requirement: If (fact A) this type of agreement is entered into, it will be presumed that (fact B) these mutual duties are agreed to as well. But an expression by the parties that fact B is not true will rebut the presumption raised by the existence of fact A.

⚿ 3.5 Form Contracts

There is a remarkable dissonance between contract theory and practice on the subject of form contracts. In practice, form contracts are ubiquitous. From video rentals to the sale of automobiles, form contracts are everywhere. Yet contracts professors are nothing if not suspicious of such contracts. Indeed, I would wager that a plurality of contracts teachers would favor a judicial refusal to enforce form contracts altogether—or could not explain exactly why they would reject such a suggestion.

3.5.1 Form Contracts and the Modern Objective Approach

If we take a purely objective approach toward discerning the existence of a promise, then form contracts are unproblematic. Just look at the signs employed in the form and give them their normal public meaning. Not only would this approach treat form and nonform agreements alike, it would treat individual form terms exactly the same as separately negotiated terms within an agreement. All would be judged by the objective meaning of the words employed.

However if, instead of adhering strictly to the public meaning of the signs used, one asks what one party would reasonably have thought the other party meant by his words and deeds, then form contracts run into a serious problem. If the promisee knows or has reason to know that a particular promise went unread, then would it not be unreasonable for the promisee to think that the promisor objectively manifested assent by signing a form contract, or clicking "I agree" after a box of text, that everyone knows no one ever reads?

Moreover, we have already seen that the modern objective approach has a subjective twist. Recall *Embry v. Hargadine, McKittrick Dry Goods Co.* discussed in section 3.1. Not only must a reasonable person have thought that the promisor intended to enter a contract, but the promisee must subjectively have believed the promisor to be contracting. It is hard to see how a promisee could really believe that a person signing a lengthy form contract, which was never read, had subjectively agreed to its terms, simply because he signed his name on the dotted line.

Consequently, ever since Friedrich Kessler dubbed them "contracts of adhesion,"[18] form contracts have been under a scholarly cloud. The reason is straightforward: How can someone have promised to do something in a writing he or she has not read and was not expected to read? Because most terms in a form contract are rarely read—and those who write form contracts know this as well as anyone—it is considered a fiction to think one has promised—either subjectively or objectively under the modern view—to perform according to a term that the other party knows good and well was unread.

Despite this, most contract law professors and practitioners also know that form contracts make the world go round. Psychologists tell us that the human mind will strive mightily to resolve the dissonance between two incompatible ideas. In this case, some resolve the conflict between theory and practice by rejecting form contracts because consent is lacking, while others are led to reject consent as the basis of contract and then, because consent is unnecessary, they too reject form contracts in favor of government-supplied terms. By either route—and despite their obvious social value—form contracts have come to be disdained.

3.5.2 Todd Rakoff's Defense and Critique of Form Contracts

Nowhere was this dissonance between the theory and practice more tellingly displayed than in Todd Rakoff's influential article, *Contracts of Adhesion: An Essay in Reconstruction.*[19] It is almost as though Rakoff's piece is comprised of two separate articles.

---

18. Friedrich Kessler, *Contracts of Adhesion—Some Thoughts about Freedom of Contract*, 43 COLUM. L. REV. 629 (1943).

19. Todd D. Rakoff, *Contracts of Adhesion: An Essay in Reconstruction*, 96 HARV. L. REV. 1174 (1983).

The first explains at length all the reasons why form contracts, so disparaged by his peers, are beneficial if not essential to a market economy. "Firms create standard form contracts," he wrote, "in part to stabilize their external market relationships, and in part to serve the needs of a hierarchical and internally segmented structure."

Rakoff identifies three ways that form contracts promote efficiency within large complex organizations. First, the standardization of terms in form contracts facilitates coordination among departments. "The costs of communicating special understandings rise rapidly when one department makes the sale, another delivers the goods, a third handles collections, and a fourth fields complaints. Standard terms make it possible to process transactions as a matter of routine." The blank spaces in standard forms "make it possible to locate rapidly whatever deal has been struck on the few customized items."

Second, "standardization makes possible the efficient use of expensive managerial and legal talent. Standard forms facilitate the diffusion to underlings of management's decisions regarding the risks the organization is prepared to bear, or make it unnecessary to explain these matters to subordinates at all."

Third, "the use of form contracts serves as an automatic check on the consequences of the acts of wayward sales personnel. The pressure to produce may tempt salesmen to make bargains into which the organization is unwilling to enter." Economists came to call this last situation the "agency problem." In a firm in which agents are unavoidably entering into transactions with third parties that will bind their firm, how does the firm constrain the ability of agents to serve their own interests? For example, how do they stop agents from boosting their sales by offering extravagant terms of which their principals will unavoidably be unaware? Simple—a firm binds both its own agents and third parties to the unwaivable terms in a form contract. Business on a scale that benefits everyone would simply be impossible if firms were unable to use form contracts to control the terms their agents could offer to those with whom they are doing business.

But what about the welfare of the other parties doing business with a firm using its own form contracts? Here, Rakoff anticipated what came later to be called "rational ignorance," which was previously mentioned in section 3.4.1. For a large proportion of terms in almost any contract, the low probability of the term ever being invoked in some future lawsuit, combined with the relatively low stakes of many such contracts, makes it irrational for form-receiving parties to spend time reading, much less understanding, the terms in the forms they sign. "[F]or most consumer transactions, the close reading and comparison needed to make an intelligent choice among alternative forms seems grossly arduous."

Moreover, "many of the terms in form contracts concern risks that in any individual transaction are unlikely to eventuate." Rakoff notes how "notoriously difficult" it is "for most people, who lack legal advice and broad experience concerning the particular transaction type, to appraise these sorts of contingencies. And the standard forms—because they are drafted to cover many such contingencies—are likely to be long and complex, even if each term is plainly stated." For all these reasons, "it is clear that the near-universal failure of adherents to read and understand the documents they sign cannot be dismissed as mere laziness. In the circumstances, the rational course is to focus on the few terms that are generally well publicized and of immediate concern, and to ignore the rest."

This leads to a twofold problem for a theory of contract based on consent. First, clearly the person signing such a contract did not subjectively, consciously assent to terms that went unread. Second, no one offering such terms can reasonably have thought that the other party subjectively assented. Therefore, according to the modern objective theory, there was no objective assent either. That is, no one who hands a form contract to another to sign, knowing full well that it will largely go unread, can reasonably believe that the other party has consciously assented to each of the terms therein.

Another of Rakoff's advances on previous scholarship was his disassociation of form contracts from the pejorative concept of unconscionability. As we shall see in Chapter 6, unconscionability involves the problems of unequal bargaining power, unfair surprise, and substantively unreasonable terms. In contrast with other contracts scholars before or since, Rakoff insisted that none of these concerns is at the core of the problem with form contracts.

Instead, for Rakoff, the problem with form contracts was not whether terms were bargained for but whether they could be "shopped" elsewhere; not whether some terms constituted an "unfair surprise" but whether it was rational for the form-receiving party to read any of them; not whether the terms were substantively objectionable but whether there is a lack of assent caused by rational ignorance. After all, most forms are signed by agents of large companies doing business with agents of other large companies, neither of whom can complain about the problems typically handled by unconscionability doctrine.

Rakoff also made a key distinction between what he called the "visible" and "invisible" terms of an agreement. Visible terms are terms that are in the parties' interest to focus on and shop; invisible terms are terms for which it was not in the interest of rational cost-minimizing persons to shop elsewhere or even to read. "Considered by themselves, then, the visible terms of a contract of adhesion are most often those that would constitute the entire explicit contents of a very simple ordinary contract, with the price term (dickered or not) being the paradigmatic example. The invisible terms are, quite simply, all the rest."

While Rakoff's identification of these two types of terms was an important advance, his decision to call the former "visible" and the latter "invisible" was unfortunate. After all, the terms one may rationally fail to read are not literally invisible; rather, they were unread and unshopped. Unread terms could be read if a party so chose; literally invisible terms cannot.

Rakoff's rhetoric choice reflects how he resolves the dissonance between the benefits of form contracts, which he took pains to explain, and the unread nature of so-called invisible terms. In what seems almost like a second and different article, he argued that only visible terms should be enforced as written. Invisible terms should presumptively be supplanted by terms supplied by statute or by the courts.

There are a great many things one can say about this recommendation. For one, it assumes that courts, legislatures, or the American Law Institute are capable of writing gap-filling terms that better serve the interests of both contracting parties than is the author of the form. Imposing terms more favorable to one of the parties to the form will raise the cost of the transaction to the other party and may thereby raise the price. This could ultimately disserve the party who is supposed to be the beneficiary of the intervention. And, it is not just price.

One-sided contracts can empower companies to deal summarily with unreasonable consumers while voluntarily treating reasonable consumers more generously. Lisa Bernstein examined the benefits of one-sided legal provisions tempered by more generous "extra legal" concessions.[20] Sometimes "transactors allocate aspects of their contracting relationship to the extralegal realm because the transaction costs of including a sufficiently well-specified written provision in their contract would exceed the benefits." Other times, "they do so because nonlegal sanctions such as reputation bonds are strong enough in the relevant market to ensure that an obligation will be performed, making a legally enforceable provision unnecessary."

Another reason to allocate aspects of a contractual relationship to the extralegal realm concerns legal system costs. "Legal system costs are those costs that arise from the fact that litigation is costly, prone to delay, and subject to judicial error." For example, in computer software markets, legal system costs may lead both manufacturers and consumers to prefer shrink-wrap agreements that disclaim all warranties and state that no licenses will be granted,

---

20. *See* Lisa Bernstein, *Merchant Law in a Merchant Court: Rethinking the Code's Search for Immanent Business Norms*, 144 U. PA. L. REV. 1765 (1996).

but manufacturers promise, in some legally unenforceable way, to fix defective products and grant licenses where appropriate. Bernstein interviewed one manufacturer whose shrink-wrap contained broad warranty disclaimers and restrictive license provisions who explained:

> [M]ost software houses are willing to be less restrictive in practice, but with suits being brought for almost any reason, valid and otherwise, and with such suits being expensive to defend . . . [s]oftware houses will probably continue to use similar wording in warranties and licenses, if for no other reason than to avoid attorney fees rather than responsibility.

If manufacturers used provisions that stated more precisely when licenses would be granted and the software repaired, these "provisions would increase the likelihood that manufacturers would have to defend against nuisance suits and would create a substantial risk that, even if a manufacturer met its obligations, a court might err and force it to pay a large judgment." Such clauses would be "of limited benefit to consumers, who would, in most instances, find them prohibitively expensive to enforce," and would be better off relying on the relatively accessible information about manufacturers' reputations for repairing their products and granting licenses. "As a consequence, both manufacturers and consumers may prefer lower-priced software with broad disclaimers and the manufacturer's extralegal, reputation-bond-backed promise to grant licenses and repair products in appropriate circumstances to higher-priced software with detailed, legally enforceable warranty and license provisions."

Finally, contracting parties may want to conclude a deal with two well-developed sets of contractual provisions, one legally enforceable and one purely extralegal, because one party may not know at the outset of a contracting relationship if the other party is trustworthy. "Although he would find it ideal to include two sets of written provisions, one that would apply if the transactor turned out to be trustworthy and another if he turned out to be untrustworthy, trustworthiness is not something the contract can condition on because it is unverifiable." For this reason, one contracting party "may find it desirable to include terms in the contract that are the best terms if the other" contracting party turns out to be untrustworthy, "while making extralegal commitments, many of which will, over time, ripen into self-enforcing agreements, that will govern the relationship if the other party turns out to be trustworthy." In this situation, the one-sided form contract functions as a *bond* in case the relationship goes poorly, whereas the extralegal relational agreement provides the terms of the relationship so long as it remains healthy.

For all these reasons, it might work to the ultimate advantage of the "adherent" to consent to a one-sided term and rely on the other party to deliver voluntarily what may not be required of it under the terms of the form. It is very hard for third parties, such as courts or legislatures, writing terms of contracts to know whether they are really improving the situation for the adherent. However, if we lack confidence that any particular legal intervention is actually beneficial to the adherent, the principal justification of intervention is greatly weakened to say the least.

Of course, terms that are imposed on the parties by judicial decisions or statutes are even more removed from the transaction than is a form. The problem of rational ignorance will be exacerbated as parties would no longer be weighing the probability of a potential lawsuit against the cost of reading the form in front of them. Instead, they would have to weigh the likelihood of a lawsuit against the cost of hiring a lawyer to tell them what is in case law or a statute and predict, if possible, how a background rule will be applied by a future court.

Regardless of whether one finds Todd Rakoff's reform proposal appealing, he undoubtedly provided important and previously overlooked reasons why form contracts are useful and why they do not automatically implicate the same problems addressed by the doctrine of unconscionability. And, his terminology notwithstanding, the substance of his distinction between visible and invisible terms in form contracts is a highly useful one, as we shall now see.

3.5.3 The Consensual Basis for Enforcing Form Contracts

In this section, I want to challenge the conventional wisdom that form contracts, or the "invisible terms" within them, are not consented to because they are largely unread and explain how consent to unread terms can be quite real. To appreciate this, we need to separate (1) the terms of a party's promise or commitment from (2) whether that party has manifested his consent to be legally bound to perform that commitment.

An illustration of this separation is provided by the Uniform Written Obligations Act, which has been in effect in Pennsylvania since 1927: "A written release or promise, hereafter made and signed by the person releasing or promising, shall not be invalid or unenforceable for lack of consideration, if the writing *also* contains an additional express statement, in any form of language, that the signer intends to be legally bound."[21] Here the promise is enforceable if accompanied by a separate statement indicating that the signatory intends to be legally bound, so the promise and the consent to be legally bound are clearly demarcated into two different commitments.

Now think of click license agreements on websites. When one clicks "I agree" to the terms in the box, does one usually know what one is doing? Absolutely. There is no doubt whatsoever that one is objectively manifesting one's assent to the terms in the box, whether or not one has read them. The same observation applies to signatures on form contracts. Clicking the button that says "I agree," no less than signing one's name on the dotted line, indicates

---

21. Uniform Written Obligations Act, Pa. Stat. Ann. tit. 33, § 6 (West 1997) (emphasis added).

unambiguously: I agree to be legally bound by the terms in this agreement.

When considering consent to be bound to perform one's promise, rather than the terms of the promise, such consent seems to exist when one signs a form contract or clicks "I agree." Even under the modern objective theory, there is no reason for the other party to believe that such subjective assent is lacking. If a party clicking "I agree" does not subjectively intend to be bound, he knows, or should know, that the other party will take this conduct as indicating his consent to be bound thereby.

Suppose I say to my dearest friend, "Whatever it is you want me to do, write it down and put it into a sealed envelope, and I will do it for you." Is it categorically impossible to make such a promise? Is there something incoherent about committing oneself to perform an act the nature of which one does not know and will only learn later? To take another example, is there some reason why soldiers cannot commit themselves to obey the commands of a superior (within limits perhaps), the nature of which they will only learn about some time in the future? Hardly. Is there any reason to conclude that these are not real promises? If not, then what is true of these promises is also true of contractual consent in the case of form contracts.

If contractual enforcement is about legally committing oneself to perform the act described in the envelope, there is no reason, in principle, why this consent cannot be considered real, not fictional. There is no reason, in principle, why such consent cannot be objectively manifested to another person. This reveals the "nested" nature of contractual consent. The particular duty consented to—the promise or commitment—is nested within an overall consent to be legally bound. The consent that legitimates enforcement is the latter consent to be legally bound.

Suppose now that instead of the promise being in an unopened envelope, it is contained in an unread scroll box on a computer screen. Is the act of clicking "I agree" below the box any less a manifestation of consent to be bound by the unread terms therein than was the promise to perform the unknown act described in the envelope? Whether or not it is a fiction to say someone is making the promise in the scroll box, it is no fiction to say that, by clicking "I agree," a person is consensually committing to these (unread) promises.

True, when consenting in this manner one is running the risk of binding oneself to a promise one may regret when later learning its content. But the law does not, and should not, bar all assumptions of risk. Hard as this may be to believe, I know of people who attach waxed boards to their feet and propel themselves down slippery snow- and tree-covered mountains, an activity that kills or injures many people every year. Others, for the thrill of it, freely jump out of airplanes expecting their fall to be slowed by a large piece of fabric that they carry in a sack. (I am not making this up.) Or, they ride bicycles on busy streets with automobiles whizzing past them. It seems to me that if people may freely and legally chose or consent to engage in such unnecessarily risky activities, they may freely and legally choose or consent to run the much lesser, and more necessary, risk of accepting a term in an unread agreement they may later come to regret.

3.5.4 Limits on Enforcing Form Contracts

The justification for enforcing form contracts based on the existence of a manifested intention to be legally bound does not entail, however, that any and every term in a form contract is enforceable. To begin with, as with negotiated terms, there are limits to what the obligation can be. As we saw in Chapter 3, for example, a commitment to transfer or waive an inalienable right may not itself be enforceable. But form terms may be subject to additional constraints on enforcement that would not apply to expressly negotiated terms.

Although assent to a form manifests consent to unread terms as well as read terms, there is a qualification implicit in every such manifestation. Call it the "your-favorite-pet" qualification. Suppose a term of the sort that Rakoff calls "invisible"—meaning it is rational to remain ignorant of its content—specifies that, in consequence of breach, one must transfer custody of one's beloved dog or cat. The promisor could surely contend that "while I did agree to be bound by terms I did not read, I did not agree to *that*." As Andrew Kull explained in the context of the defenses of mistake, impossibility, and frustration (to which we will return in Chapter 6), "[t]he force of the implicit claim is hard to deny: I did not mean my promise to extend to this circumstance; nor did you so understand it; to give it that effect would therefore be to enforce a contract different from the one we actually made."[22]

If clicking "I agree" realistically means "I agree to be legally bound to unread terms *that are not radically unexpected*," then that, and nothing more, is what has been consented to objectively. To appreciate this better, consider these three possible interpretations of clicking "I agree."

1. By clicking "I agree," I am expressing my intent to be bound only by the visible price and quantity terms and none of the terms in the box above. (In the case of free software, I am agreeing to nothing whatsoever when I click "I agree," though I know perfectly well that the other party does not wish me to use the software without agreeing to these terms).

2. By clicking "I agree," I am expressing my intent to be bound by any term that is in the box above no matter how unexpected such a term may be.

3. By clicking "I agree," I am expressing my intent to be bound by the terms I am likely to have read (whether or not I have done so) and also by those unread terms in the agreement above that

---

22. Andrew Kull, *Mistake, Frustration, and the Windfall Principle of Contract Remedies*, 43 HASTINGS L.J. 1, 38–39 (1991).

I am not likely to have read but that do not exceed some bound of reasonableness.

Options 1 and 2 have the advantage of certainty but are unlikely to reflect the subjective and, for this reason, the objective meaning of "I agree."

If Option 3 is the most likely meaning of clicking "I agree," then two things follow. First, in Rakoff's terminology, those "invisible" terms that are unlikely to be read but are not unexpected, as well as all "visible" terms whether unexpected or not, can be consented to and should be enforced. Second, "invisible" terms that are beyond the pale should not be enforced unless they are brought to the attention of—that is, made "visible" to—the other party who then manifests a separate agreement to them. Although Option 3 does require judicial scrutiny of the unexpectedness of invisible terms, it requires much less judicial scrutiny than Option 1—the option preferred by Rakoff and probably most contracts scholars—that permits courts to provide all the terms of the agreement beyond the few that are visible.

Discerning whether or not an "invisible" term is unexpected would require an inquiry resembling that employed in law and economics. Namely, is this the sort of term that a reasonable person would have agreed to had the matter been expressed? If most reasonable persons would not have agreed to such a term, then the other party cannot assume consent to be bound to such a term unless it is made visible. In this way, what is sometimes called "hypothetical consent" is perhaps the best way to determine the actual objective or manifested consent to unread terms. If objective consent is a message that is communicated by one person to another, a hypothetical consent analysis may identify the substance of this message.

Option 3 was the approach taken by the Supreme Court in *Carnival Cruise Lines v. Shute*,[23] a case involving a forum selection

---

23. 499 U.S. 585 (1991).

clause in a form contract on the back of a cruise ticket. The Court rejected the proposition that a nonnegotiated forum-selection clause is never enforceable simply because it is nonnegotiated. But it then emphasized that such "clauses contained in form passage contracts are subject to judicial scrutiny for fundamental fairness." In essence, the Court rejected Options 1 and 2 in favor of Option 3. Inquiring into the "fundamental fairness" of a term is a way to identify those terms that are highly unexpected. No one expects a fundamentally unfair provision in the unread "invisible" terms of a form.

Does an inquiry into the fundamental fairness of terms in form contracts reflect a rejection of freedom of contract? Hardly. We must never forget that it is a form contract the court is expounding. The issue is what the parties have *objectively* agreed to. On the one hand, parties who sign forms or click "I agree" are manifesting their consent to be bound by the unread terms in the forms. They would rather run the risk of agreeing to unread terms than either (1) declining to agree or (2) reading the terms. Refusing to enforce all of these terms would violate their freedom *to* contract. On the other hand, parties who click "I agree" are *not* realistically manifesting their assent to radically unexpected terms or terms that are fundamentally unfair. Enforcing such an unread term would violate their freedom *from* contract.

Refusing to enforce a term that a court finds to be radically unexpected or fundamentally unfair does not prevent both parties from contracting on that basis. All a party who seeks to have such an unexpected term enforced need do is make it visible to the other party. The term would then be expected and, unless another limiting doctrine such as unconscionability applies, it should be enforced.

This is analogous to the rule of *Hadley v. Baxendale*, which requires that special notice be given of any consequences of breach that are unusual and therefore not normally foreseeable or expected. Like the rule in *Hadley*, the "fundamental fairness" test helps distinguish between what was actually consented to and what was radically unexpected and therefore not objectively agreed to. In other words, rather than being vehicles for overriding the consent of the parties, both the fundamental fairness evaluation of invisible terms and the rule in *Hadley* are attempting to discern realistically the scope of a party's manifested consent.

This analysis of terms that are unread because of rational ignorance can also be applied to terms that are unread because they are supplied later. This issue was raised in the cases of *ProCD, Inc. v. Zeidenberg*[24] and *Hill v. Gateway 2000, Inc.*[25] *ProCD* involved what is called a shrink-wrap or box-top agreement in which the terms are contained inside a box and cannot be read until after you purchase the software and open the box. In *ProCD*, the court held that the terms of the software license were agreed to.

In *Gateway*, the buyer purchased a computer over the phone. The written terms of the sale were later delivered to the buyer in the box along with the computer, both of which he was free to accept or reject by returning the computer to the seller. In *Gateway*, the court upheld the enforceability of the agreement that followed the telephone transaction. In both of these transactions, then, there was an initial "agreement"—the store purchase and the phone order—and terms that followed later.

At first blush, there is one seemingly big difference between clicking "I agree" to unread terms in a scroll box and agreeing to unread terms in a form one has not yet received. With the scroll box a party *could* read the terms and reject them by refusing to click "I agree." With terms arriving later in a box, one cannot read them until one receives them. Unlike terms in a scroll box, before they arrive, these terms are literally invisible. In such a case, it seems appropriate that one be given the opportunity to decline such terms by returning the goods.

---

24. 86 F.3d 1447 (7th Cir. 1996).

25. 105 F.3d 1147 (7th Cir. 1997).

In his opinions for the majority in both *ProCD* and Gateway, Judge Frank Easterbrook emphasized the existence of this option. The act of purchasing software or ordering a computer over the phone is realistically portrayed as the first step of a process of consent that is not finalized until there is an opportunity to inspect the terms. By insisting on this, the court in *ProCD* and *Gateway* can be seen as viewing the manifestation of consent as a two-step combination of the initial purchase or phone order and the act of retaining the software or computer.

That a manifestation of consent has two steps at two different times is far from novel. In the famous case of *Hobbes v. Massasoit Whip Co.*[26] the seller sent eel skins used to make whips to the buyer who then kept them without using them. The Supreme Judicial Court of Massachusetts found that this constituted acceptance of the eel skins because of the prior relationship or understanding of the parties, and the fact that the skins conformed to the previous specifications of the buyer. "The plaintiff was not a stranger to the defendant," wrote Justice Holmes, "even if there was no contract between them." In their prior dealings, "[h]e had sent eel skins in the same way four or five times before, and they had been accepted and paid for.... [I]t was fair to assume that ... there was a standing offer to him for such skins." Given this background, "the plaintiff was warranted in sending the defendant skins conforming to the requirements, and even if the offer was not such that the contract was made as soon as skins corresponding to its terms were sent, sending them did impose on the defendant a duty to act about them." The defendant's silence combined with its retention of the skins "warrant[ed] the plaintiff in assuming that they were accepted, and thus to amount to an acceptance."

In *Gateway*, as in *Hobbes*, the parties were not strangers to each other. In the absence of the phone order, Gateway could not simply send the buyer a computer and take his failure to return it as

---

26. 33 N.E. 495 (Mass. 1893).

consent to the purchase. By placing the phone order, the buyer undertook a duty to accept or return the computer and accompanying terms. And, also like *Hobbes*, the transaction must be viewed in its entirety to assess the reasonable meaning of the buyer's silence.

From this perspective, the only genuinely controversial issue of *Gateway* is whether the court should have upheld the enforceability of the form contract in the absence of some express notice to phone buyers that a form would be sent to them later. There are some compelling reasons for requiring that such notice be given. If most consumers would be surprised by the existence of additional form terms in the box, a default rule requiring notice that a form will follow later is more likely to lead to manifestations of assent that reflect the subjective assent of the parties than a contrary rule requiring no disclosure.

We can expect that repeat-player-sellers such as Gateway will have low-cost access to a default rule requiring them to notify buyers that a form agreement will follow later in the box. In contrast, one-time-player-buyers are unlikely to know of a background rule permitting forms to follow without notice, and for this reason are unlikely even to ask whether such will occur. Therefore, a default rule requiring disclosure by sellers is more likely to reduce any gap between objective consent and subjective assent and is preferable for that reason.

To obtain enforcement, all sellers like Gateway need do is to tell consumers on the phone that the form will follow in the box. They no more need to read aloud all the terms to follow than the software company needs to read aloud all the terms in the scroll box above the button labeled "I agree." Both formalities perform the same function: putting the other party on notice that it is agreeing to other terms that it may or may not choose to read.

In sum, just as persons can manifest their intent to be bound by terms they have not read in a scroll box, they can manifest their intent to be bound by terms they will receive later in the box containing the goods they are buying. The empirical question is whether or not they have so consented. The presence of notice that more terms are to follow resolves any uncertainty as to the existence of consent and greatly reduces the risk of any misunderstanding. And if repeat-player-sellers know that one-shot-player-buyers would be surprised to learn additional terms are forthcoming, they cannot take the failure to return the computer as an objectively manifested consent to the terms in the box.

We may conclude from this discussion that one can consent to be legally bound even to terms in form contracts of which one is rationally ignorant, whether the unread terms are in a box on a computer screen, in a box purchased in the store and opened later, or in a box sent later by Federal Express. Nothing in principle prevents a competent individual from assuming the risk that they later will dislike one of the unread terms in the box, though there are limits on what one can consent to in this manner. Such terms should not be enforced if they are shown to be radically unexpected or fundamentally unfair, or some other defense applies. In the absence of such a showing, the enforcement of even the "invisible" terms of form contracts can be justified on the basis of consent— real consent, properly understood, not a fiction.

Some contracts professors may challenge this analysis by asking which communication is the offer and which is the acceptance? But, as was observed at the beginning of this chapter, it is widely acknowledged that offer and acceptance is only one way of manifesting mutual assent. Section 2-204 of the UCC famously says that "[a] contract for the sale of goods may be made in *any manner sufficient to show agreement*, including conduct by both parties which recognizes the existence of such a contract (emphasis added)." There is no reason in principle why contracts cannot be formed in stages, provided the circumstances or prior practice makes this clear or adequate notice is provided.

Of course, some may question either the justice or utility of enforcing consensual agreements. In the next chapter, I will explain why freedom of contract—which in this context includes both the freedom *to* consent to form contracts and the freedom *from* having other terms imposed on both parties by judges or legislatures—is needed to solve the pervasive social problems of knowledge and interest. What the analysis presented here is intended to do, and nothing more, is refute the commonplace notion that form contracts, including click agreements, or contracts with terms that follow later are illegitimate by their very nature because they lack actual contractual consent.

3.5.5 UCC Section 2-207 and the Battle of the Forms

With the rise of form contract came the following situation: One commercial firm places a purchase order using its form; the seller then confirms the order using its form. What happens when the terms on these forms differ from each other?

Traditionally, under what was called "the mirror image rule," when the terms of an acceptance differ substantially from the terms of an offer, there is a failure of assent and no contract. In some circumstances this remains the law. For example, in *Ardente v. Horan*,[27] the Supreme Court of Rhode Island, refused to enforce the sale of a home where the terms of the acceptance differed from that of the offer. "To be effective, an acceptance must be definite and unequivocal," the court stated. "The acceptance may not impose additional conditions on the offer, nor may it add limitations." It then quoted from a previous decision in which it had held that: "An acceptance which is equivocal or upon condition or with a limitation is a counteroffer and requires acceptance by the original offeror before a contractual relationship can exist."

In *Ardente*, neither party had performed under the contract. But what happens if one or both parties start performing as though a contract existed? Would the fact of performance change the result? For one thing, it is much more difficult to find the absence of a

---

27. 366 A.2d 162 (1976).

contract as was done in *Ardente*. Performance by one party now seems to require some sort of remedy, if only restitution, rather than simply refusing to award a remedy as was done in *Ardente*.

There are then two distinct issues created by a situation in which a purported "acceptance" contains terms materially different than the original offer. First, is there a contract at all? The mirror image rule says there is no contract until the acceptance "mirrors" the previous offer. But performance by one party makes it more difficult to find no contract when it appears that one or both parties themselves acted as though there was a contract. Recall *Sun Printing*, where the parties' own actions recognized the existence of a contract. We have already seen how UCC section 2-204 allows the enforcement of contracts with open terms, provided that the parties "intended to make a contract."

Second, assuming a contract existed and can be enforced, what are its terms? When there are open terms, the UCC fills the silence with gap-filling default rules. But what happens when the terms in a purported acceptance do not mirror those in the original offer? The UCC attempted to address this issue in section 2-207. Section 2-207 was designed to prevent mirror-image-rule type problems from allowing one party to escape liability from the contract when it suited its purposes—think of Judge Crane's opinion of the Remington Paper and Power Company's behavior in *Sun Printing*. But it raises many well-known vexatious questions.

Paragraph (1) reads:

(1) A definite and seasonable expression of acceptance or a written confirmation which is sent within a reasonable time operates as an acceptance even though it states terms additional to or different from those offered or agreed upon, unless acceptance is expressly made conditional on assent to the additional or different terms.

In case of a conflict between a term in an "expression of acceptance" or confirmation and the same term in an "offer," is it the offeror's term that governs, or do the two terms cancel or "knock out" each other so there is a gap to be filled by the UCC or by the Court? Commentators and courts differ on this; though Allan Farnsworth, for one, thought that the offeror's term would or, at least, should govern.[28] How different can an acceptance be from offer while still forming a contract? Perhaps if there is too great a difference, the "acceptance" is not really an acceptance (with "different" terms).

Paragraph (2) reads:

> (2) The additional terms are to be construed as proposals for addition to the contract. Between merchants such terms become part of the contract unless:
>
>   (a) the offer expressly limits acceptance to the terms of the offer;
>
>   (b) they materially alter it; or
>
>   (c) notification of objection to them has already been given or is given within a reasonable time after notice of them is received.

Between merchants this section allows the silence of the offeror to constitute acceptance of different terms by the offeree, provided that the terms do not "materially alter" the offer. So if the terms in the acceptance *do* materially alter the terms of the offer, then they do *not* become part of the agreement. The official comments to section 2-207 refer to terms that "so result in surprise or hardship without express awareness by the other party." Farnsworth says that "a vast amount of litigation" has surrounded what terms result in "surprise or hardship."[29]

An offeror can prevent even nonmaterial differing terms from the offeree from becoming part of the agreement if the "offer

---

28. *See* E. ALLAN FARNSWORTH, CONTRACTS § 3.21 (4th ed. 2004).

29. *Id.*

expressly limits acceptance to the terms of the offer." In response to this, an offeree may decide to take advantage of paragraph (1)'s option to make "acceptance . . . expressly . . . conditional on assent to the additional or different terms." But what happens if both parties use forms that expressly limit their assent to the acceptance by the other party of the terms in their form, and then both parties proceed to perform under the "contract" without resolving this contradiction? Does the contract fail, as in *Ardente?*

In this situation, paragraph (3) then applies, which says:

> (3) Conduct by both parties which recognizes the existence of a contract is sufficient to establish a contract for sale although the writings of the parties do not otherwise establish a contract. In such case the terms of the particular contract consist of those terms on which the writings of the parties agree, together with any supplementary terms incorporated under any other provisions of this Act.

This means that, even when "the writings of the parties *do not otherwise establish a contract*," a court can still find and enforce a contract if there is "[c]onduct by both parties which recognizes the existence of a contract." In which case, according to Farnsworth, the offeree is bound by "a contract consisting of terms common to both writings, together with any others supplied by the Code."[30] Farnsworth suggests that offerees flatly reject the offer and then make an entirely new offer. By so doing, the offeree has arguably avoided section 2-207 altogether because there would be no "definite and seasonable expression of acceptance" under paragraph (1), and paragraph (3) would not apply.

In *ProCd v. Zeidenberg*, Judge Easterbrook thought that section 2-207 did not apply because, in that case, there were not two conflicting forms. "Our case has only one form," he wrote, and therefore

---

30. *Id.*

"UCC section 2-207 is irrelevant." However, in *Klocek v. Gateway*,[31] another case involving the enforceability of terms supplied by Gateway in the box in which it shipped a computer ordered over the phone, a federal district court in a different circuit disagreed. "By its terms, section 2-207 applies to an acceptance or written confirmation. It states nothing which requires another form before the provision becomes effective." Judge Kathryn Vratil then noted that the official comment to section 2-207 provides that paragraphs (1) and (2) apply "where an agreement has been reached orally . . . and is followed by one or both of the parties sending formal memoranda embodying the terms so far agreed and adding terms not discussed."

Yet, in applying section 2-207 to the terms in a form provided later, the court in *Klocek* allows firms like Gateway a relatively easy way out. In a footnote, it says:

> The Court is mindful of the practical considerations which are involved in commercial transactions, but it is not unreasonable for a vendor to clearly communicate to a buyer—at the time of sale—either the complete terms of the sale *or the fact that the vendor will propose additional terms as a condition of sale*, if that be the case (emphasis added).

According to the court in *Klocek*, then, section 2-207 would be satisfied by this simple statement presumably because it would show that Gateway's consent was "expressly conditioned" on the acceptance of the additional terms to follow. In short, the court is requiring the express notice that I suggested in section 3.4.4 was appropriate when terms follow later.

---

31. 104 F. Supp. 2d 1332 (2000).

FOUR

Enforceability

Summary: The second element of a contract is to distinguish those manifestations of assent that will be enforced from those that will not. Historically, there have evolved three doctrines to address this issue. The first was formal contracts—that is, a contract in writing and under seal. The second was the enforcement of informal contracts supported by the doctrine of consideration. The third was the doctrine of promissory estoppel to protect reliance on the informal commitments of others in the absence of bargained-for consideration. This chapter explains these three doctrines. This chapter also considers the consensual basis of enforcing formal contracts, why the bargain theory of consideration arose to distinguish enforceable from unenforceable informal manifestations of consent, and how promissory estoppel can be understood as protecting reliance on the consent of the other party to be legally bound even in the absence of a bargain. Cases discussed include: *Hamer v. Sidway*, *Mills v. Wyman*, *Stilk v. Myrick*, *Alaska Packers v. Domenico*, *Ricketts v. Scothorn*, *Allegheny College v. National Chatauqua Co. Bank*, *Feinberg v. Pfeiffer*, *Greiner v. Greiner*, *Goodman v. Dicker*, and *Hoffman v. Red Owl Stores*.

At several junctures in the earlier chapters, I mentioned the consensual nature of contractual obligation. This chapter begins with an explanation of why consent is the central focus of contract law, but also why and how reliance needs to be protected (section 4.1). Viewing contractual obligation as consent based does not, however, automatically provide workable doctrines for distinguishing enforceable from unenforceable consensual commitments, so also examined are the three doctrines that have arisen to address this question: consideration (section 4.2), formalities (section 4.3), and promissory estoppel (section 4.4).

〽 4.1 The Social Function of Consent

Earlier, in section 3.1, I suggested that property law identifies the rights we have to use and enjoy scarce physical resources, while tort law defines what actions constitute a wrongful interference with the rights of others. In contrast, contracts can be viewed as the means by which people consensually alter their legal relations with others by alienating their preexisting rights. In this section, I explain why this is socially beneficial: It helps address two pervasive social problems that must somehow be solved: the problems of knowledge and interest.[1] This section is intended for those who want to know why consent is and ought to be at the heart of contract law. Those who are not interested in this issue may proceed to section 4.2. Students should also be advised that this explanation is likely to be unfamiliar to their professors, and is not the only way that the importance of consent can be understood.

4.1.1 Using Resources: The First-Order Problem of Knowledge

Human beings confront myriad ways of using physical resources, including their own bodies. Knowledge of the uses to which resources may be put is both radically dispersed among the persons

---

1. Section 4.1 is based on the analysis presented at greater length in RANDY E. BARNETT, THE STRUCTURE OF LIBERTY: JUSTICE AND THE RULE OF LAW (1998).

and associations that comprise a society, and highly contingent on the particular circumstances facing each person. The problem of a person or association making knowledgeable choices among alternative uses of physical resources is compounded by other persons and associations striving to make their own choices based on their own knowledge. This radical dispersion of knowledge gives rise to what can be called the "first-order problem of knowledge," a problem that was famously identified by F. A. Hayek.[2]

The first-order problem of knowledge arises because access to the vast range of knowledge possessed by individuals and associations is restricted. For example, each person has knowledge of his particular situation—including knowledge of his abilities, his interests, his preferences, and his opportunities—but access to this knowledge by others is extremely limited. When persons seek to act on the basis of the knowledge in their possession, such actions necessarily involve the use of physical resources, including the use of their bodies. Many of these actions will conflict, in the sense that attempts by some to use physical resources to put their knowledge into action will inevitably interfere with the efforts of others to do the same. This problem of knowledge does not arise because one person necessarily has "better" information than another, although this may well be the case. Rather, the first-order problem of knowledge unavoidably arises because each person and association of persons possesses knowledge that is inaccessible to others.

The radical dispersion of knowledge may be either *personal* or *local*, depending on the degree of its accessibility. Individuals have access to their own personal knowledge that others necessarily lack. Only I know what I am thinking and feeling as I write this passage; only I can observe the room I am working in from this vantage point; only I know that I am thirsty at this moment. The same is

---

2. *See* F. A. Hayek, *The Use of Knowledge in Society*, in INDIVIDUALISM AND ECONOMIC ORDER (1948). For additional discussion of the knowledge problem *see* DON LAVOIE, NATIONAL ECONOMIC PLANNING (1985), and DON LAVOIE, RIVALRY AND CENTRAL PLANNING (1985).

true for you who are now reading this passage. No one else knows, or could know, what is running through your mind.

A list of one's personal knowledge would be both endless and impossible to compile. One's personal knowledge includes knowledge of one's personal preferences, but it also includes knowledge of one's physical and emotional needs, one's particular circumstances, and one's opportunities or alternative courses of action. Indeed, it is impossible to enumerate precisely all the types of knowledge each of us possesses, much less the knowledge itself.

In contrast to personal knowledge, local knowledge is knowledge that is publicly accessible, though this access is still quite limited. Instead of being confined to a single person, access to local knowledge is limited to particular associations of persons. A dinner conversation between two people in a crowded restaurant is accessible to both participants, but not to everyone in the restaurant. Even persons at the next table may be hard-pressed to understand what is being said. What is happening in a classroom is known to the dozens of persons who are present but unknown to those who are outside the room. Knowledge need not be limited to a few people to be "local." Sixty-thousand people viewing a football game in a stadium have local knowledge of the game in the sense that the rest of the world does not have access to what they can observe about the game in progress. Even if millions more are watching on television, such knowledge would still be local because billions lack access to it.

In sum, as used here, personal knowledge refers to an individual's knowledge that is inaccessible to others. Local knowledge refers to knowledge to which only certain associations of persons have access. These terms refer not to the substance or origin of knowledge, but to the limited access that persons have to it. This radical dispersion of personal and local knowledge creates what I am calling the first-order problem of knowledge. This problem has two aspects or dimensions: First, to pursue happiness, a person must be able to act on the basis of his own personal knowledge as well as the local knowledge to which he has access as a member of an association. Second, when so acting he must somehow take into account the knowledge of others of which each person is hopelessly ignorant.

The dispersal of personal and local knowledge can be pictured as a "knowledge glass" that is both half-full (what each of us knows) and half-empty (what each of us is ignorant of). The first-order problem of knowledge facing any society is how to put to use the half that is full while at the same time taking into account the half that is empty.

For persons to survive and flourish in society with each other, they must be able to develop and act on their own personal and local knowledge. Their actions, however, are likely to affect others in ways that can scarcely be known. And, the first-order problem of knowledge is magnified because what each of us knows and wishes to put into action is dwarfed by our ignorance. Rather than being half-full, everyone's knowledge glass is more like a swimming pool with but a precious molecule of what each knows against the vastness of what each does not.

The first step in addressing this problem is to recognize that it is the *use* rather then the mere possession of personal and local knowledge that creates a problem when persons live in society with others. Only a person's actions can interfere with the ability of others to act on the basis of their own knowledge. Ideally, what is sought is a relational or social order in which the use of everyone's knowledge is possible. Although differing preferences and opinions can lead to conflicting actions, we need not control preferences and opinions themselves to handle the problem of conflicting action. We need only control actions, and only those actions that impede the ability of others to put the knowledge in their possession to good use. In sum, solving the first-order knowledge problem requires what Hayek called an "order of actions,"[3] not an order of preferences.

---

3. F. A. HAYEK, 1 LAW, LEGISLATION, AND LIBERTY 96 (1974).

A relational order of actions requires some scheme in which conflicts among actions are minimized. Human action must occur during particular periods of time and in particular physical spaces; this imperative is reflected in the term "order" itself. An order of actions initially suggests a scheme of temporal priority. ("First her actions, then his.") But spatial priority is another dimension of order. ("She acts over here; he acts over there.") Thus, to achieve an order of actions requires that the use of physical resources somehow be regulated.

A relational order of actions is achieved when the individual or associational uses of physical resources are temporally and spatially coordinated so as to reduce or eliminate the possibility that two persons or associations will attempt to use the same resource at the same time. If human actions can be suitably regulated, then we need not attempt to remold or coordinate personal or local knowledge itself. Not just any relational order will do, however. We want an order of actions in which personal and local knowledge can be developed, disseminated, and acted on, and some ordering methods will perform this function better than others.

Two quite different methods of achieving a relational order of actions are centralized and decentralized ordering. Although both methods are essential to attaining a relational order of actions in any society, they are not equally suited to address the first-order problem of knowledge.

Centralized Ordering

The idea of centralized ordering of society as a whole is both attractive and plausible in light of its familiarity. The family is organized in this way, with parents making decisions about the disposition of family assets among the family members. Larger commercial firms are also organized this way, with a hierarchical association of persons called "management" making decisions concerning the use of company resources subject to the approval of a board of directors. The military, with its extremely well-defined chains of command, is perhaps the paradigm of centralized ordering.

Centralized ordering is undoubtedly a valuable method of capitalizing on both personal and local knowledge. One individual acting as a central director or planner can effectively order the actions of other persons so as to capitalize on the planner's personal knowledge. For example, centralized ordering can harness a parent's personal knowledge of the needs of his or her child, an entrepreneur's personal knowledge of an unfulfilled demand in a market, or a field officer's personal knowledge of a tactical situation in combat. Or centralized direction can capitalize on the local knowledge of an association. For example, it can use the local knowledge of spouses, the talented managers of a corporation, or a military command.

Yet, despite its undeniable advantages, centralized ordering is completely unsuited to handle the first-order problem of knowledge. Suppose we delegated to some person or association the responsibility for coordinating resource use in accordance with the diverse knowledge of all persons and associations in society. To achieve an overall order of actions with such a strategy, some person or identifiable set of persons would somehow have to (1) obtain the personal and local knowledge of all persons and associations; (2) incorporate this knowledge into a coherent or coordinated plan of human actions; and (3) transmit instructions on resource use consistent with this plan to everyone in the society so that persons could act accordingly. Intractable problems arise at each step in this process.

The very strength of centralized direction in capitalizing on the personal and local knowledge of central directors is at once its weakness as a strategy for solving the first-order problem of knowledge. Centralized ordering is especially effective when those in charge of the ordering scheme have access to useful personal or local knowledge. But, although central directors have access to their own personal and local knowledge, they plainly lack access to the ever-changing totality of personal and local knowledge dispersed throughout an entire society.

In sum, centralized direction cannot solve the first-order problem of knowledge in society at large because central directors cannot possibly have access to the personal and local knowledge that such an ordering strategy requires. They are hopelessly ignorant of the knowledge needed to achieve an order of actions that would permit persons to put to use their personal and local knowledge. Moreover, they lack the capacity to integrate the necessary knowledge into a coherent plan and to communicate to all their allocated roles. Together, the three essential requirements of a centralized ordering strategy are unobtainable when this method is applied to govern resource use in an entire society. For this reason, centrally planned economies have, without exception, failed miserably to serve the public welfare.

Decentralized Ordering

How could the first-order problem of knowledge possibly be addressed by anything except central direction without immediately descending into chaos or disorder? The answer involves the concept of *jurisdiction*. A jurisdictional strategy attempts to handle the first-order problem of the radical dispersion of personal and local knowledge by using the idea of "bounded individual and associational discretion." This method of social ordering defines a jurisdiction or domain within which an individual or association is free to act on the basis of personal and local knowledge.

Implicit in this jurisdictional strategy is a crucial distinction between the judgment maker and the judgment to be made. To use the language of American sports, such a strategy distinguishes the jurisdictional question, "Who makes the call?" from the substantive question, "What is the correct call?" To answer each question requires substantially different knowledge. Answering the second question requires personal and local knowledge of particular circumstances—knowledge that is inaccessible to centralized mechanisms. Answering the first question requires only that we know who is in the best position to have this knowledge.

This quality of "being in the best position to know" is one important aspect of institutional or personal *competence*. The knowledge needed to make a correct decision differs substantially from the knowledge needed to identify a competent decision maker. Even when we do not know the correct call, we may know who is most likely to have the knowledge that such a call requires. Instead of gaining access to the personal and local knowledge needed to make the decision in question, such an assessment requires only that we determine who is in the best position to obtain this knowledge. In baseball, for example, we may know that the umpire is in the best position to assess whether or not a pitched ball is in the strike zone without knowing anything about a particular pitch.

The earlier discussion of personal and local knowledge suggests that individuals and associations have a comparative advantage over centralized mechanisms. They have access to types of knowledge that centralized mechanisms lack. The fact that individual persons and institutions are generally in the best position to make the right call does not, however, mean that they will always make good use of their access or that others are never in a better position to make a particular call. Nor does it mean that an analysis of personal and institutional competence would never benefit from a substantive assessment of the right call to make. We may, in fact, bolster our assessment of personal and institutional competence by sampling a few decisions to see if they appear to reflect the knowledge we expect these persons and institutions to possess. A pattern of egregious decisions would call into question the competence of the decision maker. And, as we shall see in Chapter 6, contract law restricts the power of persons who have been found to be incompetent to consent to contracts.

Still, the possibility of second-guessing the decisions of those in the best position to make a call does not change the basic analysis. Given that no decision-maker is perfect, we need to make a comparative and generalized judgment when allocating jurisdiction to make decisions. The fact that others sometimes know better does not entail an institutional competence to make correct calls for others systematically. The concept of competence does not rest on an ability to make every decision better than anyone else; it rests on generally being in a better position than anyone else to make knowledgeable decisions.

The idea of jurisdiction based on "bounded individual and associational discretion" is, of course, far too general to define actual conduct as permissible or impermissible. Nor does it specify the extent of the boundary. Nonetheless, even in the abstract, such a strategy is revealing. First, it identifies discretion—or *liberty*—as an essential means of capitalizing on knowledge that cannot be transmitted through a chain of command to central directors. Second, it gives discretion to individuals, who are most likely to possess personal knowledge, and to associations, which are most likely to possess local knowledge. Finally, it immediately suggests that discretion must somehow be bounded, albeit in a manner that does not undermine the purpose for adopting the jurisdictional strategy.

Allocating bounded discretion to individuals and associations involves two issues: (1) how individuals may use particular physical resources and (2) how they may transfer their jurisdiction over physical resources to others. The first of these components is addressed by the concept of private property. To have property in a physical resource, including one's body, means that one is free to use this resource in any way one chooses provided that this use does not infringe upon the rights of others. The issue of transferring jurisdiction over property is addressed by the concept of "freedom of contract."

As was discussed in section 3.4.1, freedom of contract is comprised of two distinct principles: freedom *to* contract and freedom *from* contract. Freedom to contract holds that persons may consent to legally enforceable transfers of their preexising rights; freedom from contract holds that transfers of preexisting rights should not be imposed upon them without their consent. In other words, freedom to contract *permits* consensual transfers, whereas freedom from contract *requires* them.

Against a backdrop of private property rights, these two aspects of contractual freedom regulate the transfers of preexisting rights. The manifested consent of the rights-holder is normally sufficient to transfer a property right; and property rights may not normally be transferred without the consent of the rights-holder. Permitting and requiring consensual transfers addresses both dimensions of the first-order problem of knowledge discussed above: (1) one must be able to act on the basis of one's own personal knowledge or the local knowledge one has access to as a member of an association; (2) when so acting, one must somehow take into account the knowledge of others of which each person is hopelessly ignorant.

First, permitting consensual transfers of jurisdiction—freedom to contract—enables persons to act on the basis of their personal and local knowledge by allowing them to exchange jurisdictions they currently have for jurisdictions they believe they can put to better use. In this way, a transfer of a person's jurisdiction reflects his or her local and personal knowledge.

Second, requiring that all transfers of jurisdiction be by consent—freedom from contract—addresses the second dimension of this knowledge problem by compelling persons to take into account the knowledge of others when making their decisions. For changes in boundaries to reflect the knowledge of all affected parties, such revisions must be based on the manifested consent of all the individuals or associations whose boundaries are being changed. By requiring consent, each party to a transfer of rights is compelled to take the knowledge of the other into account. For example, even though a prospective buyer lacks access to the personal knowledge of the current owner, the buyer must figure out a sum of money that the owner thinks he can put to better use than the resource he is being asked to give up.

But freedom from contract addresses the knowledge problem far more profoundly than this simple "micro" example suggests. Requiring consensual transfers also makes possible the evolution of a powerful "macro" institution that enables personal and local knowledge to be *encoded* and transmitted worldwide in a form that can be easily understood by others and incorporated into their decisions without centralized direction. The term we use for this code is *price.*

Prices are by far the most neglected form of knowledge we have. This is because the knowledge embedded in prices is not explicit; we are never conscious of it as knowledge. It is encoded knowledge, and we are conscious only of the code. Prices reflect the vast personal and local knowledge of the many competing uses to which any physical resource may be put. My computer is constructed of plastic, various metals, and other resources. My desk is made of wood. These resources could have been used in a variety of other ways by people throughout the globe. I have not the slightest way of knowing even a small fraction of the specific alternative uses that others might find for these resources. Without a comprehensive knowledge of all the alternative uses of these resources, how can a knowledgeable decision be made on how these resources should be used?

Resource prices condense the personal and local knowledge of each one of us into a simple form of local knowledge—an amount of money—that can be integrated into the personal knowledge of all of us. For example, a trip to Europe has a resource price attached to it. When you consider this choice, you must consider the subjective cost of paying this price. This cost is the most highly valued set of opportunities that you will forgo by choosing to go to Europe. In other words, you must consider what you will have to sacrifice to make the trip. Of course, even with a market price of zero, there is no such thing as a truly cost-free trip to Europe, because such a trip will require you to forgo other potential uses of your time. But the monetary price to travel to Europe will strongly influence the subjective cost to you of such a trip. And this monetary price incorporates into your decision the uses to which others may put the same resources it takes to get you to Europe. This is only true, however, if resource prices result from freedom from contract.

Prices are able to communicate information about dispersed personal and local knowledge only if the consent of those with jurisdiction over particular resources is required before jurisdiction may be transferred to another. If you could compel the airline to fly you to Europe without its consent, you would not have to integrate how its resources might be used by others into your own decision to make the trip. By requiring the consent of a property owner, anyone wishing to obtain and use property owned by another must offer the present owner something the present owner subjectively believes he or she would put to better use. The exchange price reveals that the subjective value the current owner placed on the resource was less than the subjective value of the resources offered. Without the requirement of consent, this subjective information would never be manifested, and meaningful market prices could not arise.

Confronted with a set of market prices for scarce resources, every person must decide whether to use a resource, save it for later use, or exchange it for another resource, while taking into account the knowledge and preferences of countless others that are encoded in the market price for the good. If the market price is higher than the value one places on the resource then one will be induced to exchange it. If the market price is lower, one will either use the resource or conserve it for later use or exchange.

The process is dynamic in that jurisdiction holders are continually incorporating price signals—a form of local knowledge—into the personal knowledge on which they base their decisions. In turn, each person's decision to hold or sell will influence the price signals received by others to be incorporated into their personal knowledge. For example, my ongoing decision not to sell my house both influences the market price of housing and, simultaneously, is influenced by the market price of my house and by the market price of alternative housing. True, the effect of my decision alone is unlikely to "move the market," but the current market price is an aggregation of everyone's decision either to sell or not to sell. This process of knowledge generation and transmittal would be impossible if individual rights to resources could be transferred without the consent of the rights-holder.

In sum, freedom to contract enables persons to exchange their rights on the basis of their knowledge that other rights would better serve their purposes. Freedom from contract protects the expectations of current rights-holders, permitting them to put their knowledge into effect over a period of time free from the interference of others. Without adherence to the principle of freedom from contract, resource prices would not arise. Nonconsensual transfers of rights "short-circuit" the price system of knowledge transmittal and make it literally impossible for individuals and associations to take the knowledge of others into account when putting their own knowledge into action.

The dispersed nature of personal and local knowledge gives rise to a knowledge problem of such enormous proportions that less information is preferable to more. That is, even if a central planner had direct access to all the knowledge required for coordination, the sheer volume of such personal and local knowledge would prevent the planner from putting it to use. We need somehow to condense this widely dispersed knowledge into a usable form that can be integrated into each person's personal knowledge. And this process of condensation need not be perfect to be superior to the only alternative—near-total ignorance that results from the general inaccessibility of personal and local knowledge. This vital social function is performed by the device of resource prices made possible by contractual consent. This is a pretty darned important reason why consent is at the heart of contract law.

4.1.2 Two Problems of Interest

The first-order problem of knowledge is not the only important social function performed by freedom of contract. Even if no knowledge problem existed, we would still face serious social *problems of interest* that spring from the common tendency of persons to make judgments or choose actions that they believe will serve their subjective preferences. In this section, I consider two distinct problems of interest: the *partiality problem* and the *incentive problem*. The ability of freedom of contract to handle these pervasive problems provides an independent and reinforcing reason for respecting contractual consent. Those who urge that contractual consent be abandoned or highly qualified must explain how these problems can be handled successfully in some other manner. In my judgment they cannot, and in my experience they do not even try.

The Partiality Problem

The term "partiality" refers to the tendency of people to make decisions that favor their own interests or the interests of those who are close to them at the expense of others. A partiality *problem* arises when persons whose viewpoints are influenced by their own interests are called upon to make decisions that are supposed to take into account the interests of persons remote to them. This type of impartial or objective assessment is required when systems of resource allocation require some person or group to make a general or society-wide determination of how all resources are to be used. It is next to impossible for human beings to set their own interests in proper perspective to make an impartial assessment on behalf of everyone.

The partiality problem refers to the difficulty of making decisions concerning resource use that take into account all available personal and local knowledge, along with the interests of others, without succumbing to the tendency of persons to give priority to their own knowledge and interests. Even if persons with centralized jurisdiction over resources could gain sufficient access to the personal and local knowledge of others to address the knowledge problem, we would still need to confront the problem of partiality. What assurance do we have that the decisions of these planners concerning resource use will be based impartially on this knowledge, rather than on a partial judgment of what is in their own interest, or the interests of those who are close to them?

By requiring the consent of a current rights-holder, freedom from contract forces prospective rights-holders, whether they like it or not, to take both the interests and knowledge of current holders into account when deciding whether to effectuate a transfer. By becoming part of the prospective owner's cost of obtaining control over the resource, the interests and knowledge of the current rights-holder are brought to bear on the allocation decision. In this way, the system of resource prices that results from contractual consent addresses not only the first-order problem of knowledge but also the partiality problem.

The Incentive Problem

Using freedom to contract to address the first-order problem of knowledge assumes that people will have sufficient interest to actually employ their access to knowledge of how resources may be used to make value-enhancing transfers. What if right-holders lack adequate incentives to put their knowledge to use?

Imagine a world of private property where control over resources was decentralized as it largely is today. Now imagine that all the benefits accruing from a knowledgeable exercise of control were routinely siphoned off and given to others, for example, through a steeply progressive income tax or a confiscatory wealth tax. The inability to reap the benefits from acting on one's personal and local knowledge would greatly reduce the incentive to do so. Some incentive to act productively might remain if an activity were intrinsically rewarding. As the inherent interest in doing a job declined, however, even this residual incentive to put one's knowledge into action would diminish. For this reason, just as the distribution of control over resources should correspond to the distribution of knowledge in society, so too the distribution of benefits should closely correspond to the distribution of control.

Yet another reason for respecting both freedom to and freedom from contract is that both aspects of contractual freedom address the incentive problem. The principle of freedom from contract ensures that changes in control of resources reflect the knowledge of the original right-holder. Only if the right-holder consents to a transfer will it be recognized as valid. Consent will not be given unless the right-holder subjectively values the distribution of rights resulting from the transfer more highly than the original distribution of rights. Without a requirement of consent, the incentive to use one's knowledge to improve the resources within one's rightful jurisdiction would be undercut by the prospect that others could dispossess the right-holder and gain the improved resources without his or her consent.

The principle of freedom to contract provides incentives for beneficial transactions by enforcing agreements motivated by the prospect of receiving a benefit or profit. This prospect creates powerful incentives to investigate and discover previously unknown opportunities for beneficial transfers. *Entrepreneurship* is the ability to identify previously unknown or neglected opportunities for beneficial transactions. If contracts producing so-called "speculative" *gain* were unenforceable, then the incentive for such entrepreneurial activity would be eliminated.

Conversely, the prospect of incurring a *loss* induces a level of caution in people's actions. One has an incentive to be more careful about putting one's knowledge into action if one incurs the full cost of any mistaken transaction. The only way to eliminate the costs of mistakes is to transfer resources to the actor who has made the bad bargain from others who have not. In the absence of consent by the person to whom the loss is shifted—for example, by a consensual risk-pooling or insurance scheme—taking their resources to compensate others for their bad bargains will create adverse incentives for those from whom this compensation is confiscated. Nonconsensual transfers also create what economists call a "moral hazard" when people engage in risky behavior that they alone will benefit from if things go well, but others who were more cautious will pay for the losses if things turn out badly.

Freedom of contract, then, both encourages beneficial transfers and discourages transfers that adversely affect interest. Freedom to contract—that is, consensual transfers are valid—makes entrepreneurship possible by ensuring that positive incentives exist for beneficial rights transfers. Freedom from contract—that is, nonconsensual transfers are invalid—ensures that rights transfers will not create negative incentives. In these ways, contractual consent addresses the problems of interest as well as the first-order problem of knowledge.

4.1.3 Protecting Reliance: From Subjective to Objective Consent

The consent that addresses the problems of knowledge and interest is subjective—what some view as the only "real" assent. But subjective assent encounters the following difficulty: Because every person's intentions are part of his or her personal knowledge, and because these intentions are inaccessible to observers, subjective assent is an impractical basis for determining rights transfers. Lacking any direct access to these intentions, a party to a rights transfer can never be entirely sure that the other party has subjectively assented. Third parties seeking to adjudicate conflicting claims of rights also have difficulty making such an assessment after the fact.

This may be viewed as a *second-order problem of knowledge*: the problem of knowing the legal rights that define the extent and limits of one's liberty to act. It is "second order" because it must be addressed only after one acknowledges that the private property and freedom of contract are the solutions to the first-order problem of how to allocate and use scarce resources. The jurisdictional solution to the first-order problem of knowledge will simply not work unless each person knows where the boundaries lie.

Without a manifestation of assent that all affected parties can know, the system of bounded individual discretion will fail to address the underlying problems of knowledge and interest. At the time of a transaction, it will have failed to identify clearly and communicate to both parties, and to third parties including adjudicators, the rightful boundaries that must be respected. Without such communication, parties to a transaction, and third parties, cannot know what constitutes rightful conduct and what constitutes a commitment on which they can justifiably rely. In sum, to handle this secondary knowledge problem—knowledge of one's rights—everyone needs to be able to "rely on the appearances" with respect to their own domains and those of others.

Only a general reliance on objectively ascertainable assertive conduct will enable a decentralized system of rights to perform its allotted boundary-defining function. In contract law this is known as the "objective theory of assent," which we examined in Chapter 3. We hold persons to the *reasonable* or normal meaning that their conduct conveys to others. For example, signing a written contract or clicking "I agree" on webpage conveys the message, "I am transferring some of my rights to the other party."

The imputation of meaning to conduct requires reference to a conventional system of language that is shared by the relevant community. So, for example, "yes" means *yes*, and "no" means *no* within the community of English-speaking people. Asking what "yes" means to a reasonable person is to ask what meaning a normal participant in the English-speaking community would attach to this sound, given the context in which it was uttered. A person who did not speak English would be unable to express an opinion, however "reasonable" this person might otherwise be. The objective approach acknowledges the conventional nature of language. Contracts based on manifested consent, then, operate similarly to resource prices by converting the personal knowledge of each party into a form of local knowledge that is accessible to both parties. Subjective assent becomes a manifested consent.

Understanding the communication function that an objective approach to consent plays also enables us to appreciate the limits of this approach. For example, suppose it can be shown that one party to a contract actually knew or had reason to know that the other party attached an idiosyncratic meaning to a linguistic utterance that would normally mean something quite different to a "reasonable person." In such a case, the purpose for which we adopt the objective approach—to enable persons to rely on the appearances created by others because subjective intentions are generally inaccessible—is satisfied by actual knowledge that the appearances here are deceiving. Therefore, in contract law, we protect a party's reliance on objective appearances, unless it can be shown that the parties shared a common subjective understanding of a term.

Although many law professors may question whether freedom from and freedom to contract deserve to be the central animating principles of contract law, there is little doubt that these principles account for the structure of contract law as it has evolved. Where contract law doctrines are thought to be inconsistent with freedom of contract, this is usually because the interrelational nature of contractual freedom is not sufficiently appreciated. Freedom of contract is as much about being able to rely on the apparent consent of another as it is on one's own will or intent to make such legally binding commitments. Every contract has (at least) two parties, and contract law exists to protect both promisors and promisees alike.

Contractual freedom, in short, embraces both will and reliance, and by so doing helps identify the limits of both potentially conflicting considerations. Moreover, those academics who are hostile to contractual freedom do not adequately acknowledge that contractual freedom, like all individual rights or jurisdictions, is bounded by the rights or jurisdictions of others. In Chapter 2, we saw how freedom of contract is also bounded by the inalienability of some rights, which entails that these rights cannot be transferred to another even if the rights holder so consents. When a right is inalienable, the rights holder can always change his or her mind about performance. In Chapter 6, we will examine contract defenses that have long been available to avoid the imposition of contractual obligation notwithstanding a previous manifestation of consent to be bound. As we shall see then, these doctrines are quite consistent with the principle of freedom of contract.

Finally, even if a consensus existed that respecting the principles of private property and freedom of contract was the best way to address the pervasive social problems of knowledge and interest, another aspect of the second-order problem of knowledge would still remain. These principles are simply too abstract to guide individual conduct directly. Abstract principles of private property and freedom of contract cannot address the problems of knowledge and interest unless people know how to act consistently with them. In other words, people must somehow learn what justice requires them to do or refrain from doing.

The second-order problem of knowing what specific conduct is consistent with abstract principles of justice is traditionally handled by *law*. Legal doctrine in the form of rules and principles evolve to address the complexities of human interaction in a way that can be applied to particular cases. Lawyers trained in legal doctrine can give legal advice, and judges trained in legal doctrine can resolve disputes. While the abstract principles discussed in this section are important to understanding the underlying structure of contract law, these principles are no substitute for the legal rules and principles that comprise contract doctrine.

※ 4.2 The Doctrine of Consideration

No legal system enforces all promises. In *Consideration and Form*,[4] Lon Fuller explained why: "There is a real need for a field of human intercourse freed from legal restraints, for a field where men may without liability withdraw assurances they have once given. Every time a new type of promise is made enforceable, we reduce the area of this field." Fuller thought that the "need for a domain of 'free-remaining' relations" was not merely spiritual but served an important economic purpose as well. "Business deals can often emerge only from a converging series of negotiations, in which each step contains enough assurance to make worthwhile a further exchange of views and yet remains flexible enough to permit a radical readjustment to new situations." Therefore, to "surround with rigid legal sanctions even the first exploratory expressions of intention would

---

4. Lon L. Fuller, *Consideration and Form*, 41 COLUM. L. REV. 799 (1941).

not only introduce an unpleasant atmosphere into business nego-tiations, but would actually hamper commerce."

Another famous nineteenth-century contracts theorist, Morris Cohen, earlier made a very similar observation.[5] "It is indeed very doubtful whether there are many people—not necessarily diplo-mats—who prefer a world in which one would be obliged to keep all one's promises instead of the present more viable system, in which a fair proportion is sufficient." Part of this preference is personal. "Many of us indeed would shudder at the idea of being bound by every promise, no matter how foolish, without any chance of letting increased wisdom undo past foolishness. Certainly freedom to change one's mind is necessary for free intercourse between those who lack omniscience." But business too would become "more complicated and would become too risky if we were bound by every chance promise that escapes us. Negotiations would be checked by such fear." In these circumstances, "men do not want to be bound until the final stage, when some formality like the signing of papers gives one the feeling of security, of having taken the proper precautions."

Stated in so general a manner, these considerations argue that a line between enforceable and unenforceable promises must be drawn somewhere, but do not specify exactly when contractual enforcement is desirable and when it is not. So we now turn to the first of three doctrines that have evolved to distinguish the commit-ments that are enforceable from those that are not: the doctrine of consideration. All three can be understood as effectuating freedom of contract—both freedom to and freedom from contract—and the ability to rely on the commitments of others.

4.2.1 The Origins of the Doctrine of Consideration

When the writ of assumpsit was adopted to allow enforcement of promises, there arose two problems of *over*enforcement—that is,

---

5. Morris R. Cohen, *The Basis of Contract*, 4 HARV. L. REV. 553 (1933).

the enforcement of promises that should not be enforced. The first problem concerned fraudulent claims that a promise had been made. This problem was handled by the enactment in 1677 of the first Statute of Frauds that required some promises be in writing to be enforced, although they need not be under seal. Enhanced formality was required for contracts for land, for goods worth more than a stipulated amount, and contracts whose performance would take more than a year. All these contracts would impose a great burden on anyone falsely accused of having made a promise. As with the presumption of innocence in criminal cases, the evil of overenforcement in these situations was thought to be greater than that of underenforcement.

The second problem concerned distinguishing those informal promises that merited enforcement from those that did not. For, as Fuller and Cohen observed, no legal system has ever enforced *all* promises. The doctrine adopted to address this question was called, the "doctrine of consideration." The doctrine got its name from its original focus on the reasons or "considerations" that motivated the making of the promise. Expressed statements of these considerations were included in formal contracts long before there was a *doctrine* of consideration. Legal historian A. W. B. Simpson describes the original meaning of "consideration" this way: "The consideration, or considerations, for a promise meant the factors which the promisor considered when he promised, and which moved or motivated his promising. Although not a precise equivalent, 'motive' is perhaps about as near as one can get by way of synonym."[6]

When the doctrine of consideration first developed, explained Simpson, it was based on "the idea that the legal effect of a promise should depend upon the factor or factors which motivated the promise. To decide whether a promise to do X is binding, you need to know why the promise was made." For example, "one might or might not accept love of charity, or a future marriage, or a past

---

6. A. W. B. SIMPSON, A HISTORY OF THE COMMON LAW OF CONTRACT: THE RISE OF THE ACTION OF ASSUMPSIT 321 (1975).

payment, as sufficient in law to impose promissory liability. Whatever decisions are made about such matters as these can be fitted into the basic analysis."

Originally these "*good* considerations" included promises made after the promisee had received a benefit. Courts also started to enforce promises that were intended to induce a detriment to the promisee. This conception of "benefit-detriment" consideration can still be glimpsed in some of the cases taught in contracts courses. For example, in *Blatt v. University of Southern California*[7] a court found that the alleged promise of a law school to admit the defendant to the Order of the Coif if he achieved a specified grade point average was not enforceable because "[t]here was no benefit flowing to defendants as a result of plaintiff's hard work or his class ranking. Any benefit that occurred inured to the plaintiff. Consequently there was no consideration for any alleged promise or representations of defendants." But as we shall now see, this is aberrational. Beginning in the late nineteenth century, the benefit-detriment theory of consideration was eventually supplanted by what is known as the bargain theory.

4.2.2 The Bargain Theory of Consideration

To understand why the "benefit-detriment" theory of consideration was ultimately abandoned, consider the famous case of *Hamer v. Sidway*,[8] in which an uncle "promised his nephew that if he would refrain from drinking, using tobacco, swearing and playing cards or billiards for money until he became 21 years of age, he would pay him the sum of $5,000." The uncle died before paying the money.

When the nephew lodged his claim against the uncle's estate, the executor of the estate denied there was consideration for the

---

7. 5 Cal. App. 3d 935, 85 Cal. Rptr. 601 (1970).

8. 124 N.Y. 538, 27 N.E. 256 (1891).

promise of the deceased on the ground "that the promisee by refraining from the use of liquor and tobacco was not harmed, but benefitted; that which he did was best for him to do independently of the uncle's promise." Therefore "it follows that unless the promisor was benefitted, the contract was without consideration." Because (1) the nephew incurred no detriment but benefitted by his performance, and (2) the uncle was not benefitted by the return performance of the nephew, the nephew's performance did not constitute good consideration for the uncle's promise. In sum, if the doctrine of consideration requires either *detriment to the promisee* or *benefit to the promisor*, neither existed here.

The court rejected this argument on the ground that courts "will not ask whether the thing which forms the consideration does *in fact* benefit the promisee or a third party, or is of any substantial value to anyone (emphasis added)." The only requirement is "that something is promised, done, forborne or suffered by the party to whom the promise is made as consideration for the promise made to him." The court also rejected the executor's claim that the uncle received no benefit from the nephew's promise. "Consideration means not so much that one party is profiting as that the other abandons some legal right in the present or limits his legal freedom of action in the future as an inducement for the promise of the first." The Court then concluded that "it is of no moment whether such performance actually proved a benefit to the promisor, and the court will not inquire into it."

The concept of subjective value discussed in Chapter 2 helps explain this development. What's the best evidence that the nephew's performance was a "benefit" to the uncle? Is it not that he was willing to give $5000 to secure it? He cared about his nephew's well-being enough to pay him a reward to live virtuously. In other words, the uncle subjectively preferred knowing that his nephew abstained from drinking to keeping his $5000, which means the uncle was subjectively benefitted by the nephew's abstinence. Why would the essential subjectivity of value lead a court to refrain from assessing whether abstinence by the nephew was in fact a "detriment" to him? Because whether the nephew was harmed would depend on the nephew's own preferences about the matter—not some external person's judgment about what the nephew's true interests were.

But recognizing the inherent subjectivity of benefits and detriments posed a practical problem for contract law doctrine. If *any* subjective benefit or detriment is enough to support contractual enforcement, then *every* promise will be enforceable and the doctrine of consideration will fail to distinguish enforceable from unenforceable promises. No one makes a promise voluntarily unless they gain some sort of subjective benefit from doing so. For this reason, the benefit-detriment theory of consideration proved unworkable in practice.

In the late nineteenth century, the benefit-detriment theory of consideration was supplanted by what is called "the bargain theory of consideration." In the words of one of the theory's biggest advocates, Oliver Wendell Holmes, Jr.: "No matter what the actual motive may have been, by the express or implied terms of the supposed contract, *the promise and the consideration must purport to be the motive each for the other*, in whole or at least in part."[9] According to Holmes, "[i]t is not enough that the promise induces the detriment or that the detriment induces the promise, if the other half is wanting."

Under the bargain theory, it does not matter *what* the consideration is—or whether there was a benefit to the promisor or detriment to the promisee—but only whether each party's promise or performance was the inducement for the other party's promise or performance. The *Restatement 2nd*, section 71(1) defines consideration in terms of a bargain. "To constitute consideration, a performance or a return promise must be bargained for." Section 71(2) then defines bargain just as Justice Holmes did: "A performance or return promise is bargained for if it is sought by the promisor in

---

9. *Wisconsin & Michigan Railway*, 191 U.S. 379, 386 (1903) (emphasis added).

exchange for his promise and is given by the promisee in exchange for that promise."

The bargain theory has an obvious advantage over a benefit-detriment theory of consideration. No inquiry into whether there was an actual subjective benefit to the promisor or detriment to the promisee is required. All that is needed is a mutual inducement. Apart from its greater workability, a bargain theory has two other advantages as well.

First, in most contexts, formal bargaining usually manifests an intention to be legally bound. When two commercial parties each say to the other, "I'll do this for you, if you do that for me," they typically contemplate and desire that their commitment will be enforceable. In this way, the bargain theory of consideration does a reasonably good job of identifying when parties have exercised their freedom to contract, and screening out promises that were not intended to be enforceable, thereby protecting the parties' freedom from contract. As we shall see below, however, because the bargain theory is imperfect in achieving these ends, it needs to be supplemented by other doctrines of enforceability.

Second, apart from its instrumental value in identifying the intentions of the parties and protecting contractual freedom, the enforcement of bargains can be viewed as a socially beneficial end in itself. No one has explained this more clearly than Adam Smith. Although we think of Smith as an economist, he was actually a philosopher whose expertise included legal philosophy. In his *Lectures on Jurisprudence*,[10] he observed that bargaining makes possible what economists today call the "division of labor," which Smith explains is not "the effect of any human policy, but is the necessary consequence of a natural disposition altogether peculiar to men, viz. the disposition to truck, barter, and exchange." He identifies human interdependency and the need for a division of labor as the

---

10. ADAM SMITH, LECTURES ON JURISPRUDENCE 347 (R. L. Meek et al. eds), Oxford Univ. Press, 1978) (1762–63).

reason why bargains are essential to human existence. "Man continually standing in need of the assistance of others, must fall upon some means to procure their help." There are two ways to obtain the assistance of others: ask for it as a gift—what Smith refers to as "coaxing and courting"—or offer something in return. Ordinarily, a person does not expect your assistance "unless he can turn it to your advantage or make it appear to be so. Mere love is not sufficient for it, till he applies in some way to your self love." Smith concludes that "[a] bargain does this in the easiest manner."

In his most famous work, *The Wealth of Nations*,[11] in which he explains why some nations are rich and others poor, he offers a more colorful formulation of the central social importance of bargains, as well as a very useful definition of "**bargain**":

> Whoever offers to another a bargain of any kind, proposes to do this: *Give me that which I want, and you shall have this which you want, is the meaning of every such offer*; and it is in this manner that we obtain from one another the far greater part of those good offices which we stand in need of. It is not from the benevolence of the butcher, the brewer, or the baker, that we expect our dinner, but from their regard to their own interest. We address ourselves, not to their humanity but to their self-love, and never talk to them of our own necessities but of their advantages. (emphasis added)

Notice that Smith's defense of bargaining is not premised on so-called atomistic individuals whose welfare is wholly independent of others. To the contrary, it is premised on the inherent dependency of each person on the assistance of others. Nor is his discussion of "self love" a defense of selfishness. To the contrary, he defended bargains because they compel each party to take the subjective welfare

---

11. ADAM SMITH, AN INQUIRY INTO THE NATURE AND CAUSES OF THE WEALTH OF NATIONS 18 (Edwin Cannan ed., Univ. Chicago Press, 1976) (1776).

of the other party into account. To obtain the assistance of some-one else, bargaining requires that you figure out a way to leave them better off as well.

As noted above, according to legal historian A. W. B. Simpson, that a promise was to pay for benefits previously received, or was made from a sense of moral obligation, were originally deemed to be "good considerations" for its enforcement. By the nineteenth century, however, the enforceability of such promises was shaky.

For example, in the 1825 case of *Mills v. Wyman*,[12] the Massachusetts court denied the enforceability of a man's promise to reimburse the expenses of an innkeeper who had cared for his grown son after the son had fallen ill. "The kindness and services towards the sick son of the defendant were not bestowed at his request." The result in *Mills* is consistent with the benefit-detriment theory: The promisor could be said to have received no benefit in return for his promise to the innkeeper and the innkeeper, having already rendered services, incurred no detriment.[13]

After the bargain theory developed, it too could explain the result in *Mills*. If the father did not promise to pay in order to induce the innkeeper to perform, but did so out of a sense moral duty, the assistance to the son was not bargained for and the promise not supported by consideration. This reasoning was employed by Holmes himself in *Moore v. Elmer*.[14] In this case, Josephine Moore, a fortune teller doing business as Madame Sesemore, predicted that Willard Elmer would die before the end of the year. Hearing this, Elmer promised in writing to pay off Moore's mortgage if her predic-tion came true. When Elmer died as predicted, Moore sought to enforce the promise. In his opinion for the Supreme Judicial Court

---

12. 20 Mass. (3 Pick.) 207 (1825).

13. It turns out that the father's promise may well have been made, not to pay for past services, but to induce the innkeeper to continue to assist his son. *See* Geoffrey R. Watson, *In the Tribunal of Conscience:* Mills v. Wyman *Reconsidered*, 71 TUL. L. REV. 1749 (1997).

14. 180 Mass. 15, 61 N.E. 259 (1901).

of Massachusetts, Holmes denied there was consideration for the promise. Because the fortune-telling session had already been performed when the promise was made, "the consideration was executed and would not support a promise made at a later time."

Today, although the *Restatement 2nd*, section 86 allows for the enforcement of promises to pay for benefits already received "to the extent necessary to prevent injustice," this is treated, not as consideration, but as an exception to the requirement of bargained-for consideration specified in section 71.

4.2.3 Distinguishing Bargained-For Exchanges from Conditioned Gifts

If a promise is not bargained for but is a gift, then it is not enforceable if the donor refuses to perform as promised. Sometimes, however, a promise of a gift—sometimes called a "gratuitous promise"—can be made conditional on the occurrence of some event. One of the trickiest aspects of consideration is to distinguish a bargained-for exchange that is enforceable from a "conditioned gift" that is not. Consider some variations on the facts of *Hamer v. Sidway*.

Suppose that Willie's uncle sees his nephew walking on the other side of the street. Feeling generous he shouts, "If you come across the street, I'll pay you $1000." Is there a "bargained-for exchange"? Did the nephew cross the street to obtain the payment of the money? Yes. Was the uncle's promise made to induce the nephew's "performance" of crossing the street? No. Crossing the street was merely a condition that needed to be satisfied for the nephew to collect his gift. The key is that *getting the nephew to cross the street* was no part of *the reason* why the uncle made the promise of $1000.

To be bargained for a promise must be made, at least in part, to induce the performance of the other party, although the inducement of the performance need not be the only motivation for making the promise. To be a bargain, then, the nephew must have been induced to cross the street because of the promise, which he was, *and* the uncle must have made the promise, at least in part, to induce the nephew to cross the street, which he did not. The uncle merely wanted to make a gift.

To find a conditioned gift you must conclude that the promise was not made, even in part, to induce "the condition." To decide whether this was the case, a court may consider whether the return promise or performance benefitted the promisor. In the hypothetical, did the nephew's crossing the street benefit the uncle even psychologically? No. The lack of any subjective benefit to the uncle suggests he did not make the promise to induce the "performance" of crossing the street.

In the actual case of *Hamer v. Sidway* did the nephew's performance of his promise benefit the uncle? Psychologically yes—the uncle made the promise because he wanted the nephew's performance; he gained a subjective benefit from seeing the nephew avoid vices. But, in the hypothetical, didn't the uncle get a subjective benefit from giving the nephew the $1000? Why else did he make the promise? This is not the issue. The issue is whether *the crossing of the street* was bargained-for or whether it was merely a condition placed on a gift. So the question is whether the uncle made his promise of $1000 *to induce* the nephew to cross the street. One way of figuring this out is to ask whether the uncle received a subjective benefit from the nephew's performance, which would have motivated the uncle to make his promise to pay the nephew $1000.

This does not mean that benefit to the promisor is a requirement of consideration. We are still applying a bargain theory. Benefit to the promisor is merely an indication that the promise was made to induce the performance. By the same token, the degree of detriment imposed on the promisee may also indicate the existence of a bargain. The smaller the detriment to the person performing, the less likely it was bargained for. For example, why would the uncle offer to pay so much money to get the nephew to perform so trivial an act? *This does not mean that detriment to the promisee is a requirement of consideration.* Degree of detriment to the promisee is merely an indication that the promise was made to induce the performance.

A change in the hypothetical may make this even clearer. Suppose the uncle made the promise of $1000 if the nephew would cross a busy eight-lane expressway. We might then suspect both that the uncle was benefitting from the sadistic entertainment of seeing his nephew trying to cross the street, and that the detriment to the nephew explains why it was necessary to promise so much money. Both benefit and detriment would indicate the existence of a bargained-for exchange in which the uncle made the promise to induce the nephew to cross the expressway, and the nephew was induced to cross the expressway by the uncle's promise.

Again, why does it matter whether a transaction is a conditioned gift or a bargained-for exchange? Because, an offer or promise of a gift, whether conditioned or not, is unenforceable and generally revocable by the donor until the thing promised is actually delivered. A bargained-for contractual commitment is both enforceable and irrevocable by the promisor.

4.2.4 Preexisting Duties

The bargain theory of consideration's requirement of mutual inducement has led to a number of doctrines that sometimes produce troubling results. I have already mentioned the refusal to enforce so-called "past" and "moral" consideration on the ground that a promise for a benefit already received, or motivated by moral obligation, cannot have been bargained for and lacks mutual inducement. Another similar doctrine is the "preexisting duty rule" that finds a lack of consideration when a promise is made to obtain a performance already due the promisor.

For example, in *Stilk v. Myrick*,[15] after several sailors were lost because of death and illness, a captain promised extra pay to those sailors who would continue the voyage. Afterwards, a court refused

---

15. 6 Esp. 129, 170 Eng. Rep. 1168 [1809].

to enforce the promise on the ground that the sailors already owed the captain a duty to sail notwithstanding any loss of crew. Similarly, in *Alaska Packers v. Domenico*,[16] when fishermen in Alaska refused to fish unless paid more than they were promised when they signed on in San Francisco, the manager on the scene agreed. Later, a court refused to enforce the promise on the ground that the fisherman already had a duty to perform, and there was no consideration for the new promise.

These cases are species of a more general problem known as opportunistic contracting behavior. At formation both parties are ordinarily in a position to agree to a bargain or walk away.[17] During the course of performance, however, one party may have relied on the other party's commitment to such an extent that he or she is in no position to resist when the other person threatens to withhold performance. In this situation, one party is vulnerable to threats by the other to withhold performance unless a premium is promised.

Both *Stilk v. Myrick* and *Alaska Packers* can be understood as cases in which this type of opportunistic behavior might have existed to a greater or lesser degree. Although both opinions describe what appears to be opportunistic behavior, neither purports to rest its decision directly on this issue. Instead, each uses the requirement of consideration as an indirect method of policing this sort of abuse.

When considering the enforceability of modifications to an ongoing contract, the "preexisting duty rule" has been widely criticized as a poor device for indirectly policing opportunistic behavior. At formation, although the existence of a formal bargain is good evidence that the parties manifested their intention to be legally bound to perform their commitments, it is not a very good indicia

---

16. 117 F.99 (1902).

17. Situations in which a party's ability to refuse its consent is improperly restricted at formation are handled by such contract defenses as duress and unconscionability, which we will discuss in Chapter 6.

of the existence of coercion. Proof that a bargain existed will not reveal whether or not it was a product of coercion or duress. Because coercion is extraordinary, we place the burden on the party asserting such a defense to prove that it occurred; and such proof of duress is wholly apart from the presence or absence of consideration.

Adjustments of contractual obligations during performance are often necessary or desirable. In *Alaska Packers*, for example, the fisherman complained that the nets they were given by the company were deficient and, as a result, they could not catch the quantity of fish they assumed when they agreed to the original contract. If the agent of the employer who was on the scene accepted this reasoning, he may well have freely agreed to modify the agreement.[18]

There is no reason why one party cannot freely agree to pay more to the other party who is in the middle of performance when a variety of unexpected events occur. Furthermore, in the contract modification situation, every promise that changes the agreement is likely to have been made with the intention to be legally bound, regardless of whether it was separately bargained for. So the normal evidentiary function played at formation by bargained-for consideration, which was discussed in section 4.2.2, is unnecessary.

Although coercion at the time of formation is highly unusual, the existence of opportunistic behavior because of an imbalance of performance makes it more likely to happen in the middle of a deal when it is much harder for one party to walk away from a contract and sue for damages or specific performance. On the one hand, enforcing all modifications would lead to overenforcement insofar as coerced modifications would be enforced. On the other hand, refusing to enforce all modifications lacking separate consideration to police this behavior would lead to underenforcement. That is,

---

18. For an investigation into this and other issues raised in *Alaska Packers, see* Deborah I. Threedy, *A Fish Story:* Alaska Packers' Association v. Domenico, 2000 UTAH L. REV. 185.

every such modification would be unenforceable, even those many modifications that are freely made.

For this reason, most contracts scholars now believe that opportunistic behavior should be policed directly rather than through the mechanism of the doctrine of consideration. This entails, however, that at least some contract modifications lacking separate bargained-for consideration should be enforceable. If so, then manifestations of intention to be legally bound should sometimes be enforceable even in the absence of bargained-for consideration. Let us now turn to this issue.

🕮 4.3 The Use of Formalities

As was discussed in Chapter 1, even before the doctrine of consideration was developed, nonbargained-for promises could be enforced if they were in writing and under seal. That a promise was in writing and under seal unmistakably manifested an intention to be legally bound. What else could it mean? While the rise of assumpsit and the doctrine of consideration initially provided an alternative to the seal, eventually it came to undermine its use. A. W. B. Simpson observed, "there has always in the common law been a tendency towards a sort of doctrinal monism." With this mind set, "there must be *one* test for the formation of contract (offer and acceptance), *one* principle governing possession, *one* test for the actionability of promises. Hence the adoption of good consideration as the requirement for *all* promises."[19]

Courts soon came to say that "a seal imports a consideration" rather than a seal was an alternative to consideration. In the nineteenth century, statutes were passed in the United States abolishing the *requirement* that some writings be under seal. Eventually most states also abolished the legal effectiveness of having a

---

19. SIMPSON, *supra* note 6, at 325.

sealed writing. In these states, in the absence of consideration, a writing was unenforceable whether or not it was under seal. With respect to the sale of goods, UCC section 2-203, entitled, "Seals Inoperative," reads: "The affixing of a seal to a writing evidencing a contract for sale or an offer to buy or sell goods does not constitute the writing a sealed instrument and the law with respect to sealed instruments does not apply to such a contract or offer."

At least part of the reason for the abolition of the seal as a basis for enforcement grew out of practical considerations. Originally, a seal was made by impressing a metal form into hot wax that was dripped onto a parchment. Eventually, adhesive wafers were affixed to a document. Although both conveyed the unmistakable message of intention to be legally bound, wax seals and stickers could fall off over time, thereby destroying the enforceable effect. More importantly, many statutes required that certain official forms be under seal. To ease the burden of these requirements and to allow for printed pads of form contracts, other statutes were passed that allowed for the word "seal" and even the initials "L.S." to satisfy the requirement of a seal. A few words of text hardly sufficed to convey to the parties that they were binding themselves legally to an agreement. By this point, the seal had ceased to perform its function of meaningfully manifesting an intention to be legally bound.

The effective abolition of the seal by statutes, and the absence of any other formal alternative to bargained-for consideration, however, leads to a problem of underenforcement when a promisor manifests an intention to be legally bound, although bargained-for consideration is lacking. In the absence of some legally recognized formality, a person cannot make a legally enforceable promise without bargaining for something in return. And casting a gratuitous promise in the form of a bargain will not work either. If I promise to give you my car in "consideration" of $1, this will be considered a "pretense" of consideration and would generally be unenforceable. The *Restatement 2nd*, section 71, comment b says that "a mere pretense of bargain does not suffice, as where there is a false recital of consideration or where the purported consideration is merely nominal."

Recognizing this deficiency with the doctrine of consideration, Samuel Williston, the reporter for the first *Restatement of Contracts* and champion of the bargain theory of consideration, devised the Uniform Written Obligations Act, which was mentioned in section 3.4.3. It provides that: "A written release or promise, hereafter made and signed by the person releasing or promising, shall not be invalid or unenforceable for lack of consideration, if the writing also contains an additional express statement, in any form of language, that the signer intends to be legally bound."[20]

In urging its adoption by the National Conference of Commissioners on Uniform State Laws,[21] Williston observed: "I don't see why a man should not be able to make himself liable if he wishes to do so." Although the Commissioners recommended the Act to the states, just two adopted it: Utah, which later repealed it for reasons unknown, and Pennsylvania, where it is still in effect. Pennsylvania decisions employing the Act reveal few problems with its application, and it seems to fill a gap between the doctrines of consideration and promissory estoppel.

Outside of Pennsylvania, contract law does not provide a general way to make one's nonbargained-for promise enforceable. Still, the *Restatement 2nd* does recognize the enforceability of certain types of contracts in the absence of both consideration and reliance. For example, although it is not clear how many courts follow it, section 90(2) allows for the enforcement of formal promises made to charities without either bargained-for consideration or proof of reliance: "A charitable subscription or a marriage settlement is binding . . . without proof that the promise induced action or forbearance." Section 87(1)(a) allows nonbargained-for option contracts to be enforced when there is either a nominal consideration or a recital of

---

20. Uniform Written Obligations Act, Pa. Stat. Ann. tit. 33, § 6 (West 1997).

21. *See* Handbook of the National Conference of Commisioners on Uniform State Laws and Proceedings of the Thirty-Fifth Annual Meeting, Detroit, Michigan, Seventh Session, Friday, Aug. 28, 1925, pp. 193–215.

purported consideration: "An offer is binding as an option contract if it . . . is in writing and signed by the offeror, recites *a purported consideration* for the making of the offer, and proposes an exchange on fair terms within a reasonable time" (emphasis added). The UCC section 2-205 adopts a similar rule for what it calls "firm offers":

> An offer by a merchant to buy or sell goods in a signed writing which by its terms gives assurance that it will be held open is not revocable, for lack of consideration, during the time stated or if no time is stated for a reasonable time, but in no event may such period of irrevocability exceed three months; but any such term of assurance on a form supplied by the offeree must be separately signed by the offeror.

These scattered recognitions of formal intentions to be legally bound are typically ignored in contracts courses. Also commonly overlooked is the generally accepted effect of express disclaimers of intention to be legally bound. Such disclaimers are common in employee handbooks. In one case, a Colorado court upheld the effectiveness of the following language: "IMPORTANT. This Handbook is not a contract but merely a condensation of various Company policies, procedures, and employee benefits to assist you in the conduct of Company business . . . Management has the right to change the policies and benefits of the Company in accordance with the needs of the business without notice."[22] Indeed, disclaimers are recognized by the *Restatement 2nd*, section 21, which is entitled "Intention to Be Legally Bound": "Neither real nor apparent intention that a promise be legally binding is essential to the formation of a contract, *but a manifestation of intention that a promise shall not affect legal relations may prevent the formation of a contact* (emphasis added)."

---

22. Ferrera v. A.C. Nielsen, 799 P.2d 458 (1990).

Given the effectiveness of such disclaimers, what are we to make of the first half of section 21 affirming that "'[n]either real nor apparent intention that a promise be legally binding is essential to the formation of a contract"—a principle favored by Samuel Williston and included in the first *Restatement* for which he was the reporter? Given that Williston also proposed the Uniform Written Obligations Act, however, section 21 should probably not be taken as a rejection of the enforcement of contracts where the promisor manifested an intention to be legally bound. Instead, it merely establishes that, *if there is bargained-for consideration* then there is no need for any *additional* proof of intention to be legally bound, though an express disclaimer of such an intention can deny a bargain of enforceability. In other words, section 21 affirms that, on the one hand, the existence of bargained-for consideration is sufficient to find a promise enforceable without any other proof of intention to be legally bound; on the other hand, an express disclaimer of intention to be bound can deprive even a bargain of its enforceability.

Despite these exceptions, modern contract law, at least as normally taught, eschews enforceability based on formalities. What ought to matter, however, is whether a formality is the sort of action that manifests an intention to be legally bound. The initials "L.S." on a printed form clearly do not. A wax seal might do so, but is impractical for reasons discussed above. In contrast, casting one's promise in the form of a bargain, for example, by paying nominal consideration of $1, seems to unambiguously convey an intention to be legally bound.[23] So too does clicking an on-screen button saying "I agree" or "I accept" beneath a scroll box of terms before one is able to download or install some free software.

---

23. *See* Joseph Siprut, *The Peppercorn Reconsidered: Why a Promise to Sell Blackacre for Nominal Consideration Is Not Binding, But Should Be*, 97 Nw. U.L. Rev. 1809 (2003).

✍ 4.4 The Doctrine of Promissory Estoppel

4.4.1 Section 90 of the First and Second Restatements

In 1932, the first *Restatement of Contract* supplemented the bargain theory of consideration with the following provision:

> § 90. Promise Reasonably Inducing Definite And Substantial Action.
>
> A promise which the promisor should reasonably expect to induce action or forbearance *of a definite and substantial character* on the part of the promisee and which does induce such action or forbearance is binding if injustice can be avoided only by enforcement of the promise. (emphasis added)

Although it did not use the name, this doctrine is commonly referred to as *promissory estoppel*. The term was borrowed from the doctrine of *equitable estoppel.* Equitable estoppel bars a person in litigation from contradicting his or her past statements of fact, even where those statements were false, when doing so would be unfair to another person who relied on the original, if erroneous, statement.

Equitable and promissory estoppel share in common the idea of detrimental reliance. Whereas equitable estoppel concerned reliance on statements of fact, the doctrine of promissory estoppel concerns reliance on a promise or commitment to do or refrain from doing something. However, equitable estoppel was a doctrine that prevented a person from later contradicting a prior factual claim; it was not itself a cause of action for which a person could be held responsible. In contrast, promissory estoppel provides a cause of action for a breach of promise that is not supported by bargained-for consideration.

In 1979, the *Restatement 2nd* changed section 90 in several respects:

§ 90. Promise Reasonably Inducing Action *Or Forbearance*

(1) A promise which the promisor should reasonably expect to induce action or forbearance on the part of the promisee *or a third person* and which does induce such action or forbearance is binding if injustice can be avoided only by enforcement of the promise. *The remedy granted for breach may be limited as justice requires.*

(2) *A charitable subscription or a marriage settlement is binding under subsection (1) without proof that the promise induced action or forbearance.* (emphases added)

I have italicized where the two provisions differ from each other. The revised section 90 (1) eliminated the requirement that reliance be "of a definite and substantial character"; (2) added protection for third parties who rely on a promise to another; (3) allowed for recovery less than full enforcement of the promise, that is, allowed for damages based on the reliance rather than expectation interest; and as discussed in section 4.3, (4) allowed for the enforcement of charitable subscriptions or marriage settlements in the absence of reliance.

These changes reflected a shift in thinking about the basis of enforcing contracts that took place between the 1920s when the first *Restatement* was drafted and the 1970s when the second *Restatement* was published. In the 1920s, Samuel Williston, the reporter for the first *Restatement*, conceived of a contract as an enforceable promise. So section 90 provided a reliance-based substitute for the existence of bargained-for consideration. Call this the *consideration substitute* conception of promissory estoppel. According to this conception, promissory estoppel provides an alternative route to enforceability of a contract in the absence of consideration; and presumably all the other doctrines governing mutual assent would still apply—such as the requirement that a commitment be sufficiently definite or satisfy the statute of frauds.

By the time of the second *Restatement*, detrimental reliance on a promise was also thought to justify recovery all on its own, even without the sort of promise that satisfied the contract doctrines regulating mutual assent. Call this the *alternative to contract* conception of promissory estoppel. According to this conception, promissory estoppel was not only a substitute for the doctrine of consideration that justifies enforcing a promise in the absence of a bargain; it was also a reliance-based alternative to contract itself. And if promissory estoppel is operating when there is no contract, then the other doctrines of contract law need not be satisfied; and money damages could be limited to compensating for the reliance loss incurred rather than for the expectation of full performance. Under this theory, the object of promissory estoppel is to rectify injuries caused by promissory misbehavior in the same way that tort law rectifies injuries caused by physical misbehavior.

Debating the merits of this shift was once all the rage among contracts professors.

4.4.2 Grant Gilmore and the Death (and Rebirth) of Contract

In *Consideration and Form*,[24] Lon Fuller offered the following definition of what he called "private autonomy" which, along with the principles of reliance and unjust enrichment, constituted the substantive basis of contractual enforcement. "Among the basic conceptions of contract law," Fuller wrote, "the most pervasive and indispensable is the principle of private autonomy." What Fuller meant by this sounds a lot like the idea of consent discussed in section 4.1: "This principle simply means that the law views private individuals as possessing a power to effect, within certain limits,

---

24. Fuller, *supra* note 4.

changes in their legal relations. The man who conveys property to another is exercising this power; so is the man who enters a contract." Fuller viewed this as a form of private law making. "When a court enforces a promise it is merely arming with a legal sanction a rule or *lex* previously established by the party himself. This power of the individual to effect changes in his legal relations with others is comparable to the power of a legislature." In the 1950s and 1960s, this conception of contract law went into a steep decline.

By the mid-1970s, it was an article of faith among many legal academics that contract was not properly conceived as a means by which persons could, by their own choice, make law for themselves to govern their relations. Instead, contract was thought best conceived as the rectification of injuries persons may have caused by their verbal conduct in much the same way as persons have a tort duty to rectify the injuries caused by their physical acts. The injuries caused by promissory misbehavior consisted of detrimental reliance on the words of another. As Charles Fried colorfully summarized this approach: "My statement is like a pit I have dug in the road, into which you fall. I have harmed you and should make you whole."[25] So conceived, both contract and tort duties are imposed by law, and do not arise from the parties' consent, and contract law is conceptually indistinguishable from tort law.

The potential doctrinal implications of this reliance-based conception of contract were threefold. First, if duties are imposed by law rather than being the product of the parties' consent, then many of the niceties of finding mutual assent in the formation stage should not be a concern. Second, if the basis of a cause of action is the existence of reliance injury, then the enforcement of wholly executory agreements where neither party had yet to perform or rely would be called into question. Third, if reliance is the basis of contract, then the normal expectation measure of recovery should also be suspect—justified, if at all, as an indirect way to protect

---

25. CHARLES FRIED, CONTRACT AS PROMISE: A THEORY OF CONTRACTUAL OBLIGATION 10 (1981).

what Fuller and Perdue labeled the "reliance interest in contract damages." Indeed, it says much about the conventional wisdom during the 1960s and 1970s that Fuller and Perdue's 1936 "reliance interest" article received far greater attention and regard and than did Fuller's later *Consideration and Form*.

The thesis that contract law primarily concerns rectifying detrimental reliance was bolstered by two claims—one historical and the other doctrinal—contained in Grant Gilmore's highly influential 1974 monograph, *The Death of Contract*.[26] Historically, Gilmore claimed that contract law had been artificially separated from tort law in the nineteenth century due largely to the creative efforts of Christopher Columbus Langdell and Oliver Wendell Holmes, Jr. "Speaking descriptively, we might say that what is happening is that 'contract' is being reabsorbed into the mainstream of 'tort,'" Gilmore contended. "Until the general theory of contract was hurriedly run up late in the nineteenth century, tort had always been our residual category of civil liability. As the contract rules dissolve, it is becoming so again." In a footnote to this passage Gilmore observed that "[i]t is an historical truism that assumpsit, from which our theories of contract eventually emerged, was itself a split-off from the tort action of trespass on the case. Until the late nineteenth century the dividing line between 'contract' and 'tort' had never been sharply drawn."

Gilmore's second claim was doctrinal: By combining the bargain theory of consideration and the reliance-centered section 90, a fundamental contradiction was introduced into the *Restatement*. This contradiction would ultimately be resolved by reliance-based obligation imposed by law, as in torts, swallowing any distinct concept of contract as consent-based obligations originating with the parties. This is what constituted the "death of contract" as a distinct category of legal analysis. As always, Gilmore made his point colorfully: "We have become accustomed to the idea, without in the least

---

26. GRANT GILMORE, THE DEATH OF CONTRACT (1974).

understanding it, that the universe includes both matter and anti-matter. Perhaps what we have here is Restatement and anti-Restatement or Contract and anti-Contract." For Gilmore, it was clear "that these two contradictory propositions cannot live comfortably together: in the end one must swallow the other up."

Gilmore's historical argument that contract was a nineteenth-century offshoot of torts, although widely accepted, was always a curious half-truth. True, "[u]ntil the late nineteenth century the dividing line between 'contract' and 'tort' had never been sharply drawn," as Gilmore stated, but that was because until the mid-nineteenth century all lawsuits were governed by the various forms of action, not by *concepts* such as contracts *or* torts. As legal historian G. Edward White observed when describing the intellectual history of torts,[27] "[t]he emergence of Torts as an independent branch of law came strikingly late in American legal history." Like contracts, "Torts was not considered a discrete branch of law until the late [nineteenth] century. The first American treatise on Torts appeared in 1859, Torts was first taught as a separate law school subject in 1870, the first Torts casebook was published in 1874."

Gilmore's claim was, therefore, both true and misleading because virtually *all* the concepts, categories, and distinctions we now use to understand causes of action were "invented" or developed in the nineteenth century. Legal categories such as contracts and torts replaced the forms of action that had defined causes of action since the Middle Ages, but were abolished in the nineteenth century. Thus, it is as anachronistic to refer to assumpsit as a "tort" action as it is to refer to debt, detinue, or covenant as "contract" actions. Of course, we are free to categorize them as such, but only by retroactively applying concepts developed in the late nineteenth century. Contract law no more grew out of torts than did tort law grow out of contracts.

---

27. G. Edward White, *The Intellectual Origins of Torts in America*, 86 YALE L.J. 671, 671 (1977).

Somewhat amazingly, given the widespread sympathy for a reliance-based conception of contract,[28] from the 1930s to the 1970s no contracts scholar ever published a comprehensive reliance theory of contract that attempted to reconcile or reform existing contract law doctrine. By the 1980s, it had begun to be realized that the much-ballyhooed reliance revolution in contract law was not to be. As Allan Farnsworth observed,[29] "[t]he expansion of the role of reliance . . . did not continue in the 1980s. Indeed, . . . the trend appears to be in the other direction." The 1980s "did not witness the death of contract. Academic attempts to merge contracts into torts in courses called 'contorts' failed to flourish and it may be argued that contracts, through liberal application of third-party beneficiary doctrine, invaded the domain of tort during the 1980s." So striking were these developments that at the 1981 annual meeting of the Association of American Law Schools, Gilmore himself attempted to provide "an explanation of why this field of law, which somebody or other said was dead, some time ago, is not only alive and well but bursting at the seams."[30]

The prediction by Gilmore and others that a solely reliance-based, tort-like conception of contract would eventually completely supplant a consent-based conception should always have been more suspect than it was. After all, as early as 1933,[31] Morris Cohen observed that "[c]ontractual obligation is not coextensive with injurious reliance because (1) there are instances of both injury and reliance for which there is no contractual obligation, and (2) there are cases of such obligation where there is no reliance or injury." Tellingly, Cohen noted that "[c]learly, not all cases of injury resulting

---

28. *See, e.g.,* P. S. Atiyah, The Rise and Fall of Freedom of Contract (1979).

29. E. Allan Farnsworth, *Developments in Contract Law During the 1980's: The Top Ten,* 41 Case W. Res. L. Rev. 203, 219–20 (1990).

30. Charles Kelso, *The 1981 Conference on Teaching Contracts: A Summary and Appraisal,* 32 J. Legal Educ. 616, 640 (1982) (quoting a speech by Gilmore).

31. Morris R. Cohen, *The Basis of Contract,* 4 Harv. L. Rev. 533, 579 (1933).

from reliance on the word or act of another are actionable, and the theory before us offers no clue as to what distinguishes those which are."

Cohen's observation brings to the fore the fundamental weakness of promissory estoppel as embodied in the *Restatement* and the reason why law students find it so frustrating: It simply fails to identify when a legal remedy is available and how much recovery is due. Section 90 does not purport to compensate for all losses incurred in reliance on a promise. Instead, it authorizes compensation for reliance by the promisee that "the promisor should reasonably expect" or foresee. More typically, courts speak of "reasonable" or "justified" reliance. But whether reliance is foreseeable, reasonable, or justified must depend on some other factor or factors apart from the existence of reliance itself, and section 90 does not offer a clue as to what these other considerations (no pun intended) might be.

Nor does section 90 tell us "when justice requires" the full enforcement of the promise or "when justice requires" merely the award of reliance damages. Indeed, the "new and improved" version of section 90 in the *Restatement 2nd* appeals to "justice" twice— once when deciding whether a nonbargained-for promise should be enforced and again when deciding how much damages are due. In short, section 90 begs the doctrinal question of when and how a nonbargained-for promise that has been relied upon by the promisee should be enforced. This seems a pretty major omission.

Perhaps not coincidentally, then, the 1980s also witnessed a scholarly reexamination of the doctrine of promissory estoppel by an ideologically diverse group of contract scholars to see if it could be integrated into a comprehensive theory of contract, rather than used as a fulcrum to move contracts over into torts. Some concluded that promissory estoppel actually reflected not one but two distinct doctrines—one sounding in contract, and the other in tort. These doctrines are not mutually exclusive. In other words, part of the confusion caused by the doctrine of promissory estoppel resulted from the attempt to jam two distinct doctrines into a single formulation. Although promissory estoppel is not always taught this way, one can sort the more famous promissory estoppel cases into one of these two categories.

4.4.3 Promissory Estoppel *as Contract*: Consent to be Legally Bound

To appreciate how promissory estoppel can provide an alternative to consideration, it is necessary to clarify two different roles that reliance might play in the doctrine of promissory estoppel. The first is the tort-like role identified by Grant Gilmore in which the *inducement of detrimental reliance* may be held to justify a remedy to compensate for the detriment incurred, in the same way that the infliction of physical harm justifies a remedy in tort. Call this the "injurious reliance model" of promissory estoppel. The second is to focus on protecting a promisee's *right to rely* on promises, even in the absence of a bargain, where the promisor has manifested his or her intention to be legally bound. Call this the "consent model" of promissory estoppel.

Although contracts professors sometimes blur these two conceptions, the difference between them is crucial. According to the injurious reliance model, it is the existence of detrimental reliance or injury that justifies the enforcement of a contractual obligation. According to the consent model, it is the existence of a manifested intent to be legally bound that justifies protecting reliance. Thus according to the first model, we enforce contracts because reliance on the promises of another has occurred; whereas according to the second model, we enforce the manifestation of intent to be legally bound, at least in part, to enable people to rely in confidence on the nonbargain promises of others.

According to the consent model, although the protection of reliance is one purpose of contract, the existence of detrimental reliance alone does not tell you when reliance will be protected. Rather, reliance by a promisee is "reasonable" or "justified" only when the promisor manifests an intention to be legally bound. As we saw in section 4.2, to be enforceable, traditionally a promise must have been bargained for. Everyone is entitled to rely on a bargain. Promissory estoppel can be viewed as a way of expanding enforcement beyond bargaining by identifying additional factors that manifest an intention to be legally bound the way bargaining does. When such factors exist, reliance on a nonbargained-for or gratuitous promise will be *justified* and therefore protected.

Promissory estoppel originally developed in a number of specific situations in which one party has good reason to make a gratuitous promise he wants to be enforceable, and he manifests to the other person an intention to be legally bound: commitments made by one family member to another, by persons to charities, and by employers to employees. In a fourth situation, the silence of the promisor in the face of substantial reliance by the promisee also manifests an intention to be legally bound.

Family Promises

In *Ricketts v. Scothorn*,[32] to enable his granddaughter to quit her job if she chose, a grandfather delivered a promissory note reading: "May the first, 1891. I promise to pay to Katie Scothorn on demand, $2,000, to be at 6 per cent. per annum. J.C. Ricketts." When the grandfather died before making the payment, his estate contested the claim on the ground that the note lacked consideration, which it surely did. (Many famous promissory estoppel cases arose from alleged promises by a deceased person that are contested by executors of estates who have a fiduciary duty to the beneficiaries of a will to preserve the assets of the estate from claims against it.)

Although it was not bargained for, the formality of the promise in *Ricketts* clearly indicated the promisor's intention to be

---

32. 57 Neb. 51, 77 N.W. 365 (1898).

legally bound. An injurious reliance model of promissory estoppel would enforce the note only if the granddaughter relied to her detriment by quitting her job and would only award damages for any detrimental reliance actually incurred. A consent model of promissory estoppel recognizes the enforceability of the formal gratuitous promise that would give the granddaughter the security of the promise whether or not she chose to quit. It would protect her *right to rely* on the promise, which would be fully enforceable. As it happens, in the actual case, the promise was held to be fully enforceable without any specific showing of detrimental reliance.

Charitable Subscriptions

In *Allegheny College v. National Chatauqua Co. Bank*,[33] a promisor executed a formal *charitable subscription* to pay the college $5000 after her death: "In consideration of my interest in Christian Education, and in consideration of others subscribing, I hereby subscribe and will pay to the order of the Treasurer of Allegheny College, Meadville, Pennsylvania, the sum of Five Thousand Dollars; $5,000." Despite the fact that Judge Cardozo found the presence of consideration and discussed promissory estoppel only in dicta, contracts professors have doubted his consideration analysis and typically teach it as a promissory estoppel case.

According to Curtis Bridgeman,[34] however, Cardozo's consideration analysis was not only plausible, it was correct. Bridgeman notes that, "if a party does give a promise, at least in part, in order to induce a return promise or action, then the promise (and the return promise) is enforceable, even though the primary motivation for the promise may be altruistic." This, he contends, is what happened in *Allegheny College*. In essence, where other professors consider the

---

33. 246 N.Y. 369, 159 N.E. 173 (1927).

34. *See* Curtis Bridgeman, *Allegheny College Revisited: Cardozo, Consideration, and Formalism in Context*, 39 U.C. Davis L. Rev. 149, 152 (2005).

pledged donation to be a conditioned gift, Bridgeman finds the existence of a bargain between the promisor and the college.

Of course, whether or not it was bargained for, the formality of the written pledge, including its recitals of "consideration," manifests an intention to be legally bound, so such a promise would be readily enforceable using a consent model of promissory estoppel. As noted above, *Restatement 2nd*, section 90(2) provides for the full enforceability of such promises *in the **absence of reliance**.* "A charitable subscription or a marriage settlement is binding under subsection (1) without proof that the promise induced action or forbearance." Although Bridgeman also contends that "[c]ontra the Second Restatement, purely donative promises are not enforceable without reliance, even when made to charities," perhaps they should be. In any event, section 90(2) can neither be explained nor justified by an injurious reliance model of promissory estoppel.

Promises of a Pension

In *Feinberg v. Pfeiffer Co.*,[35] a company promised its bookkeeper a pension after retirement in gratitude for her long service to the company. Because the promise did not request or require her to retire at any given time and was made after her service had been rendered, it was not bargained for. The board of directors passed a formal resolution:

> [I]n view of the length of service which she has contributed provision should be made to afford her retirement privileges and benefits which should become *a firm obligation* of the corporation to be available to her whenever she should see fit to retire from active duty, however many years in the future her retirement may become effective (emphasis added).

---

35. 322 S.W.2d 163 (1959).

It then voted that

> Mrs. Feinberg would be given the privilege of retiring from active
> duty at any time she may elect to see fit so to do upon a retire-
> ment pay of $200.00 per month for life, with the distinct under-
> standing that the retirement plan is merely being adopted at this
> time in order to afford Mrs. Feinberg security for the future and
> in the hope that her active services will continue with the corpo-
> ration for many years to come.

Later, after Mrs. Feinberg retired and the president of the company died, his widow discontinued the pension payments. Although
the court upheld the enforceability of the promise on the ground
that Mrs. Feinberg had become too old and ill to obtain substitute
employment thereby satisfying the "injustice" requirement of section 90, this entailed that the promise would not otherwise be
enforceable if she were still fit to resume working. Moreover, her
illness did not result from her reliance on the promise. A consent
model of promissory estoppel would protect her *right to rely* on the
commitment on the ground that the formality by which it was
made by the board of directors clearly manifested an intention by
the employer to be legally bound.

Promises to Convey Land

In *Greiner v. Greiner*,[36] a mother promised to convey a parcel of land
to one of her sons who was deliberately left out of his father's will.
After the son moved his family onto the parcel and invested in
its improvement, the mother repudiated her promise in response
to protests and threats by her other son who had been favored in
the will. *Greiner* is both another example of a gratuitous family
promise and also illustrates how silence in the face of substantial
reliance can substitute for bargaining or the sort of formalities

---

36. 131 Kan. 760, 293 P. 759 (1930).

that were present in the previous cases. Why? Because the silence of the promisor in the face of so substantial a reliance indicates or manifests to the promisee an intention by the promisor to be legally bound. Under the circumstances, a promisor who did not intend to be bound would be expected to have spoken up and warn the other person that he was relying at his own risk.

We can identify the following elements in the facts of *Greiner* when a promisor's failure to warn a promisee may manifest an intention to be legally bound: (1) a promise is made, (although when made, it may be unclear whether or not there is an intention to be legally bound); (2) the promisee then relies in a way that would be unlikely if he did not view the promise as binding (that is, reliance must be substantial); (3) the promisor is aware of this reliance (otherwise her silence would not manifest any particular intention because she would not have known there was anything to warn about); (4) the promisee knows of the promisor's awareness (otherwise the promisee would not expect the promisor to warn if she did not mean to be bound); and (5) the promisor remains silent (that is, she did not warn promisee).

The analysis of these factual situations in which promissory estoppel first developed suggests that there are at least two ways that a promisor making a nonbargain promise might manifest an intention to be legally bound. The first is when the presence of a formality indicates an intention to be legally bound. An old-fashioned seal was one way of doing this, but nominal consideration of a dollar or a promissory note written by the promisor that says it is binding would perform the same function. Although the law does not recognize the legal effectiveness of these formalities, promissory estoppel has expanded the enforcement of promises to embrace these and other indicia of intention to be legally bound. The second circumstance manifesting an intention that a nonbargain be legally enforceable is where a promisor remains silent in the face of substantial reliance.

Notice that under these situations, (1) to gain enforcement you do not need reliance if the formality is serious enough; and (2) you do not need formality if the reliance is serious enough. Of course, the application of promissory estoppel has not been limited to these factual situations in which it originally arose. Although rarely asserted successfully, a promissory estoppel claim can potentially apply to any promise.

In a massive empirical study of promissory estoppel cases, Sidney DeLong attempted to identify the factors that lead courts to protect detrimental reliance on a nonbargain promise.[37] His data suggest the existence of two types of reliance that he called "performance reliance" and "enforcement reliance." *Performance reliance* refers to the trust that a promisee puts in the promisor to perform his or her promise. For many reasons, wholly apart from the prospect of legal enforceability, the promisee reasonably believes that the promise will be performed. *Enforcement reliance,* by contrast, refers to reliance on a promise that a promisee reasonably believes to be made with the intention of being legally enforceable.

DeLong suggests a norm may be developing that limits promissory estoppel recoveries to enforcement reliance. "Many of the opinions reported in 1995 and 1996," he concluded, "lend support to the thesis that, in order to prevail on a promissory estoppel claim, a commercial promisee must now demonstrate not only that her reliance was reasonable in light of the likelihood that the promisor would perform, but also that she had a reasonable belief that the promise was legally enforceable when made." If so, to succeed in making a promissory estoppel claim you need *detrimental reliance plus something*—and that "something" is a manifested intention to be legally bound. "[T]he 1995–96 case sample contains several decisions suggesting that a manifestation of consent to be legally bound may be becoming essential to liability under [s]ection 90." In other words, a manifested intention to be legally bound may be what

---

37. *See* Sidney W. DeLong, *The New Requirement of Enforcement Reliance in Commercial Promissory Estoppel: Section 90 as Catch-22,* Wis. L. Rev. 943 (1997).

separates the detrimental reliance that justifies legal relief from the detrimental reliance that does not.

4.4.4 Promissory Estoppel *as Tort*: Promissory Misrepresentation

One of the problems with the injurious reliance model of promissory estoppel was its doctrinal monism. That is, it sought a single explanation for a category of cases whose only common characteristic was the absence of a bargain. Instead, promissory estoppel can more accurately be viewed as serving two of the functions served by traditional contract and tort remedies available to parties in consensual relationships: the enforcement of some promises intended as legally binding and the imposition of liability to compensate for harm caused by some misrepresentations.[38]

Tort law provides a remedy for some negligent or reckless misrepresentations of fact. In almost all jurisdictions, liability will lie in tort if the speaker made a misrepresentation of fact negligently or with reckless disregard for the truth in order to induce desired reliance provided that the plaintiff reasonably relied in the desired manner. In almost all American jurisdictions, tort law also provides a remedy for some promissory misrepresentations made to induce reasonable reliance desired by the speaker.

For liability to lie in tort, however, a promissory misrepresentation must be a lie when made. If, at the time the promise is made to induce desired reliance, the promisor has no intention of performing, liability will be established. Liability will not lie in tort, however, if the promisor made the promise to induce desired reliance and

---

38. The analysis in this section is based on Randy E. Barnett & Mary E. Becker, *Beyond Reliance: Promissory Estoppel, Contract Formalities, and Misrepresentations*, 15 HOFSTRA L. REV. 443 (1987). *See also* IAN AYRES & GREGORY KLASS, INSINCERE PROMISES: THE LAW OF MISREPRESENTED INTENT (2005).

hoped that the promise would be fulfilled. Thus, tort affords no general remedy for breach of a promise made to induce desired reliance even when the promisor knows that the promisee will consider the promise more reliable than it actually is.

In one famous case, courts used "estoppel" to impose liability when traditional tort doctrines would also have afforded a remedy for the misrepresentation. In *Goodman v. Dicker*,[39] the local distributor of a franchisor was held liable for the plaintiffs' reliance on its assurance that the franchisor had decided to award plaintiffs their own franchise. The plaintiffs had written the franchisor, the Emerson Radio & Phonograph Corporation, inquiring about a franchise. Emerson referred the plaintiff's query to the defendant, who was its local distributors in Washington. The defendant then responded to the plaintiffs and, after some discussions, sent them a franchise application, which required the defendant's approval. The plaintiffs submitted the application to the defendant, who signed the application, noting its approval, and forwarded it to Emerson.

Later, the defendant told the plaintiffs that their application had been approved by Emerson. The defendant offered this assurance to induce the plaintiffs to hire salesmen and to begin selling Emerson radios prior to the receipt of a formal franchise certificate. Contrary to the defendant's assurance, however, Emerson had not decided to award the plaintiffs a franchise, and eventually rejected the application. The plaintiffs sued the defendant for losses sustained in reliance on their assurance that the franchise had been awarded.

Perhaps it is significant that the court in *Goodman* used the term "estoppel" and not "promissory estoppel" to find liability. The defendant's mistaken assurance could well be regarded as a false statement of fact; that Emerson had made an affirmative decision when it had not. Although its wording is not reproduced in the court's

---

39. 169 F.2d 684 (D.C. Cir. 1948) (applying D.C. law).

opinion, in the letter informing the plaintiffs that a franchise would not be awarded, the defendant virtually admitted the misrepresentation: "During the numerous times that we have spoken about your franchise, your application was being held up for approval at the factory. *I led you to believe that it had been accepted* although I was trying to convey to you the fact that the application had been sent in to the factory, and usually, they accept same without hesitation" (emphasis added).[40] Both then and now, tort law would afford a remedy for this misstatement of fact because the defendants made the misrepresentation negligently or recklessly; the defendant had no basis for thinking that Emerson had made any decision.

In another famous case involving a franchise, promissory estoppel was used to afford a remedy for misrepresentation beyond those available under either traditional contract or tort doctrines. In *Hoffman v. Red Owl Stores*,[41] the plaintiffs, Mr. and Mrs. Hoffman, owned and operated a bakery in Wautoma, Wisconsin, but were interested in a franchise for a Red Owl grocery store. The defendant's agents repeatedly assured Mr. Hoffman that Red Owl would give the plaintiffs a franchise in Chilton for a total cash outlay of $18,000. Although the terms of the franchise were never worked out, the agents encouraged Mr. Hoffman to rely on their assurances in many specific and potentially costly ways desired by Red Owl. Apparently, the agents had made the representation that $18,000 would be enough without consulting Red Owl's credit manager regarding Hoffman's financial standing and the financing of the store. When the credit manager was consulted, the cash needed by Hoffman increased dramatically, and the deal fell through.

Liability would lie in the consent model of promissory estoppel discussed in section 4.4.3 only for Hoffman's reliance on what he reasonably thought was an enforceable contract. Much of Hoffman's

---

40. Joint Appendix at 17-18, Goodman (No. 9786) (emphasis added).

41. 26 Wis. 2d 683, 133 N.W.2d 267 (1965).

reliance occurred, however, at a very early point in negotiations prior to the parties agreeing on such basic terms as the town the store would be in. When negotiations finally broke down, long after most of Hoffman's reliance, the parties had yet to agree on the specifications for the new store or many of the terms of the lease. It is unlikely, even at that late date, that Hoffman reasonably thought that he and Red Owl had a legally binding franchise agreement.

Furthermore, unlike *Goodman v. Dicker*, liability cannot be explained by the then-existing tort standard for promissory misrepresentation. At the time that they assured Hoffman that $18,000 cash would be enough, the agents for Red Owl sincerely hoped that it would be enough. As the court noted, a tort action for misrepresentation "cannot be predicated on unfulfilled promises unless the promisor possessed the present intent not to perform." The court, without much explanation, imposed liability on the basis of promissory estoppel.

If, however, tort liability is deemed appropriate when a promisor makes a promise in order to induce desired and detrimental reliance with the knowledge, or under circumstances such that the promisor should know, that the promisee will consider the promise more reliable than it actually is, then holding Red Owl liable is justified. Red Owl's agents apparently assured Hoffman that $18,000 cash would be enough without talking to the Red Owl employee who would ultimately decide how much cash would be required. The agents were, or should have been, more familiar than Hoffman with the allocation of authority within the Red Owl organization. They knew, or should have known, that the assurance would appear to Hoffman to be more reliable than it actually was.

Hoffman is the first of a small line of cases in which courts have used promissory estoppel to afford a remedy for negligent promissory misrepresentation—that is, to afford relief when a promise is made to induce a promisee to rely in a desired way in circumstances such that the promisor knows, or should know, that the promise will appear to be more reliable than it is. In each of these cases, the plaintiff relied detrimentally on the defendant's promises.

Consistent with this model of promissory estoppel—that it is based on misrepresentation of the reliability of the promise—courts have generally denied relief for losses sustained during ordinary preliminary negotiations no matter how reasonable the reliance.

The courts using promissory estoppel to impose liability for negligent promissory misrepresentation could reach the same result under tort, by changing the standard for promissory misrepresentation from lie-when-made to negligent or reckless. For more than a hundred years, however, common law courts have repeatedly held that tort liability for promissory misrepresentation requires that the promise be a lie when made. Given its vagueness, the doctrine of promissory estoppel offers an alternative basis for liability. But it would be less confusing simply to expand misrepresentation doctrine in tort to include negligent promissory representation just as the tort of factual misrepresentation has been expanded to include negligent representations as well as lies when made. By recognizing the tort of *negligent promissory misrepresentation*, court and parties would be able to focus on whether reliance on this type of misleading conduct had occurred.

In *Red Owl*, the court dismissed the defendant's claim that the promise was too indefinite to be enforceable under traditional doctrines governing mutual assent. The court's rejoinder is provocative and revealing: "We deem it would be a mistake to regard an action grounded on promissory estoppel as the equivalent of a breach-of-contract action." This statement seemed to validate the view of promissory estoppel as an alternative to breach of contract. But the court's rejection of the defendant's claim could equally be consistent with there being not one but two distinct doctrines of promissory estoppel—one lying in contract and the other lying in tort, with *Red Owl* being an example of the latter.

In all the classic promissory estoppel cases that can be considered contractual insofar as there was a manifestation of consent to be legally bound, the promise itself was fully enforced using the expectation measure of damages. In contrast, in both *Goodman* and *Red Owl*, the court refused to enforce the promise of the franchises either by specific performance or by awarding the expectation measure of damages. Instead, out-of-pocket reliance losses were awarded.

We saw in Chapter 2 that courts sometimes enforce contracts by awarding the reliance measure of damages. Nevertheless, this is another indication that there is a contract version of promissory estoppel in which the contractual *promise is being enforced* and a tort version of promissory estoppel in which reliance *injuries are being compensated.* For this reason, it is useful to study remedies before formation, if only to appreciate how the differing remedies in these cases suggest differing underlying conceptions of promissory estoppel.

One last point deserves emphasis. Claims based solely on promissory estoppel are rarely successful. The doctrine of promissory estoppel is emphasized in contracts courses largely because of its theoretical implications rather than its practical importance. For this reason, I have not dwelled on the nuances of how promissory estoppel is used in practice. Instead, my aim is to provide some balance to the picture of promissory estoppel as "anti-contract" so colorfully drawn in the 1970s, a picture that captured the imagination of generations of contracts professors and is still projected in some contracts classes.

4.4.5 An Alternative to Section 90

The bargain theory of consideration results in the underenforcement of nonbargain promises where the promisor manifested an intention to be legally bound in some manner other than by bargaining. In its current form, promissory estoppel can provide courts with a flexible means of protecting a right to rely on such commitments, as well as providing a remedy for some promissory misrepresentations. Still, perhaps it would be better to move beyond the vagueness of section 90 to a more specific doctrine that, when combined with an expanded tort of promissory misrepresentation, would better describe this residual category of contractual obligation. Maybe something like this:

§ 90. ENFORCEABILITY OF NONBARGAIN PROMISES

In the absence of consideration as defined in section 71, a promise is binding if

(1) the promise is accompanied by a formality that manifests an intention to be legally bound, such as:

    (a) a seal, or

    (b) the recital of a nominal consideration, or

    (c) an expression of intention to be legally bound, or

    (d) copies of a writing bearing the signatures of both parties; or

(2) with the knowledge of the promisor, the promise induces reliance by the promisee

    (a) that is so substantial it would be unlikely in the absence of a manifested intention by the promisor to be legally bound and,

    (b) the promisee expects the promise to be enforceable and is aware that the promisor has knowledge of the promisee's reliance, and

    (c) the promisor remains silent concerning the promisee's reliance.

FIVE

Performance and Breach

SUMMARY: Once the elements of a contract have been established, a remedy is not forthcoming unless the contract has been breached. This chapter discusses two vexatious doctrines: the duty of good faith performance and the doctrine of material breach. Special attention is paid to the theories of Steven Burton and Eric Anderson according to which the doctrines of good faith performance and material breach reflect the consent of the parties at the time of formation. Cases discussed include: *Kirke La Shelle Co. v. Paul Armstrong Co.*, *Goldberg 168-05 Corp. v. Levy*, *Stop & Shop v. Ganem*, *Mutual Life Insurance Co. of New York v. Tailored Woman Inc.*, *Hochster v. La Tour*, and *Kemp v. Reebok*.

To make out a cause of action for breach of contract, one must first establish the existence of a contract. Whether or not a contract exists can be broken down into two elements. In Chapter 3, we examined the element of mutual assent; in Chapter 4, we considered the element of enforceability. If a contract exists, one must then show that it was breached. In this chapter, we examine the *scope of performance* against which a breach is assessed—in particular, the duty to perform one's commitment in good faith. We then turn to the problem of determining *whether* that duty has been breached and what *type* of breach has occurred.

※ 5.1 The Duty of Good Faith Performance

5.1.1 The Concept of the Duty of Good Faith Performance

The notion that all contracts contain an implied covenant to perform in good faith is commonly traced to the New York Court of Appeals opinion in *Kirke La Shelle Co. v. Paul Armstrong Co.*[1] where the court stated that: "By entering into the contract and accepting and retaining the consideration therefor, the respondents assumed a fiduciary relationship which had its origin in the contract, and which imposed upon them the duty of utmost good faith." It identified "the principle that in every contract there is an implied covenant that neither party shall do anything which will have the effect of destroying or injuring the right of the other party to receive the fruits of the contract, which means that in every contract there exists an implied covenant of good faith and fair dealing." This principle has been generally adopted by the Uniform Commercial Code. Section 1-203 reads: "Every contract or duty within this Act imposes an obligation of good faith in its performance or enforcement."

What constitutes "good faith"? Does enforcing such a duty represent a restriction on or an extension of contractual freedom? Put another way, is this duty imposed upon all contracting parties despite their consent, or is it an inescapable aspect of their consent? Like the doctrine of promissory estoppel, as formulated by the *Restatement 2nd*, the duty of good faith performance is so vague that some theory is needed to get a handle on how it applies to particular cases.

---

1. 263 N.Y. 79, 188 N.E. 163 (1933).

5.1.2 The Summers-Burton Debate

When I teach the doctrine of good faith performance, I assign an exchange between two distinguished contracts scholars, Robert Summers and Steven Burton, that has come to be known as the "Summers-Burton" debate. This debate is interesting not only for the contrasting views of its protagonists concerning the doctrine of good faith but also because of the generational shift in modes of scholarship it represents.

In the 1950s and 1960s, contracts scholars, like so many others, rejected so-called "conceptualist" or "formalist" approaches that attempted to dictate the outcome of cases using general concepts and rules. Contract scholarship became dominated by supposedly "realist" inquiries into the complexities of actual commercial practice, seeking to identify the multiple factors or considerations that judges do or should take into account when deciding cases. Usually it was denied that these factors could or should be weighted or organized in some manner in advance of a legal dispute. Any effort to reduce the vast complexity of the real world of commercial practice to some verbal formula was dismissed as "reductionist" or "simplistic."

The Oxford English Dictionary defines "reductionist" as "one who attempts to analyse or account for a complex theory or phenomenon by reduction."[2] And it defines "simplistic" as "[o]f the nature of, or characterized by, (extreme) simplicity. Now usu[ally] with the connotation of excessive or misleading simplification."[3] An 1881 example of its usage nicely captures the realist spirit that eventually gripped the imagination of legal scholars: "The facts of nature and of life are more apt to be complex than simple. Simplistic theories are generally one-sided and partial."

---

2. 13 OXFORD ENGLISH DICTIONARY 437 (2d ed. 1989).

3. *Id.* at 501.

Summers is of the generation of legal academics that was taught by the vanguard of realist professors—a generation that took their teacher's gestalt and terminology to heart. For example, in his seminal 1968 article, *"Good Faith" in General Contract Law and the Sales Provisions of the Uniform Commercial Code*,[4] Summers proposed a series of six categories of bad faith performance: (1) evasion of the spirit of the deal, (2) lack of diligence and slacking off, (3) willfully rendering only "substantial performance," (4) abuse of a power to specify contract terms, (5) abuse of a power to determine compliance, (6) interfering with or failing to cooperate in the other party's performance.

In terms that embodied the spirit of the realist generation and their proteges, Summers explicitly denied that any more general conception of good faith was helpful or even possible because "any but the most vacuous general definition of good faith will . . . fail to cover all the many and varied specific meanings that it is possible to assign to the phrase in light of the many and varied forms of bad faith recognized in the cases." For this reason, he contended, "general definitions of good faith either spiral into the Charybdis of vacuous generality or collide with the Scylla of restrictive specificity." A judge, he advised, "should not waste effort formulating his own reductionist definitions. Instead, he should characterize with care particular forms of bad faith he chooses to rule out."

In the 1970s and 1980s, this attitude toward scholarship began to change. Legal scholarship shifted away from realist modes in favor of what is now called "legal theory." Contracts scholarship, like other fields, came to be dominated by scholars who risked the epithets of "reductionist" and "simplistic" in search of unifying theories of legal doctrine. One example of this phenomenon, discussed in Chapter 4, was the search for a theory of promissory estoppel specifying what previous scholars had insisted had to be an

---

4. Robert Summers, *"Good Faith" in General Contract Law and the Sales Provisions of the Uniform Commercial Code*, 54 VA. L. REV. 195, 232–43 (1968).

open-ended doctrine. As a result, realist-style lists of multiple factors that judges, in their discretion, needed somehow to take "into account," began to give way to more systematic theories and approaches.

One of these was a comprehensive theory of good faith performance developed by Steven Burton, which he presented in his 1980 article, *Breach of Contract and the Common Law Duty to Perform in Good Faith*.[5] Burton contended that without "an operational standard that distinguishes good faith performance from bad faith performance," the general requirement of good faith as contained in the Uniform Commercial Code "appears as a license for the exercise of judicial or juror intuition, and presumably results in unpredictable and inconsistent applications."

Burton specifically took issue with Summers' "list of factors" approach: "No effort is made to develop a unifying theory that explains what these categories have in common. Indeed, the assertion is made that one cannot or should not do so." In contrast, Burton argued that "[r]epeated common law adjudication . . . has enriched the concept of good faith performance so that an operational standard now can be articulated and evaluated." Burton's unifying theory was based on a survey of more than 400 cases in which courts explicitly referred to good faith performance.

Summers did not remain silent in the fact of this challenge, and his response was as methodological as it was substantive: "My view is that all such efforts to define good faith . . . are misguided." Summers contended that such "formulations provide little, if any, genuine *definitional* guidance. Moreover, some of them may restrictively distort the scope of the general requirement of good faith." Lastly, "the very idea of good faith, if I am right, is simply not the kind of idea that is susceptible of such a definitional approach."[6]

---

5. Steven J. Burton, *Breach of Contract and the Common Law Duty to Perform in Good Faith*, 94 HARV. L. REV. 369 (1980).

6. Robert Summers, *The General Duty of Good Faith—Its Recognition and Conceptualization*, 67 CORNELL L. REV. 810, 829–30 (1982) (emphasis in original).

Burton in turn responded with a thoughtful reply in which he highlighted the generational difference in their methodologies.[7] "We want our language to call our attention to the facts that matter—those that legitimately establish similarities with or significant differences from the precedents.... We want to know which facts shall count for more than their truth because they are legally significant." Burton denied that his approach was "definitional." Instead, he was trying to formulate a "general description or model—a simplified representation of a complex reality." In contrast with Summers' lists of factors, "the general description technique encourages us to focus on complex webs of relationships among the facts." Or, in the words of P. J. O'Rourke: "Complexities are fun to talk about, but, when it comes to action, simplicities are often more effective."[8] The world is simply too complex for humans to gasp in its entirety. To *understand* the world necessarily requires simplifications to bring it within the scope of human comprehension.

5.1.3 Recapturing Forgone Opportunities

So what is Burton's simplifying theory? According to him, the problem of good faith performance arises (1) when a contract gives one party a degree of discretion in performing, and (2) this discretion is then used by that party to recapture an opportunity foregone at contract formation. "Good faith limits the exercise of the discretion in performance conferred on one party by the contract.... Bad faith performance occurs precisely when discretion is used to recapture opportunities forgone upon contracting—when the discretion-exercising party refuses to pay the expected cost of performance."[9]

---

7. Steven J. Burton, *More on Good Faith Performance of a Contract: A Reply to Professor Summers*, 69 IOWA L. REV. 497, 509 (1984).

8. P. J. O'ROURKE, EAT THE RICH: A TREATISE ON ECONOMICS 209 (1998).

9. Burton, *supra* note 5, at 372–73.

Or conversely, "[g]ood faith performance . . . occurs when a party's discretion is exercised for any purpose within the reasonable contemplation of the parties at the time of formation—to capture opportunities that were preserved upon entering the contract, interpreted objectively." The good faith performance doctrine therefore "directs attention to the opportunities forgone by a discretion-exercising party at formation, and to that party's reasons for exercising discretion during performance."

To understand Burton's theory, we must begin with the notion of *contractual discretion.* Contractual discretion can arise in two ways: "The parties may find it to their mutual advantage at formation to defer decision on a particular term and to confer decision-making authority as to that term on one of them." For example, they may adopt output or requirements contracts, floating-price contracts, conditions of satisfaction and other conditions within the control of one party. "Discretion also may arise, with similar effect, from a lack of clarity or from an omission in the express contract." Good faith performance is required in every contract because the problems of omission and lack of clarity can arise in every contract.

Burton's theory rests on the idea that, when one enters into a contract, one forgoes the opportunity to enter into the next best alternative, which in section 2.3.3 we called the "opportunity cost" of action. "The economic cost of any action—including the act of contracting, the act of performing, and the act of breaching a contract—should be viewed descriptively as the value of the next best opportunity necessarily forgone by taking that action." Every breach of contract can be viewed as an attempt by one party to recapture opportunities forgone upon contracting. When a party uses the discretion afforded by the contract to reclaim a lost opportunity, courts invoke the duty good faith performance to describe why this breaches the contract.

According to Burton's theory, "a party fails to perform in good faith when it uses such discretion [it is given under the contract] to recapture forgone opportunities." So to determine whether a party has acted in bad faith, one must engage in a two-step analysis.

First, identify an opportunity *objectively* foregone by the promisor at the time of formation; second determine whether the promisor used the discretion afforded to him by the contract with the *subjective* intention of recapturing this forgone opportunity. The theory is best understood by considering some examples.

In *Goldberg 168-05 Corp. v. Levy*,[10] the plaintiff agreed to rent a store to the defendant, Levy. Levy was to pay a minimum annual rent or 10 percent "of the gross receipts of the business conducted by the tenant on the leased premises" whichever was higher. The lease also provided that "in the event that the total gross sales of the Tenant for any one calendar year does not equal $101,000 . . . then the Tenant shall have the right to cancel said lease." Levy took possession of the premises and conducted a retail men's clothing business.

When Levy closed his store and terminated the lease because sales were below the specified amount, the plaintiff sued alleging that Levy had diverted sales from the leased premises to another store he operated. The court held that Levy "could not avoid liability under the lease . . . by a diversion of business to another store which he operated in the same vicinity when such diversion is effected *for the sole purpose* of bringing the gross receipts below the specified figure and thereby laying the basis for a cancellation of the lease" (emphasis added). Had he done so, Levy would have been in breach of his duty of good faith performance.

In other words, the purpose for which the diversion was made is crucial to the issue of good faith, not merely the action itself. Although Levy's employees were free under the contract to refer business to another store—imagine that they did not stock an item that was carried in their other shop—they could not make such referrals with the subjective intention of lowering sales to reduce the amount of rent owed to the plaintiff or to allow Levy to terminate the lease. By using its discretion in this way, the tenant was

---

10. 170 Misc. 292, 9 N.Y.S.2d 304 (1938).

seeking to recapture an opportunity it gave up when it entered into the lease, and was therefore in breach of its contract.

Next, consider the facts of *Mutual Life Insurance Co. of New York v. Tailored Woman Inc.*[11] In 1939, the plaintiff and defendant entered into a ten-year lease of the lower three floors of a building on Fifth Avenue in New York City. This lease included two covenants. First, the tenant was to pay the landlord 4 percent on all sales made "on, in, and from the demised premises." Second, the tenant promised that the new store would be conducted and maintained in a manner substantially similar to the tenant's present store from which it was moving.

In 1945, the defendant bought out a custom-made dress business on part of the fifth floor and entered into separate lease with the plaintiff at a flat no-percentage rent. When the fifth-floor custom-made dress department was unsuccessful, the tenant altered the building so that two elevators, which had served the first three floors from inside the main store, could also carry passengers to the fifth floor. It then moved its fur department from the lower floors, which were governed by the percentage of sales provision, to the fifth floor, which was governed by the flat rate rent.

The court refused to find the tenant to be in breach on the ground that the lease gave the tenant discretion to move departments as it saw fit. The court did not consider whether the move of the fur department was made with the intent of avoiding the 4 percent of gross sales payment to the landlord. In contrast, the dissent contended that the tenant made the move to avoid the restrictions of the percentage lease. According to Burton's theory, the court was wrong to limit its inquiry to whether the lease gave the tenant discretion to relocate its departments; it should also have inquired into whether the motive for moving the fur department was to avoid paying the percentage of fur sales to the landlord.

---

11. 309 N.Y. 248, 128 N.E.2d 401 (1955).

Finally, in *Stop & Shop v. Ganem*,[12] a grocery chain leased two buildings, one in Haverhill and one in Lawrence, under a percentage lease. The lease for the Haverhill store did not specify the purpose for which the building would be used, but various requirements appeared to contemplate its use as a grocery store. Stop & Shop operated two other stores in Haverhill, one within about a mile and the other within one-half mile from the building leased from defendant. Stop & Shop sought a declaratory judgment allowing it to cease operating the business at the leased premises and continue to pay the minimum rent due thereon without violating their lease.

After noting that the contract did not restrict Stop & Shop's discretion to open other stores as it deemed fit, the court then addressed Stop & Shop's motive for closing its Haverhill store: "The lessors do not . . . allege that the lessee acted for other than sound business reasons or for the purpose of depreciating the worth of the demised premises rather than for the affirmative advantage of doing business elsewhere."

In all three cases the contract gave the tenant substantial discretion to manage its business on the leased property, including the discretion to do what it did. In *Tailored Woman*, that is where the majority ended its analysis. In *Stop and* Show, however, the court also considered whether the lessee used its discretion for any other reason than its "sound business judgment," and concluded it had not done so. In *Goldberg*, the court found that the lessee had diverted "business to another store which he operated in the same vicinity when such diversion is effected for the sole purpose of bringing the gross receipts below the specified figure and thereby laying the basis for cancellation of the lease." It therefore concluded that "[s]uch conduct would be in direct violation of the covenant of good faith and fair dealing which exists in every contract."

The key factor that distinguishes these cases, then, is the motive for using the discretion given to a party by a contract. Were the

---

12. 347 Mass. 697, 200 N.E.2d 248 (1964).

actions taken for the purpose of running a successful business in a competitive market, or were they taken for the purpose of defeating the percentage clause of the lease? So it is not so much *what* was being done, as *why* it was being done. According to Burton, "where a lessee diverted customers to other premises for the sole purpose of bringing down gross receipts at the leased premises, . . . the lessee's reason for acting lay outside the bounds of the contract." Put another way, "it may be inferred reasonably that neither party contemplated at formation that the lessee would interfere with the flow of customers in order to reduce its own sales at the leased premises."

The doctrine of good faith performance appears to be a restriction on the party's contractual freedom because it operates to restrict the discretion apparently given by the silence in a contract. But that is only true if the parties truly retained the discretion to exercise their discretion in bad faith. Burton's inquiry into the subjective intent to recapture opportunities that were objectively forgone is merely an effort to identify what all contractual parties reasonably assume about the discretion they are afforded by their contracts. Viewed in light of Burton's approach, the duty of good faith performance is not a restriction on the freedom of the parties to contract as they see fit. To the contrary, it seeks an accurate account of the actual agreement to which the parties consented.

✺ 5.2 Anticipatory Repudiation and Material Breach

The duty of good faith performance is an effort to more closely define the scope of the performance due under the contract when a contract allocates discretion. We now consider two doctrines that are used to determine whether a breach of the duty of performance has taken place. The doctrine with which we will be most concerned is that of "material breach." Like promissory estoppel and the duty of good faith performance, material breach is extremely fuzzy.

Most law students, and probably most practicing lawyers, think a material breach is a "big" or major breach, which tells us very little about when a breach should be considered material. Neither does the *Restatement 2nd*, section 241, which merely offers a list of "significant" circumstances factors that must somehow be taken into account:

1. The extent to which the injured party will be deprived of the benefit which he reasonably expected.
2. The extent to which the injured party can be adequately compensated for the part of that benefit of which he will be deprived.
3. The extent to which the party failing to perform or to offer to perform will suffer forfeiture.
4. The likelihood that the party failing to perform or to offer to perform will cure his failure, taking account of all the circumstances including any reasonable assurances.
5. The extent to which the behavior of the party failing to perform or to offer to perform comports with standards of good faith and fair dealing.

In his article, *A New Look at Material Breach in the Law of Contracts*,[13] Eric Anderson—a long-time colleague of Steven Burton—developed a principled approach to distinguishing material from immaterial breaches. Like Burton's theory, it provides more guidance than does the multifactor approach of the *Restatement* by identifying the core question for which material breach provides the answer: When may a promissee unilaterally terminate a contract and seek substitute performance elsewhere on account of the other party's breach of contract? If a breach is deemed to be material, the contract can be terminated; but if a

---

13. Eric Anderson, A *New Look at Material Breach in the Law of Contracts*, 21 U. C. DAVIS L. REV. 1073 (1988).

breach is not material, then the victim of the breach is limited to seeking damages or specific performance for nonperformance. This leads naturally to the question, why do some breaches justify terminating a contract, whereas other breaches do not?

To answer this question, Anderson first examined the different but related doctrine of *anticipatory repudiation.* Consider the case of *Albert Hochster v. Edgar De La Tour.*[14] There, the defendant engaged to employ the plaintiff, beginning on a future date, to travel with him into a foreign country as a "courier"—a servant employed by a traveler having the duty of making all the arrangements connected with the journey. The plaintiff was to receive a monthly salary during the continuance of such service. Before the day that the plaintiff's service was to begin, the defendant renounced the agreement and refused to perform it. The plaintiff then contractually committed himself to another courier job. Although the second job was to begin after the date the first trip was scheduled to start, because of his new contract, the plaintiff was no longer free to perform as a courier under the original contract with the defendant.

When the plaintiff sued for breach of contract, the defendant contended "that if the plaintiff was not contented to dissolve the contract, and to abandon all remedy upon it, he was bound to remain ready and willing to perform it till the day when the actual employment as courier in the service of the defendant was to begin" and "that there could be no breach of the agreement, before that day, to give a right of action." So the question raised by this case is: When one party indicates to the other that she does not intend to perform, may the other party suspend his performance under the contract without himself being held in breach, and seek a substitute performance elsewhere? Must he wait until the time of performance before suing for breach? May the repudiating party later retract her repudiation and insist on the performance of the other party?

---

14. 2 E. & B. 678, 118 Eng. Rep. 922 (1853).

Hochster is considered the first case to recognize the doctrine of anticipatory repudiation. "The man who wrongfully renounces a contract into which he has deliberately entered cannot justly complain if he is immediately sued for a compensation in damages by the man whom he has injured," explained the court. From this it held that the injured party has "an option . . . either to sue immediately, or to wait till the time when the act was to be done, still holding it as prospectively binding for the exercise of this option, which may be advantageous to the innocent party, and cannot be prejudicial to the wrongdoer." In defense of this rule, the court observed that, if it were otherwise, the plaintiff "must enter into no employment which will interfere with his promise 'to start with the defendant on such travels on the day and year,' and that he must then be properly equipped in all aspects as a courier for a three months' tour on the continent of Europe." To this, the court responded that it is both "more rational" and "more for the benefit of both parties, that, after the renunciation of the agreement by the defendant, the plaintiff should be at liberty to consider himself absolved from any future performance of it, retaining his right to sue for any damage he has suffered from the breach of it." Why? Because "instead of remaining idle and laying out money in preparations which must be useless, he is at liberty to seek service under another employer, which would go in mitigation of the damages to which he would otherwise be entitled for a breach of the contract." Nor does it seem fair "that the defendant, after renouncing the contract, and absolutely declaring that he will never act under it, should be permitted to object that faith is given to his assertion, and that an opportunity is not left to him of changing his mind."

From the doctrine of anticipatory repudiation, Eric Anderson identified an underlying principle at work. Every contract, he suggested, creates two distinct "interests": (1) the interest in *present* performance and (2) the interest in *future* performance. The interest in present performance is the interest of a party "in receiving the promised performance when it comes due from the other party. When that interest is impaired because performance is wrongfully delayed, withheld, or imperfectly rendered, the victim is injured in the sense that what was received (if anything) is less valuable than what was promised."

Consider a builder who breaches his contract to build a commercial building by completing it late or imperfectly. The purchaser may lose rent from tenants, be liable to tenants for delays, or be required to spend money repairing defects. "The interest in receiving proper performance *when due* is the interest in present performance. This interest comes into existence *at the time performance is due*. It is impaired by nonfeasance or malfeasance of the performance promised by the other side" (emphases added). Impairments of the interest in present performance are routinely remedied through compensatory damages. "The victim of the breach is entitled to a judgment sufficient to pay for the loss of value that breach causes."

To this, Anderson contrasted the promisee's interest in future performance. At the moment a contract is formed, both parties have an interest "in the likelihood that the contract will be performed as agreed. The most important element of that interest is the *probability* that the other party will perform as and when agreed" (emphasis added). Wholly apart from any interest in the value of the promised performance, "[t]o the extent that *probability of performance* exists, a sense of security about the future arises upon which plans may be based and commitments made. That security is one of the primary benefits to individuals participating in contractual relationships" (emphasis added).

This "likelihood of future performance" is usually "demonstrably important to the individual entering a particular agreement." For example, "the owner who contracts for the construction of a building needs the confidence that the building will be built by the time agreed. On the basis of that confidence, the owner is willing to make commitments to the building's future tenants that it would be unwilling to make without that confidence." And the likelihood of future performance can be important for other reasons besides the probability that the other side will perform properly and on time.

"A party may have an important interest in the opportunity to per-form its own future duties." For example, a "construction company under contract to erect a building, for example, may act in impor-tant ways, such as marshaling its resources in a particular manner, because of its confidence that it will be participating in the project in the future. Moreover, public awareness that the company will engage in that performance may enhance the company's reputa-tion and prospects for other employment."

As the court in *Hochster* perceived, an impairment of a party's interest in future performance is not necessarily remedied by money damages for failure to perform collected after the promised date of performance. Rather, it may need to be remedied by cancellation of the agreement combined with damages arising in connection with cancellation. The damage caused by anticipatory repudiation is a pure example of an impairment of the interest in future performance because repudiation before the time for perfor-mance arrives *only* undermines the security that the other party has in receiving future performance.

The power to unilaterally cancel or discharge (not rescind) the contract and either stop one's own performance, seek alternative performance, or both, is the way one protects one's interest in future performance. As Anderson observed, "an anticipatory repudiation always impairs only the interest in future performance and not the interest in present performance. By definition, the person commit-ting an anticipatory breach has not failed to perform a duty when due, but has manifested either an unwillingness or an inability to perform future duties."

With this understanding of how anticipatory repudiation dam-ages the interest in future performance, we are in a position to understand the doctrine of material breach. Consider the following example. A bulldozer operated by one party to a contract negli-gently damages a structure on the other party's land during the course of performance. The interest in present performance is reflected in the damage done to the building. This damage would be rectified by compensatory damages. The interest in future performance is reflected in the worry that the future operations of the bulldozer or other heavy equipment may do additional injury. The impairment of this interest might be alleviated by cancelling the contract and finding a substitute, while assessing cancellation damages against the first party for the costs of cover. A "material" breach is one that impairs the other party's interest in future performance such that it may best be rectified by cancelling the contract; a breach that only impairs the other party's interest in present performance does not justify cancellation and is not material.

Why would not every breach undermine a party's confidence in receiving future performance and, therefore, be deemed material? If the breaching party shows a willingness and ability to address a prior breach and avoid such breaches in the future, then the confidence in receiving future performance may be restored. Suppose that, after the bulldozer incident, the construction company replaces the negligent driver with a more skillful and careful one. If this is the only thing that has gone wrong, the confidence of the other party in receiving future performance should be bolstered, and he would no longer be justified in cancelling the contract and seeking substitute performance elsewhere. If he nevertheless tries to cancel, he may well be acting in bad faith in Steven Burton's sense of subjectively attempting to reclaim an opportunity that was objectively forgone—in this case the opportunity to have another construction company build the building. This also reveals a relationship between the doctrines of good faith and that of material breach.

To see the relationship between good faith and material breach, as well as how the doctrine of material breach works in practice, consider the case of former-NBA basketball player Sean Kemp. Kemp had signed an endorsement contract with Reebok in which he promised to wear Reebok shoes exclusively; that he would not "participate in any other activity for the purpose . . . of promoting any service or product which, in the Company's reasonable opinion, is competitive with or antithetical to Company's products"; and that "at no time during and after the Term of the Agreement [would] he disparage his association with the Company, the products of

Company, its advertising agencies or others connected with Company."[15]

When Kemp was playing for the Cleveland Cavaliers, the *Akron Beacon Journal* published an article entitled, "Footnoting Prose of Pros' Footwear: Kemp and His Teammates Stroll down Memory Lane, Recalling Their Favorite Kinds of Shoes Growing Up." Near the beginning of the story was the following:

> "My all time favorite pair I would probably have to say was Air Force II by Nike," said Kemp, not caring the least that he has an endorsement deal with Reebok. "They were worn by Durell Griffith and Moses Malone. Oh, yeah, you had to have them. When I got a pair of Air Force IIs, I was the coolest kid in school. I'd wear them around just to let everybody know I'm a basketball player."

The story then included quotes from other players and concluded with this:

> Kemp says today's shoes aren't as good as the old ones, because they're made to be lighter. Kemp calls them "throwaways," because they rip so easily. "I might go back next year to (Reebok) Kamakazes," Kemp said. "They've got a real crazy design. That's the shoe I started out wearing my third year and wore when I made my first All-Star Game (in his fourth season of 1992–93)." Kemp has plenty of Kamakazes in his basement. Alas, he has no Air Force IIs.

Later that same month Reebok terminated his endorsement agreement claiming that, by making these statements, Kemp had breached the contract provisions quoted above. In its termination

---

15. The facts of this case appear as a problem in RANDY E. BARNETT, CONTRACTS: CASES AND DOCTRINE 917–18 (4th ed. 2008).

letter, Reebok's attorney stated, "[g]iven that you have been contractually obligated since 1992 to wear Reebok footwear exclusively during all athletic workouts, practices, tournaments, games, exhibitions and to otherwise fulfill your obligations under the Agreement, it is patently clear your comments could only have been directed at Reebok footwear." Under the terms of the agreement, this meant Reebok refused to pay approximately $4.1 million dollars still due for the final two and a half years of the contract.

Did Kemp materially breach his agreement with Reebok? Was Reebok justified in terminating its agreement with Kemp, or, by attempting to do so, has Reebok breached the agreement itself? Would it affect your answer (and if so why) to know that Kemp's career was in significant decline by 2000? Would it affect your answer (and if so why) to know that Reebok's basketball shoes line was selling very poorly, and it reduced its endorsement contracts from around 50 to just a few? Would proof of these facts be admissible in a suit by Kemp against Reebok for breach of contract?[16]

Anderson's approach to material breach provides answers to these questions by shifting our focus away from whether Kemp's statements to the press breached his agreement at all—which they might not have—to the issue of whether these statements (assuming they constituted a breach) undermined Reebok's confidence that Kemp would perform his obligations in the future. Once he was warned by Reebok of this alleged "breach," would Kemp be likely to make such statements in the future?

In addition, Anderson's analysis of Reebok's interest in future performance focuses our attention on a possible ulterior motivation for Reebok to allege a material breach as an excuse to cancel the contract. By 2000, Kemp's career was in significant decline and

16. Disclosure: I was retained by Sean Kemp as an expert witness, and was prepared to testify that his breach was not material for the reasons elaborated here. Because the judge did not allow expert testimony on this issue, I was not called as a witness, but I was compensated for researching and writing a letter expressing my opinion.

Reebok was doing very poorly in the sales of basketball shoes. As a result, it cut its NBA endorsement contracts from around fifty, eventually to just two: Allen Iverson and Steve Francis. These facts indicate that Reebok did not terminate its contract because of concern about receiving Kemp's future performance but instead because his endorsement was no longer worth the $4.1 million balance still due under the contract. In other words, they were trying to recapture an opportunity forgone at the time they entered into a long-term agreement with Kemp and were thereby acting in bad faith in cancelling the contract.

By highlighting the difference between good faith efforts to unilaterally terminate contracts because of concern for future performance and bad faith efforts to get out of deals now regretted, this example shows how the material breach doctrine is closely related to the concept of good faith. Would proof of these facts be admissible in a suit by Kemp against Reebok for breach of contract? Based on the foregoing analysis, the answer is yes. Unfortunately, in the actual trial of this lawsuit the trial judge excluded this evidence, likely because the connection between the concept of material breach and Reebok's motivation for terminating the contract was never argued to the court. The case was pled on the assumption that material breach equaled big breach, and that this breach was small. On this theory, however, Reebok's motives were irrelevant.

Due to the exclusion of this proof, along with Kemp's poor performance as a witness, the parties agreed to settle in a manner highly favorable to Reebok while the jury was still deliberating. Indeed, Sean Kemp ended up compensating Reebok for its litigation expenses. This case provides an excellent example of how the vagueness of the doctrine, combined with the litigating attorneys' failure to appreciate and explain to the court this theory of material breach, may well have led to a miscarriage of justice.

SIX

Defenses to Contractual Obligation

SUMMARY: This chapter organizes the most common defenses to the enforcement of an otherwise valid contract into three categories: (1) lack of contractual capacity (incompetence, intoxication, and infancy); (2) obtaining assent by improper means (misrepresentation, duress, undue influence, and unconscionability); and (3) the failure of a basic assumption (mistake of present existing fact, commercial impracticability, and frustration of purposes). When each of the circumstances described by these various defenses is shown to exist, contractual consent loses its normal moral and practical significance, and the parties' manifestation of assent will not be enforced. Cases discussed include: *Ortelere v. Teachers' Retirement Board of New York, Vokes v. Arthur Murray, Odorizzi v. Bloomfield School District, Williams v. Walker-Thomas Furniture, Sherwood v. Walker, Wood v. Boynton,* and *Laidlaw v. Organ.*

≋ 6.1 Rebutting the Prima Facie Case of Contract

The previous chapters describe the two elements that must be satisfied for a contract to exist—mutual assent (Chapter 3) and enforceability (Chapter 4)—the scope of the duty of performance and what constitutes a breach (Chapter 5), and the possible remedies for breaches of contract (Chapter 2). These chapters describe what might be called the "prima facie" case of breach of contract. *Prima facie* is Latin for "on its first appearance," or "by first instance." In law, prima facie denotes evidence that, *unless rebutted,* would be sufficient to prove a particular proposition or fact. Therefore a prima facie determination that a contract exists and that a breach of contract has occurred does not exhaust the inquiry that is required to determine the appropriateness of granting relief, if the other party seeks to rebut the prima facie case.

There are long accepted legal defenses based on factual circumstances that rebut the enforceability of an otherwise valid contract. These defenses are the topic of this chapter. Like the rest of this book, the aim here is not to present the details of these defenses but to explain how they fit within the broader structure of contract law. In particular, we will consider how these defenses relate to the concern of contract law for consent and reliance. They do not, I will suggest, represent a limitation on the freedom of contract discussed at length in Chapter 4, but instead more closely align the enforcement of contracts with the consent of the parties than would the prima facie case of contract standing alone.

The term "defense" can be used in a variety of ways. For example, a person could deny ever having signed the contract and that the signature on the document was a forgery. This type of factual defense is better termed a *denial.* The type of legal defenses discussed in this chapter are what the common law referred to as "pleas in avoidance"—the assertion of additional facts and circumstances that rebut or avoid the normal significance of the prima facie case of contractual obligation, breach, and damages.

In other words, when a party alleges the prima facie case of breach of contract, he or she is entitled to prevail *if* the claims are believed and *if* the other party offers no response to these claims beyond a denial. Even if the facts alleged are true and sufficient to establish the prima facie case of breach of contract, however, the other party might allege *additional* facts and circumstances that deprive the prima facie case of contract (even if proved) of its normal moral significance, thereby avoiding the obligation that is normally incurred when one breaches a contract. That is, even though the facts that comprise the *prima facie* case of contract are true, if the facts comprising a defense are also true, the person seeking contractual enforcement is not ordinarily entitled to a remedy. A contract defense may also be asserted affirmatively by the promisor to avoid the enforcement of a contract before any breach occurs by bringing an action for rescission.

When studying these defenses, there is something that should be kept in mind. If a legal defense is not confined to comparatively unusual or exceptional circumstances, it will effectively negate the cause of action against which it defends. For example, if the facts needed to establish a contract defense were pervasive or common, then few if any causes of action for breach of contract would prevail and whatever purpose is served by such causes of action would be defeated. Put another way, if maintaining a legal cause of action for breach of contract is desirable, then defenses to that cause of action cannot be permitted to completely undermine it. This imperative sometimes leads to what appear to be arbitrary limits on the reach of a contract defense whose underlying logic can be extended considerably farther than the doctrine allows.

Why has contract law adopted the various presumptions and burdens of proof it has? Let me offer a few suggestions. First, these burdens can reflect a judgment about what is likely and what is exceptional. Each step of the analysis represents an approximation—at each step over an increasingly smaller domain—of what we think are probably the facts of the case. So because legally binding contracts are exceptional in most relationships, we adopt an initial presumption of no contract unless proof is presented by one who alleges the existence of a contract. This is the prima facie case of contract. And, because people who contract ordinarily honor their commitments, the default presumption is to make plaintiffs prove the existence of a breach. Similarly, because incompetence, using improper means to obtain consent, or a failure of basic assumptions are comparatively exceptional occurrences, we therefore place the burden on those alleging these unusual circumstances to establish their existence.

The fact that we presume the most likely state of facts and place the burden on the other party to prove the contrary does not mean that we deny that the exceptional state of affairs may exist in a particular case. Rather, by making our presumptions rebuttable by recognized defenses and responses to defenses, we acknowledge that these exceptions do in fact sometimes happen. But we pick our initial presumptions to reflect what we think is most likely to be the case when we are completely ignorant of what is in fact the case.

Another reason for setting presumptions as we do is what Dale Nance has called the "presumption of civility."[1] To allege a breach of contract is to accuse another member of the community of violating the moral duties each member owes to all the others. A false accusation of such a breach does an injury to the accused that is itself a serious injustice. For this reason, says Nance, "the burden should be placed on the party 'affirmatively' asserting a breach of duty ('You breached') rather than the negative of such a proposition ('I did not breach')." The principle of civility is premised on giving fellow members of the community the moral benefit of the doubt. "Civility, in the law and elsewhere, is one manifestation of our commitment to a sense of community and the respect for its members that such a commitment entails."

In this chapter, we will consider three categories of contract defenses. Each category represents a different type of attack on the moral significance of the prima facie case of breach of contract. First are defenses describing circumstances in which the promisor's capacity to assent to a contract is somehow deficient, for example, the defenses of incompetence and infancy (section 6.2). Second are defenses alleging that one person obtained the contractual consent of the other by improper means, for example, the defenses of fraud, duress, undue influence, and unconscionability (section 6.3). Third are defenses alleging that there has been a

---

1. *See* Dale A. Nance, *Civility and the Burden of Proof,* 17 HARV. J.L. & PUB. POL'Y 647 (1994).

failure of a basic assumption underlying the contract—that is, one or both parties assumed a certain state of affairs to be true that, for some reason, turned out to be false—for example, the defenses of mistake, impracticability, and frustration (section 6.4). My objective will be to explain why establishing each of these defenses deprives the prima facie case of contract of its normal moral significance.

✎ 6.2 Lack of Contractual Capacity

When people manifest their assent we normally presume that this manifestation represents their actual subjective assent. We also ordinarily presume that persons are capable of making value-enhancing decisions about their lives. As was noted in section 4.1, enforcing consensual bargains tends to enhance the welfare of those who make them because each party values what is received from the other party more than what is given up. By making both parties to a bargain better off, the enforcement of contracts also benefits society as a whole. In addition, enforcing bargains enables each party to rely in confidence on the commitment of another in making his or her plans and investments. On rare occasions this presumption in favor of enforcing consensual bargains is incorrect. The defenses of infancy and incompetence describe circumstances that, if shown to exist, rebut the normal presumption that persons are capable of making decisions on their own behalf. When this occurs, an objective manifestation of assent no longer justifies legal enforcement.

6.2.1 Deficiencies in Adult Contractual Capacity

As was discussed in Chapter 4, all adults are presumed to be competent to make value-enhancing choices. Sometimes, this assumption is false. When a particular adult is shown to be incapable of making value-enhancing choices due to some demonstrable mental condition or defect, his manifestation of assent to a bargain will be held to be unenforceable. Although the appropriateness of this defense seems clear at the extremes, once the defense is recognized, borderline cases can arise in which its application is questionable.

In *Ortelere v. Teachers' Retirement Board of the City of New York*,[2] the court considered the "well-established rule is that contracts of a mentally incompetent person who has not been adjudicated insane are voidable. Even where the contract has been partly or fully performed it will still be avoided upon restoration of the status quo." In *Ortelere*, a school teacher suffering from depression changed the terms of her pension plan from the option by which she would receive a lower monthly payment with the balance of her pension going to her husband after death to the option of receiving the maximum monthly payment with no survivor benefits. When she died a month after making the switch, her husband contested the competency of her change.

The opinion of the court discussed considerable evidence indicating that the choice was carefully made, as well as expert testimony that the deceased was never mentally incompetent. For these reasons the lower court upheld the enforceability of the deceased's choice. Nevertheless, the Court of Appeals reversed the decision. The court conceded that the defendant met the traditional standard requiring that she appreciate the nature of her choice—the "cognitive" test. Yet it contended that the traditional approach failed "to account for one who by reason of mental illness is unable to control his conduct even though his cognitive ability seems unimpaired."

The court then discussed how the criminal law defense of insanity had been expanded: "The nineteenth century cognitive test embraced in the *M'Naghten* rules has long been criticized and changed by statute and decision in many jurisdictions." Notwithstanding the differences between criminal law and

---

2. 25 N.Y.2d 196, 250 N.E.2d 460, 303 N.Y.S.2d 362 (1969).

contract law, "both share in common the premise that policy considerations must be based on a sound understanding of the human mind and, therefore, its illnesses. Hence, because the cognitive rules are, for the most part, too restrictive and rest on a false factual basis they must be re-examined." Adopting the new expanded test of competence, the court concluded that Mrs. Ortelere was unable to control her conduct in a reasonable manner. "[W]hen she acted as she did on February 11, 1965, she did so solely as a result of serious mental illness, namely, psychosis."

Since *Ortelere* was decided in the 1960s, the expanded standard of insanity based on the ability to control one's conduct—sometimes called "irresistible impulse"—has been challenged. Much of the debate was provoked by the acquittal by reason of insanity of John Hinckley, who attempted to assassinate President Reagan in 1981. The evidence showed that Hinckley, who had stalked President Reagan for some time, clearly knew what he was doing and appreciated the criminality of his conduct. Rather than contest these issues, the defense successfully contended that Hinckley was unable to control his conduct. Public outrage about the verdict ensued. As a result, since *Ortelere* was decided, some jurisdictions have abolished this theory of insanity, in favor of exclusive reliance on the cognitive theory associated with *M'Naghten's Case*.

Ortelere exemplifies the imperative that contract defenses be sufficiently extraordinary so as not to undermine the significance of the prima facie case. According to the dissent, "[a]ny benefit to those who understand what they are doing, but are unable to exercise self-discipline, will be outweighed by frivolous claims which will burden our courts and undermine the security of contracts." Note how difficult it is to determine, even in principle, whether Mrs. Ortelere was able to control her conduct. In practice, after the fact it is almost impossible to distinguish between an impulse that *could not* be resisted from an impulse that *was not* resisted. By default, psychiatrists will be the ones asked to make this decision, but their ability to read people's minds is very limited. Of course, only persons with some history of mental problems will be in a position to assert the defense of incapacity. The question raised by the dissent is whether the expanded conception of incapacity adopted by the court in *Ortelere* sufficiently protects what the dissent referred to as the "reasonable expectations of those who innocently deal with persons who appear rational and who understand what they are doing."

In light of this concern, the *Restatement 2nd* qualifies the approach in *Ortelere*. In section 15(1), it allows that a person can avoid a contract "if by reason of mental illness or defect (a) he is unable to understand in a reasonable manner the nature and consequences of the transaction," or "(b) he is unable to act in a reasonable manner in relation to the transaction *and the other party has reason to know of his condition* (emphasis added)." Therefore, while the traditional conception of incompetence is sufficient to avoid the contract, the expanded approach recognized in *Ortelere* is only available if the condition was apparent to the other party.

In addition, section 15(2) denies the availability of either form of the defense "[w]here the contract is made on fair terms and the other party is without knowledge of the mental illness or defect . . . to the extent that the contract has been so performed in whole or in part or the circumstances have so changed that avoidance would be unjust." In other words, a party satisfying section 15(1)(a) or (b) cannot avoid a contract on fair terms that has already been partially or wholly performed when the party did not actually know of the incompetence. Both qualifications reflect what the comment to section 15 describes as the need to reconcile "two conflicting policies: the protection of justifiable expectations and of the security of transactions, and the protection of persons unable to protect themselves against imposition."

6.2.2 Infancy

In contrast with adults who are rebuttably presumed to be competent to enter contracts, minors are deemed to lack the capacity to contract. It is easy to see why a blanket rule would apply to those to whom we ordinarily refer as "infants." But the contract defense of infancy extends to "minors" as old as 18 or 21, which realistically shields persons who are clearly competent to make value-enhancing decisions. "Children in the Middle Ages became adults at the age of seven, at which time a boy was apprenticed to a tradesman, or otherwise sent out to find his fortune," wrote Hillary Rodham Clinton, "and a girl was trained for future domestic responsibilities. The concept of childhood gradually was expanded until children became more and more dependent on their parents and parents became less and less dependent on their children for economic support and sustenance."[3]

The overinclusiveness of this contract defense at common law probably resulted from the situation confronting the English aristocracy whose children were in line for inheritances, but who were not to have access to this wealth for the indefinite future. These so-called "expectant heirs" were often approached with deals on credit, with the expectation that the debts would be satisfied by their future inheritances. We can see why the common law courts might extend the doctrine of "infancy" past the point of literal competence as a means of protecting the estates of the parents who were the social peers of the judges. We might also question the ability or competence of those who are not yet possessed of wealth to evaluate accurately offers based on credit against their speculative patrimony. Such heirs are choosing between enjoying a real and present benefit (on credit) and a prospective and uncertain benefit in the future when and if they ever inherit.

Whatever its origin, the defense of infancy still exists in its expanded form that allows teens to escape the obligations of their agreements. This also makes it harder for any teen on his or her

---

3. Hillary Rodham, *Children's Rights: A Legal Perspective*, in CHILDREN'S RIGHTS: CONTEMPORARY PERSPECTIVES 24 (Patricia A. Vardin & Ilene N. Brody, eds. 1979).

own to enter into certain types of transactions, such as a lease of an apartment, without the cosignature of the parent. That this doctrine extends well beyond the boundaries of pure competence is reflected in a traditional exception that allows recovery for providing an infant with the "necessaries" of food, clothing, shelter, and so forth. Obviously, one would want 18 or 19 year olds living on their own to obtain such goods on credit, even those who are in line for an inheritance. But because it is considered an exception to a defense that is based on the incompetence of an infant to enter into value-enhancing exchanges, the person providing necessities is only entitled to the "fair value" of the provision, not the contract price that was bargained for.

6.3 Obtaining Consent by Improper Means

6.3.1 Why Are Some Means of Obtaining Consent Improper?

We enforce bargains to which the parties have consented, in part, because their consent ordinarily indicates that the bargain increases the welfare of both parties. Contract defenses based on lack of capacity identify circumstances where some demonstrable characteristic—for example, youth or mental condition—impairs the normal competence of adults to enter value-enhancing transactions. We now consider circumstances that undermine the rationale for enforcing manifestations of consent where both parties are fully competent.

Sometimes the manifestation of consent required by the prima facie case of contract is obtained in a manner that undermines the normal presumption that consent signals a value-enhancing transaction for both parties. The is most obvious when consent is obtained by duress or misrepresentation.

When a manifestation of consent is obtained by force or duress, the resulting agreement does not reflect the knowledge of the promisor that he subjectively prefers the benefits of the transaction to its costs. The promisor's manifested consent is the product of the threat, not his judgment. Forcible transfers also disrupt the price mechanism that is essential to dispersing information about resource use throughout the world. As was discussed in Chapter 4, prices only convey accurate information about resource use if they result from transactions that reflect the personal knowledge of individuals. The prohibition on the use of force protects the liberty of persons and associations to act on the basis of their diverse local and personal knowledge while taking into account the knowledge of others about which they are pervasively ignorant—what in section 4.1.1 was called the "first-order problem of knowledge."

The function of the prohibition against misrepresentation is related, but different. Unlike the case of force or duress, a manifestation of consent that is a product of misrepresentation *does* reflect the knowledge of the person consenting that he would prefer what he is *supposed* to be getting for what he is giving up. Although the transaction *as described* would be welfare enhancing, the performance actually received by the promisee does not conform to the description communicated by the promisor. For example, a buyer may know that he values the goods or land he is obtaining from the seller more than the money he is transferring to the seller, but the goods or land he receives do not conform to the description that was communicated to him by the other party. A gap has arisen between what was promised and what was delivered that is unjust because it results from the promisor's miscommunication. When this happens, a person can always sue for breach of contract; but another option is to seek to avoid or rescind the contract.

For example, in *Halpert v. Rosenthal*,[4] a house was falsely represented by the seller to be termite-free when in truth it was infested with termites. Despite the fact that the seller's representation

---

4. 107 R.I. 406, 267 A.2d 730 (1970).

was innocent, insofar as he claimed to have no knowledge of the termites or any evidence of their presence, the sale was avoided. Although the sale of a termite-free house in return for the contract price was value-enhancing for both parties, the same price for an infested house was not value-enhancing for the buyer.

In sum, force and misrepresentation undermine the normal significance of contractual consent in two different ways. When a seller of goods uses duress to obtain the buyer's manifestation of consent, the transfer may not be value-enhancing because it fails to reflect the buyer's knowledge. With misrepresentation, the transfer may not be value-enhancing because, although the buyer's manifestation of consent *does* reflect his knowledge, the resulting distribution of resources does not match the consent that was communicated. With this basic distinction in mind, let us consider some special problems that arise when trying to identify duress and misrepresentation in actual cases.

6.3.2 Misrepresentation

The Difference between Fraudulent and Material Misrepresentation

According to the *Restatement of the Law Second, Torts*, section 526, the tort of fraud creates a cause of action when someone detrimentally relies on a misstatement of fact and the maker of the false statement (a) "knows or believes that the matter is not as he represents it to be," (b) "does not have the confidence in the accuracy of his representation that he states or implies," or (c) "knows that he does not have the basis for his representation that he states or implies." In addition to being a tort, the existence of a fraudulent misrepresentation also provides a defense to the enforcement of a contract. Indeed the *Restatement 2nd of Contracts*, section 162(1) incorporates the same definition of "fraudulent" as the *Restatement 2nd of Torts*.

But in addition to misrepresentations that are fraudulent, a contract defense also exists for *non*fraudulent misrepresentations that are "material." According to section 162(2), a "misrepresentation is material (a) if it would be likely to induce a reasonable person to manifest his assent, or (b) if the maker knows that it would be likely to induce the recipient to do so." (Note that "material" is being used here in a different sense than with material breach.)

In *Halbert v. Rosenthal*, for example, the misrepresented fact was material because knowledge of the termite infestation would cause a reasonable person to have withheld consent to the sale. So it does not matter to the outcome whether the seller's misrepresentation was innocent or fraudulent. Had the misrepresentation been about a feature of the house that would not affect a reasonable person from buying it, it would still provide the basis for a defense if the promisee had subjectively relied on a fact that was fraudulently misrepresented.

For an example of a nonmaterial misrepresentation, consider *Byers v. Federal Land Co.*,[5] where a buyer sought to avoid the purchase of some land on the ground that real estate brokers acting as agents of the seller had misrepresented that (a) the seller had possession of the land and was capable of transferring possession to the buyer when in fact it neither had nor could transfer possession; (b) the seller already owned the land when in fact it was a party to a contract to purchase the land from another company; and (c) the land was worth $35 per acre when in fact it was worth only $15.

The court evaluated each of these misrepresentations by the broker on the assumption that they were innocently made. Although the court found the inability to transfer possession of the land to be material, it concluded that the misrepresentation of ownership was not. So long as the seller was in a position to transfer the rights to the land to the buyer, it should not matter to a reasonable buyer whether the seller already owned the land or merely had

---

5. 3 F.2d 9 (1924).

a contractual right to the land by which it could purchase the land and resell it to the buyer. (We consider the third of the misrepresentations in *Byers* in the next section discussing the difference between misrepresentations of fact versus expressions of opinion.)

Notice that materiality introduces an "objective" factor into an assessment of misrepresentation. It is not enough for a fact to subjectively make a difference to the party seeking to avoid a contract. It must also be the type of fact that would make a difference to a reasonable person *or* the party making the representation actually knew it subjectively mattered to the other party. In contrast, when a misrepresentation is fraudulent, it need only be subjectively relied on by the promisee; it need not also meet the objective standard of materiality.

Comment b to section 164 provides the following explanation for why a misrepresentation must either be fraudulent or material: "One who makes a non-fraudulent misrepresentation of a seemingly unimportant fact has no reason to suppose that his assertion will induce assent." However, when "a fraudulent misrepresentation is directed to attaining that very end," then "the maker cannot insist on his bargain if it is attained, however unexpectedly, as long as the additional requirements of inducement and justifiable reliance are met."

Statements of Fact versus Opinion

To constitute a basis for avoiding a contract, a misrepresentation must ordinarily concern a statement of fact that turns out to be other than what was asserted. Statements of opinion that turn out to be incorrect do not ordinarily justify avoidance of the contract. But if a statement of opinion was a lie when made, it could constitute a misrepresentation. After all, it would be misstating a fact about the person's state of mind who is expressing an opinion. In *Byers v. Federal Land Co.*,[6] while the court found the honest but

---

6. 3 F.2d 9 (1924).

mistaken representation that the land was worth $15 to be an expression of opinion, it also stated that a "statement of value *when the value is known to be different* from that stated is a fraudulent misrepresentation of an opinion as existing that does not exist" (emphasis added).

Statements concerning market value are sometimes considered facts and sometimes opinions. A statement of the value of property for which there is a generally accepted market price, such as bonds of the government, grain, or cattle, may be a misrepresentation of a fact. Conversely, as the *Byers* court stated, a "statement of the monetary value of property with no definite market value such as a mine, an invention, old and used goods or of lands, is generally made and understood as an expression of opinion only, and not as representation of a fact, and is not ordinarily an actionable misrepresentation."

In special circumstances, a defense of misrepresentation will also be available for a pure statement of opinion, as for example, if the person expressing an opinion is in a position of trust. A commonly studied case of this kind is *Vokes v. Arthur Murray, Inc.*,[7] in which a dance studio was alleged to have presold many hours of instruction to a student by misleading her about the progress she was making. "Thus she embarked upon an almost endless pursuit of the terpsichorean art during which, over a period of less than sixteen months, she was sold fourteen 'dance courses' totaling in the aggregate 2302 hours of dancing lessons for a total cash outlay of $31,090.45." The defendant assured, her that "she had 'grace and poise'; that she was 'rapidly improving and developing in her dancing skill'; that the additional lessons would 'make her a beautiful dancer, capable of dancing with the most accomplished dancers'; that she was 'rapidly progressing in the development of her dancing skill and gracefulness,' etc., etc." Apparently, all these assurances were false. Of particular salience was the fact that the

---

7. 212 So. 2d 906 (1968).

studio presold her far more hours of instruction than she seemingly ever could use.

In *Vokes*, the court explained that the normal rule that a defense of misrepresentation is unavailable for misstatements of opinions does not apply (a) "where there is a fiduciary relationship between the parties," (b) "where there has been some artifice or trick employed by the representor," (c) "where the parties do not in general deal at 'arm's length' as we understand the phrase, or (d) where the representee does not have equal opportunity to become apprised of the truth or falsity of the fact represented."

The opinion in *Vokes* is not without its weaknesses. For one thing the tone of the opinion was quite condescending to the plaintiff, suggesting—without so finding—a diminished capacity based on her age (though she was only 51) or perhaps the fact she was a "widow," or even that she was female. Perhaps the plaintiff knew full well she was buying more hours than she could use, but she nevertheless enjoyed the experience of being at the studio, socializing with the other students, taking the trips to other studios, and even the false compliments about her abilities. Do all teachers owe their students complete candor, even at the expense of undermining their motivation for achievement?

Still, *Vokes* well illustrates the exceptional circumstances where opinions can be misrepresentations. For one thing the opinions were allegedly lies when made. Also, the plaintiff was paying the studio for its expertise. They owed her a duty to offer opinions that served her interests. True, it may well have served her interest for them to conceal their actual opinion of her abilities and even to exaggerate her progress so as to encourage her continued efforts. But what they could not do was abuse their position of trust *to induce her to pay them more money*, as they clearly did. The plaintiff had a right to rely on the good faith of the opinions she was paying for when deciding whether to enter into additional contractual obligations to the defendant.

6.3.3 Economic Duress

It is easy to understand why a manifestation of assent obtained at gunpoint is not enforceable. Perhaps for this reason, such cases are not typically studied in contracts classes. Instead, when duress is studied, the focus is on cases involving what is called "economic duress"—a more contentious concept.

For example, in *Austin Instrument v. Loral Corp.*,[8] a supplier of components to a defense contractor threatened to withhold its performance unless the contractor agreed to pay more than the contract price and committed to buying additional components for a second transaction the contractor was negotiating with the government. After the supplier suspended delivery of the components, the contractor, being unable to secure another source, agreed to the terms lest it avoid breaching its contract with the government by missing its production deadline. When the contractor later refused to pay the increased price, the court ruled it was unenforceable because of duress.

A contrary result was reached in *United States v. Progressive Enterprises*,[9] where a contractor based its bid to the government on a price quoted by a supplier. After the bid was awarded, the supplier said it would not honor its quoted price because of unforeseen increases in its costs, and the contractor agreed to pay the higher price demanded without protest. Later, the contractor refused to pay more than the original price on the grounds that its promise resulted from duress. The court nevertheless awarded the higher price.

The doctrine of economic duress is problematic for a reason discussed at the beginning of this chapter: If a contract defense is not limited to truly exceptional circumstances, it will undermine the

---

8. 29 N.Y.2d 124, 272 N.E.2d 533, 324 N.Y.S.2d 22 (1971).

9. 418 F. Supp. 662 (1976).

institution of contract itself. It is not uncommon for a contract to be consensually modified during its performance, sometimes in response to unforeseen difficulties confronting one of the parties who asks for relief, or who even may be contemplating breaching the contract due to its economic distress. Furthermore, most everyone is subject to economic demands—including the need for food and shelter—that can afterwards be asserted to have led them to enter into undesirable bargains. If the threat of the supplier in *Austin* to breach, combined with economic pressure facing the contractor, justifies refusing to enforce the agreement to pay a higher price, why would "threats" to withhold food unless it is paid for, an apartment unless rent is paid, or wages unless work is done not also be considered improper?

Because economic circumstances can very often be said to have compelled one party to enter into agreements with others, courts have attempted to cabin the defense of duress by emphasizing, for example, the lack of alternatives available to the party being threatened (as in *Austin*) or the lack of protest by the threatened party (as in *Progressive*). Yet these limitations are difficult to apply and do not seem to explain fully when the defense should and should not be available.

Steven Burton's theory of good faith offers an alternative to thinking of these cases in terms of duress, thereby avoiding having to distinguish between the "normal" economic pressures commonly faced and "extraordinary" pressures justifying contract avoidance. With all contracts, one party can later seek a modification of its contractual obligations, and the other party is free to consent to such modifications. If a party does not merely ask for a modification but threatens to breach, as discussed in section 5.2, this could be considered an anticipatory repudiation justifying canceling the contract and seeking a substitute performance.

After a contract is formed and commenced, however, each party can become especially vulnerable to the demands of the other party since they are now relying on the promised performance. This is what Eric Anderson called a contracting party's interest in future performance. We saw this sort of "opportunistic behavior" alleged in *Stilk v. Myrick* and *Alaska Packers* discussed in section 4.2.4. Suppose instead of looking for duress, courts instead would try to identify opportunistic behavior where one party is trying to capitalize on the vulnerability created by the other party's reliance on the future performance of the contract.

In both *Austin* and *Progressive*, one party is seeking the other party's assent to a contract modification by threatening nonperformance under circumstances in which the other party is vulnerable for having relied on the contract (and perhaps for other reasons as well). We might say that every contract gives each party the discretion to seek the other party's assent to modify their agreement or waive a duty of performance. But like Burton's theory of good faith performance, this liberty or discretion is not permitted for the purpose of recapturing an opportunity that one has already bargained away.

Ordinarily by entering into a contract one has bargained away the opportunity to contract at a different price. But one remains free to ask the other party for a different price because of changed circumstances such as an increased cost of performance (when these changed circumstances would not provide a defense to contract under the failure of basic assumption defenses we will discuss in section 6.4). This change in circumstances can be viewed as providing a good business reason for seeking a modification of the agreement. In the economic duress situation, however, a party is seeking to use the leverage of the other party's reliance on the contract to reclaim an opportunity forgone at formation, without having a good business reason for refusing to perform, such as unforeseen increases in costs or other impediments to performance.

Rather than trying to identify "duress," courts could shift their focus to the party's motive for threatening to breach the existing contract unless its terms are modified. When the threat to withhold performance is subjectively motivated by a sufficient business reason—unrelated to the other party's vulnerability—as in *Progressive*, it will be upheld: When there is no legitimate business motivation, as in *Austin*, the modification will be considered opportunistic and unenforceable. When there is economic pressure on the other party to agree to the modification because it has no practical alternative to the contracted performance, courts should be suspicious of any purported business reasons for the threat. They should examine such claims with care to determine if they were sincere or were instead mere pretexts for the opportunistic exploitation of the other party's dependence on the agreement.

The court in *Progressive* endorsed this approach by noting that UCC section 2-209 changed the law governing contract modifications by eliminating the requirement of consideration. "This change from the common law of contracts supports the common business practice of adjusting the terms of agreements as conditions change." However, the UCC then emphasizes that the "ability to modify a sales agreement is limited by the general UCC requirement of good faith." The court quoted from the explanation of "bad faith" provided by the Official Comment to section 2-209: "[t]he effective use of bad faith to escape performance on the original contract terms is barred, and the extortion of a 'modification *without legitimate commercial reason* is ineffective as a violation of the duty of good faith" (emphasis added). By contrast, "such matters as a market shift which makes performance come to involve a loss may provide such a [good faith] reason even though there is no such unforeseen difficulty as would make out a legal excuse from performance."

6.3.4 Undue Influence

In *Odorizzi v. Bloomfield School District*,[10] a public school teacher was arrested for proposing to engage in homosexual activities in his own home with an undercover police officer. After being questioning by the police, he was charged and released on bail, having gone

---

10. 246 Cal. App. 2d 123, 54 Cal. Rptr. 533 (1966).

for 40 hours without sleep. Immediately upon his release, the super-intendent and principal of his school came to his apartment to obtain his resignation. They said they were trying to help him and had his best interests at heart, that there was no time to consult an attorney, and that if he failed to resign he would be suspended and dismissed with attendant publicity that would cause him "to suffer extreme embarrassment and humiliation." If he resigned quietly, he would not jeopardize his chances of securing employment as a teacher elsewhere. Odorizzi signed the resignation papers.

After rejecting the claim that his consent was obtained as a result of duress, fraud, or mistake, the California Court of Appeals held that the resignation was nonetheless unenforceable because it had resulted from undue influence. "Undue influence . . . is a shorthand legal phrase used to describe persuasion which tends to be coercive in nature, persuasion which overcomes the will without convincing the judgment." Undue influence is character-ized by high pressure, "a pressure which works on mental, moral, or emotional weakness to such an extent that it approaches the boundaries of coercion. In this sense, undue influence has been called overpersuasion."

Undue influence can be considered a hybrid defense with ele-ments of both lack of capacity and improper means. The dimin-ished capacity is less than what is required to establish a general mental impairment; the person might well be generally competent but, for some reason, be unusually vulnerable under these particu-lar circumstances. The means used to obtain consent might well be generally acceptable under ordinary bargaining situations, but become improper when applied to a person in the diminished state. Crucial to the defense of undue influence, the person applying the pressure is subjectively doing so to take advantage of the dimin-ished capacity. In this way, when a mental incapacitation (that is insufficient to make out a defense of incapacity on its own) is com-bined with the use of pressure techniques (that is insufficient to make out a defense of duress on its own) there is sufficient reason to conclude that the person being pressured was not competent to make a value-enhancing choice, and this vulnerability was being exploited by the other party.

6.3.5 Unconscionability

In the famous case of *Williams v. Walker-Thomas Furniture Co.*,[11] a welfare recipient purchased on credit a stereo costing twice as much as her monthly stipend from a store where she previously purchased furniture. The form contract she signed provided that the new balance be added to her outstanding debt for the other items she had previously bought, which meant that until she repaid her entire debt, she would still have a balance due for each item purchased. When she failed to make her payments, the furniture company attempted to repossess all the items she had purchased from the store.

The court held the contract to be unenforceable because it was unconscionable. Its lengthy opinion focused on many different aspects of the transaction, including the fact that the terms were included in a difficult-to-understand form, the lack of opportunity she had to read the form, the degree to which this purchase exceeded her income, the fact this was known to the seller, and even the fact that a stereo was a luxury item. As a result, the opinion does not make clear exactly what must be shown to find that an agreement is unconscionable. The following passage is the closest it comes to defining the defense: "Ordinarily, one who signs an agreement without full knowledge of its terms might be held to assume the risk that he has entered a one-sided bargain." However, "when [1] a party of little bargaining power, and hence little real choice, [2] signs a commercially unreasonable contract with [3] little or no knowledge of its terms, it is hardly likely that his consent,

---

11. 350 F.2d 445 (1965).

or even an objective manifestation of his consent, was ever given to all the terms."

Like the doctrines of promissory estoppel, good faith performance, and material breach, unconscionability is not very clearly defined either by the *Restatement 2nd* or the UCC. As a result, theories have arisen to fill the gap. In his classic article, *Unconscionability and the Code—The Emperor's New Clause*,[12] Arthur Leff situated the new doctrine among traditional contract defenses: "The law may legitimately be interested both in the way agreements come about and in what they provide. A 'contract' gotten at gunpoint may be avoided; a classic dicker over Dobbin may come to naught if horse owning is illegal." Leff offered a distinction between two kinds of unconscionability: *Procedural unconscionability* reflects the view that, as a result of what Leff called "bargaining naughtiness," there appears to have been a defect in the bargaining process; *substantive unconscionability* reflects a judgment that there is something "unfair" or one-sided or wrong with the substance of the terms of a bargain that was struck. In analyzing unconscionability claims, courts have widely adopted Leff's distinction and, with some exceptions, have limited the scope of the defense to procedural unconscionability.

Can the defense of procedural unconscionability, like such traditional defenses as incapacity, duress, misrepresentation, or undue influence, be reconciled with contractual consent? Writing a few years after Leff,[13] Richard Epstein attempted to justify the use of procedural unconscionability when it is difficult to prove that one of the more traditional defenses applies. Epstein began his analysis by rejecting the use of what Leff called substantive unconscionability "to allow courts to act as roving commissions to set aside those agreements whose substantive terms they find objectionable."

---

12. Arthur Leff, *Unconscionability and the Code—The Emperor's New Clause*, 115 U. Pa. L. Rev. 485 (1967).

13. *See* Richard A. Epstein, *Unconscionability: A Critical Reappraisal*, 18 J.L. & Econ. 293 (1973).

Instead, Epstein maintained, the defense of unconscionability "should be used only to allow courts to police *the process* whereby private agreements are formed, and in that connection, only to facilitate the setting aside of agreements that are *as a matter of probabilities* likely to be vitiated by the classical defense of duress, fraud, or incompetence" (emphases added). Although it is generally appropriate to place the burden of proof on those asserting such defenses, sometimes this "will create cases where contracts that should not be enforced will—for lack of proof of the defense—be enforced." Relaxing the rules of proof may sometimes be "justified on the grounds that it reduces the total error in enforcement, even though all error is not thereby eliminated."

Instead of establishing the elements of these traditional defenses directly, procedural unconscionability "looks both to the subject matter of the agreements and to the social positions of the persons who enter into them." In other words, under certain circumstances, a deal can be so substantively one sided as to call into question either the competence of the disadvantaged party, the means by which consent was obtained, or some combination of both. For Epstein, "the difficult question with [procedural] unconscionability is not whether it works towards a legitimate end, but whether its application comes at too great a price." To be safe, the doctrine should be limited "to discernable classes of contracting parties; and these classes cannot be such as to easily permit parties to bring themselves within them."

Each of the common law defenses considered by Epstein arguably involves situations where the normal or presumptive benefits incident to enforcing bargains are lacking. Normally parties have the knowledge, the interest, and the ability to look after themselves. If two parties possessing these normal characteristics reach an agreement, this agreement is very likely to be welfare enhancing for the two persons involved. Welfare effects on third parties are generally handled by tort law. Where circumstances falling under one of these recognized defenses exists, these conditions do not hold, and we cannot be sure that the bargain is welfare enhancing after all. According to Epstein's theory, procedural unconscionability is warranted (if at all) as an indirect way of proving these defenses under circumstances where direct proof is difficult.

〴 6.4 The Failure of a Basic Assumption

6.4.1 Tacit Assumptions and the Scope of Consent

In the previous sections we examined defenses that undermine the normal presumption that a consensual agreement is value-enhancing for both parties. There is another cluster of defenses aimed at something quite different. Rather than identifying circumstances that undermine the meaningfulness of consent, these defenses seek to discern realistically the scope and limits of the parties' consent.

Contracts are never entirely complete because there are always certain underlying assumptions being made by the parties that are not included in their agreement. Indeed, many of these assumptions are simply *too basic* to merit inclusion. When the salesman tells you that the loading dock where you can pick up your goods is in the rear of the building, he and you both assume that the road outside the store that connects the parking lot to the loading dock that existed when he arrived at work is still there. If the express and implied-in-fact terms to which the parties consented are the exposed portion of the iceberg, the assumptions on which their consent was based constitutes the ice that floats beneath the surface.

In his influential casebook,[14] Lon Fuller described what he called "tacit assumptions" in a passage that is worth quoting at length:

Words like "intention" "assumption," "expectation" and "understanding" all seem to imply a *conscious* state involving an

---

14. *See* Lon L. Fuller, Basic Contract Law 666–67 (1947).

awareness of alternatives and a deliberate choice among them. It is, however, plain that there is a psychological state which can be described as a "tacit assumption" that does not involve a consciousness of alternatives. The absent-minded professor stepping from his office into the hall as he reads a book "assumes" that the floor of the hall will be there to receive him. His conduct is conditioned and directed by this assumption, even though the possibility that the floor has been removed does not "occur" to him, that is, is not present in his mental processes.

Although not a part of one's consciousness, these background tacit assumptions are quite real. If you are reading these words away from your residence, you are tacitly assuming that your home or apartment has not been destroyed since you were last there. You certainly were not consciously thinking about it but, now that you are, it is no fiction to say, "Yes, that was indeed what I was assuming."

Most of the time, our tacit assumptions turn out to be true or, at least, it does not matter if they are mistaken. But sometimes, when our consent to enter into a contract is premised on such an assumption and it "fails," this could be grounds for relieving one party from what appears to have been an unqualified commitment. "Common sense," writes Andrew Kull, "sets limits to a promise, even where contractual language does not."[15] Such limits are not to be found in either the expressed or implied-in-fact meaning of the terms. "Though a promise is expressed in unqualified terms, a person does not normally mean to bind himself to do the impossible, or to persevere when performance proves to be materially different from what both parties anticipated at the time of formation."

These qualifications are not implied by what was said, but rest on the background assumptions of the parties that went unexpressed.

---

15. Andrew Kull, *Mistake, Frustration, and the Windfall Principle of Contract Remedies*, 43 HASTINGS L.J. 1, 38–39 (1991).

"Faced with the adverse consequences of such a disparity, even a person who has previously regarded his promise as unconditional is likely to protest that he never promised to do *that*." As Kull explained, "[t]he force of the implicit claim is hard to deny: I did not mean my promise to extend to this circumstance; nor did you so understand it; to give it that effect would therefore be to enforce a contract different from the one we actually made."

In his casebook, Fuller offered the example of a person "who contracts to deliver goods a year from now at a price now fixed." Such a person "certainly 'takes into account' the possibility of some fluctuation in price levels, but may feel that a ten-fold inflation was contrary to an 'assumption' or 'expectation' that price variations would occur within the 'normal' range, and that this expectation was 'the foundation of the agreement.'"

Contract law has a number of defenses to enforcement that are based on failures of basic assumption, such as mistake, frustration of purpose, and impracticability. With mistake, a *present existing fact* that was tacitly assumed by both parties to be true at the time of formation, and that was material to the assent of the party seeking to avoid the agreement, turns out to be false. With frustration of purposes, an event occurring after formation has unexpectedly *reduced the value of receiving the other party's performance* to the person seeking to avoid the contract. With impracticability, events occurring after formation have unexpectedly *increased the cost of a party's performance.* In each of these circumstances, when one party seeks to enforce the agreement, the other party is saying, in effect, "well, I did not agree to *that*."

Apart from rare exceptions, such as clerical errors in writings that have not been relied upon by the other party, defenses to enforcing contracts based on a failure of basic assumption have a common component: The assumption must be *shared by both parties.* Only if an assumption was shared by both parties, can the contract to which both parties agreed be said to have been based upon it. If it was not held in common, then we ordinarily say that a party who was unilaterally mistaken bore the risk of his own mistake and the contract can be enforced against him. (We discuss the exceptions to this in section 6.4.2.)

Even if a mistake in basic assumption is mutual, however, the party seeking to enforce the contract can respond by alleging that the mistaken party assumed the risk that the assumption might turn out to be false. For example, when one party seeks to avoid a contract because of a mutual mistake of present existing fact at the time of formation, the party seeking to enforce the contract can respond as follows: Although we both may have assumed the underlying fact to be X, and it turned out to be Y, you were aware you did not know whether it was X or Y, and you entered the contract anyway. The phenomenon of knowing that one does not know something is called *conscious ignorance.*

Assumption of risk due to conscious ignorance helps explain our intuitions about a number of famous cases alleging mutual mistake. In *Sherwood v. Walker*,[16] for example, the court found that both parties assumed that a cow named Rose the Second of Aberlone could not breed and was only fit for beef. Although the dissent questioned whether this assumption was truly mutual, even if the majority was correct, the seller likely knew he did not know for a fact whether or not the cow could breed and, therefore, assumed the risk that she could.

The existence of conscious ignorance is even clearer in the case of *Wood v. Boynton*,[17] where a woman sold a raw stone to a jeweler for $1. When the stone turned out to be a diamond in the rough, she tried to avoid the sale. The court accepted the jeweler's claim that it did not realize that the stone was a diamond— normal jewelers rarely if ever see uncut stones—so the mistake was mutual. It was evident from the facts, however, that the seller was very much aware that she did not know what sort of stone it was,

---

16. 66 Mich. 586, 33 N.W. 919 (1887).

17. 64 Wis. 265, 25 N.W. 42 (1885).

and she nevertheless took the risk that it would turn out to be something more valuable than both she and the jeweler mutually assumed.

Whereas the defense of mistake in basic assumption concerns mistakes about present existing facts—for example, the type of stone in *Wood*—the defenses of commercial impracticability and frustration of purposes concern the failure of assumptions about future events. Of course, the seeds of the future lie always in the present, so it is sometimes hard to distinguish an assumption about the future cost or value of performance from a mistake of fact existing at the time of the performance.

For example, was the mistake in *Sherwood* about the present existing state of Rose's reproductive organs or whether she was with calf at the time of the sale, or was it whether the she would breed in the future? Consider also the famous "coronation cases"[18] in which one party attempted to avoid a contract to let a room overlooking the route of a coronation parade when the coronation needed to be postponed after the king took sick. Were the parties mistaken about whether the coronation parade would proceed as planned, or about the present existing fact that the king was in good health?

Why even try drawing a line between present existing facts and future events? The principal difference between mistaken assumptions about present existing facts and mistaken assumptions about future events is that, given the inherent uncertainty about the future, we are more inclined to conclude that a party assumed the risk of unexpectedly changed circumstances. For this reason, defenses based on mistake in present existing facts are more likely to succeed.

Indeed, despite the availability of frustration of purposes as a defense, U.S. courts rarely allow a party to avoid an agreement

---

18. *See* Krell v. Henry [1903] L.R. 2 K.B. 740; and Chandler v. Webster [1904] 1 KB 493.

because it no longer values the performance it is to receive from the other party. This reluctance may well stem from the view that parties typically assume the risk that future events will render the performance of the other party less valuable than expected. After all, because the future is known to be uncertain, contracting parties can generally be said to be consciously ignorant about future events and they assume the risk of things not working out as they hope and expect.

As with *Sherwood v. Walker* and *Wood v. Boynton*, our intuitions about many of the famous cases of mistake, frustration, and impracticability, are based, not on whether the assumption was either basic or mutual, but on whether the party seeking to avoid the contract assumed the risk of a basic mutual assumption turning out to be false. This marks a difference in principle between the defenses based on the failure of basic assumption and those based on incompetence or obtaining consent by improper means. Courts do not typically say, for example that a party assumes the risk of the other party employing duress, misrepresentation, or undue influence. The persistent focus on assumption of risk signals that defenses based on the failure of a basic assumption are aimed at identifying the scope and limits of the parties' consent, rather than on reasons why the consent that would ordinarily satisfy the prima facie case of contract should nevertheless not be enforced.

6.4.2 Unilateral Mistake and Misrepresentation

Is There a Duty to Disclose Material Information?

Ordinarily a basic assumption must be mutual or shared by both parties to provide a defense to enforcement. As was just discussed, a reason for the requirement of mutuality is that only an assumption that is tacitly shared by both parties is deemed to be so basic as to go without saying. Any assumption held by just one of the parties, but not the other, cannot be considered a tacit assumption held by most everyone until it is made explicit. The element of mutuality allows us to conclude both that the party seeking to avoid the contract "did not agree to *that*," and the party seeking to enforce the contract did not reasonably think otherwise.

This explanation suggests an exception to the requirement of mutuality is warranted when one party is aware, or has reason to be aware, of a mistaken assumption being held unilaterally by the other party. When this is the case, a unilateral mistake can provide a defense to a contract. "Where a mistake of one party at the time a contract was made as to a basic assumption on which he made the contract has a material effect on the agreed exchange of performances that is adverse to him," *Restatement 2nd* section 153(b) says that "the contract is voidable by him if he does not bear the risk of the mistake ... and ... *the other party had reason to know of the mistake or his fault caused the mistake*" (emphasis added). Sensible as it may sound, this rule requires some qualification that does not appear in the *Restatement*.

Consider the case of *Laidlaw v. Organ*,[19] which involved a contract for tobacco made during the War of 1812. At the time the contract was executed, the buyer had advance information that the treaty ending the war had been signed, promising an end to the naval blockade of New Orleans that had been suppressing the price of tobacco. (Notice how this could be characterized as either a mistake in present existing fact—a peace agreement had been reached—or a mistaken assumption about the future—the blockade will be lifted.) When asked by the seller if he knew anything that might affect the price of tobacco, however, the buyer failed to disclose this information. The legal issue was whether the seller could avoid the contract because of this failure to disclose.

Laidlaw involves not one but two closely related defenses. Even if he had not been asked the question by the buyer and remained silent, the seller clearly knew that the buyer was making a mistake

---

19. 15 U.S. (2 Wheat.) 178 (1817).

about a material fact. If so, then why would the rule announced by *Restatement 2nd*, section 153(b) not apply to void the sale? In addition, the seller's silence in the face of an explicit question about any relevant knowledge clearly misled the buyer about what the seller knew and could therefore be considered fraudulent. On these facts, then, the buyer has not one but two arguments for why the contract may be avoided.

In his opinion for the Supreme Court, Chief Justice John Marshall posed the question raised by the case as "whether the intelligence of extrinsic circumstances which might influence the price of the commodity, and which was exclusively within the knowledge of the vendee, ought to have been communicated by him to the vendor?" To this, he answered that "[t]he court is of the opinion that he was not bound to communicate it." By "extrinsic circumstances," Marshall was referring to facts that affect the supply of or demand for a particular item. In contrast, an "intrinsic" fact concerns information about the item itself—for example, whether or not a house is infested with termites—which presumably must be disclosed. Marshall's distinction between extrinsic and intrinsic information is no longer used by courts, if it ever was, and is no part of the rule provided by section 153. Below, I will suggest why Marshall may well have been on to something.

Can Marshall's refusal to recognize a duty to disclose be justified? One well-known justification was offered by Anthony Kronman who defended the refusal to mandate disclosure by focusing on how the legal rule affects the incentives for the deliberate production of valuable information.[20] If a party must disclose all material information to the other party, then he cannot trade on the information for a profit. There is no incentive to expend any energy discovering valuable information, and resource prices will not reflect the true state of affairs governing the scarcity of or demand

---

20. *See* Anthony T. Kronman, *Mistake, Disclosure, Information, and the Law of Contracts*, 11 J. LEG. STUD. 1 (1978).

for goods. Conversely, Kronman contended that information that is casually obtained should have to be disclosed. Because no effort was expended to discover this information, there need be no incentives to induce discovery.

Kronman's distinction between casually and deliberately discovered information, however, misses the most important issue raised by mandating a duty to disclose such information. All speculative resource trading involves betting on price changes that are caused by extrinsic circumstances. Allowing parties to withhold information concerning the potential demand or supply of the traded resource provides substantial social benefits. True, a privilege of nondisclosure creates incentives to generate useful information deliberately, but that is only one of its advantages. Such a right also provides incentives to *disseminate* this vital information, whether it is acquired casually or deliberately.

Paradoxical as it sounds, permitting persons to conceal certain types of information from the other party best promotes the dissemination of that information to the wider market. This is because vital information is conveyed by the *actions* of persons who trade on intelligence of extrinsic circumstances. Both consenting to trade and withholding one's consent importantly affect the market price of a resource. For example, the market price of a house is influenced both by those who choose to sell at a particular price and by all those homeowners who prefer to hold on to their property rather than accept the prevailing market price.

As was discussed in section 4.1.1, the resource prices produced both by those who trade and those who decline to trade represent a summation of innumerable amounts of radically dispersed information concerning the competing alternative uses of scarce resources and the relative subjective desirability of these uses. When a person trades on casually obtained or "windfall" information, he contributes his knowledge to the aggregate market price however little he invested in discovering the information. Requiring every person to disclose material information he may possess about future market demand or supply for a resource eliminates his incentive to engage in information-revealing transactions. Consequently, a legal duty to disclose intelligence of extrinsic circumstances to the other party would greatly slow or eliminate the dissemination of this information to the society at large.

Laidlaw challenges our intuitions because news of the peace treaty was about to arrive in New Orleans in a matter of hours. Of course, if all information bearing on the supply or demand for resources would soon reach everyone, the social function performed by a privilege to withhold such information from one's trading partner would be greatly diminished. Indeed, the social function performed by all speculative trading would also be diminished. Any such scenario is, however, completely unrealistic. *Laidlaw* is a hard case that made good law.

Is Silence in the Face of a Question about One's Knowledge a Misrepresentation?

This analysis explains why Marshall was right in *Laidlaw* in refusing to find a duty to disclose information. But did not the buyer knowingly mislead the seller by remaining silent in response to the seller's question? Perhaps.

In *Laidlaw*, the seller maintained that "[s]uppression of material circumstances within the knowledge of the vendee, and not accessible to the vendor, is equivalent to fraud, and vitiates the contract." He also contended that the buyer's silence, "when such a question was asked, was equivalent to a false answer, and as much calculated to deceive as the communication of the most fabulous intelligence." The Supreme Court did not directly address this issue, instead remanding the case to the trial court to instruct the jury in a new trial to consider "whether any imposition was practised by the vendee upon the vendor."

After denying a duty to disclose information, do we want silence in the face of a question asked by the seller in *Laidlaw* to be treated as a misrepresentation that would allow the other party to avoid the sale? Perhaps not. The root of the problem stems not from the misleading nature of the buyer's answer but from the unfairness of the seller's question. When viewed in the proper context, the question can be seen as inappropriate and, therefore, the seller as simply not entitled to a truthful answer.

To understand why, suppose that every commodities trader asked every other trader whether he was in possession of any information that would affect the future supply or demand of the commodity in question. Requiring a truthful answer to such a question would undermine, if not eliminate, the institution within which both the buyer and seller are operating. Therefore, at least in this bargaining context, such questions should not be asked and, if asked, need not be answered. Silence, however misleading, is the appropriate response.

If silence in the face of the question asked in *Laidlaw* could constitute misrepresentation, why stop there? Suppose that instead of asking indirectly about the blockade, the seller in *Laidlaw* had asked the following: "Would you be prepared to pay more for the tobacco than you are offering?" Suppose further that the buyer affirmatively lied by saying, "No, this is my top offer," when in fact he would be willing to pay twice as much. Is this lie, which certainly seems material, a fraud on the seller? The answer must be no, because to hold otherwise would undermine virtually all such transactions. Every seller who agrees to a price necessarily assumes the risk that the buyer might have been willing and able to pay more, just as every buyer assumes the risk that a seller would have been willing or able to accept less. Because such ignorance, whether conscious or not, is pervasive, it cannot provide the basis for an "exceptional" defense that would undermine the normal significance of consent.

I know of no case or doctrine that sanctions affirmatively lying in the face of such a question, and I doubt such a case exists. *Laidlaw* surely says no such thing. But neither would I expect a misrepresentation defense to a contract to succeed—or even be asserted—that is based on a seller or buyer's false statement that a particular price was his "best offer" when he was really prepared to accept less or pay more. But if affirmatively lying in response to this type of question is permissible in this context, then remaining silent in the face of a similar question in a similar context should also be permissible even if it has the effect of misleading the questioner. But the context makes all the difference, which is where Marshall's distinction between information about intrinsic and extrinsic might be useful.

Bargaining or Betting?

The situation in *Laidlaw* concerned what Marshall referred to as "intelligence of extrinsic circumstances which might influence the price of the commodity." So too did the above analysis of why a refusal to mandate a duty to disclose such information is justified. But this analysis does not apply to a misstatement of fact, whether by affirmative statement or by silence, concerning some *intrinsic* characteristic of the resource itself, as opposed to knowledge of *extrinsic* circumstances affecting supply or demand for the resource.

For example, it would be misrepresentation to stand mute in the face of a buyer's statement that, "I assume that these eggs are Grade A" when the seller knows them to be of an inferior grade. Conversely, if asked a question of the sort posed by the seller in *Laidlaw*, it would not be misrepresentation for the buyer to conceal his knowledge of an important new study pronouncing eggs to be far more healthful than previously thought. Although both facts could, if disclosed, potentially affect the price of the eggs, only the first involves the description of the eggs themselves.

Chief Justice Marshall's distinction between intelligence of extrinsic circumstances concerning supply or demand and intrinsic characteristics of the item being sold reveals an important distinction between two types of motives for entering into a contract that can affect whether the contract can be avoided because of a failure of basic assumptions. One motive for entering a contract is to get the performance itself. Another motivation is to obtain a gain from future appreciation of that thing. We can summarize this as the distinction between a *bargain* and a *bet*.

Of course, oftentimes, the motives for entering into a contract are mixed. One buys a house to live in it; one also buys it to enjoy its appreciation in market value, or its usefulness as part of some other transaction. The bargain aspect of the contract is the receipt of the performance itself; the bet aspect is the chance of also gaining all the benefits that may flow from receiving the promised performance.

In *Laidlaw*, the bargain aspect of the exchange was for the tobacco itself. The bet aspect of the transaction was the chance of appreciation or depreciation of market value. The potentially mis-leading behavior of the buyer solely concerned "intelligence of extrinsic circumstances" relevant only to the betting aspect of the transaction. Had the tobacco delivered not been of the quantity or quality described, it would go to the bargain aspect of the transac-tion. When you contract to buy a car with 10,000 miles on the odometer, you are betting that the car will not have major repairs in the near future or that it will be worth a certain amount when the time comes to sell it in a year or two; you are not betting on whether the seller had rolled back the odometer from 100,000 miles before showing you the car.

Although ordinarily we are not betting on the nature of the thing itself, sometimes we are doing exactly that. When a good is sold explicitly "as is" with no returns or refunds for any reason, there is a betting aspect to what one is bargaining for. One "assumes the risk" of any defects in the good that one later discovers (although this bet would not include the deliberate concealment of a defect by the seller). Indeed, the examples of *Sherwood v. Walker* and *Wood v. Boynton*, involve elements of betting on whether Rose the Second of Aberlone was capable of breeding, or whether the rough stone was a diamond or a topaz. Bargaining in the face of conscious ignorance about the intrinsic nature of the thing itself is a sign that one is bet-ting as well. Assumption of risk, after all, is fancy way to describe a "bet."

Whether or not a defense of failure of basic assumptions is avail-able concerns the scope of whatever betting element is present in the transaction. If the event that occurs lies outside the betting aspects that typically accompany such transactions, we say that the parties did not agree to *that*. But it is possible to respond that the party seeking to avoid the contract assumed the risk of the event occurring—that is, he was betting that events would go his way and cannot escape his duty to perform when he loses his bet.

The foregoing analysis suggests that, at least when responding to a question, a duty to disclose should exist when the failure to disclose relates to the bargain insofar as it creates a disparity between what is promised and what is actually delivered. This may occur, for example, when (a) an item, as it appears, would normally have certain intrinsic characteristics, (b) a reasonable inspection will not reveal the absence of these characteristics, (c) the seller knows that these characteristics are absent, and (d) the seller has reason to know that knowledge of this fact is "material," that is, it would likely influence the manifestation of assent by the buyer. An example of this is a product with a latent defect, such as the termite-infested house in *Halbert v. Rosenthal*. When these circumstances obtain, the resources conveyed to the buyer do not conform to the substance of the rights described and conveyed by the seller. This is why houses are typically sold expressly "as is," but contingent on passing a professional inspection obtained by the buyer.

Conversely, a duty to disclose is not warranted when the seller remains silent about a fact that does not concern the nature of the performance being promised but concerns instead information that goes to the potential benefits resulting from performance. In such a case, the seller does not deliver resources that fail to conform to the performance that was bargained for. For example, to vary the facts of *Laidlaw v. Organ*, suppose a seller sells grain at a price that has greatly increased due to shortages caused by a war. Although the seller fails to communicate his knowledge that the war has ended and consequently that prices are about to decrease, he commits no misrepresentation provided he delivers grain of a quality and quantity that was communicated, which defines the rights transferred by the contract.

None of these distinctions are to be found in section 153, though it does say that a person may avoid a contract because of his or her mistake about which the other party had reason to know "if he does not bear the risk of the mistake." The distinction between a bargain and a bet, as well as between information about intrinsic properties of the item being sold and extrinsic factors relating to supply of or demand for that item, help flesh out our intuitions about when a party bears the risk of his own mistaken assumption even if the other party was aware of the mistake.

Index

About the Editor

DENNIS PATTERSON holds the Chair in Legal Philosophy and Legal Theory at the European University Institute in Florence, Italy. He is also Board of Governors Professor of Law and Philosophy at Rutgers University School of Law, Camden, New Jersey and Chair in Jurisprudence and International Trade at Swansea University, UK. Patterson is the author of *Law and Truth* (OUP 1996) and *The New Global Trading Order* with Ari Afilalo (CUP 2008). He is General Editor of *The Blackwell Companion to the Philosophy of Law and Legal Theory*. He has published widely in commercial law, trade law and legal philosophy.